Berna   d-respected author , c i sla
Middl   story, is Professor of Near Eastern
Emerit   i i ..e on University, where he has been sin   t.
Born in London in 1916, he was Professor of the I   ory of
the Middle East at the School of Oriental and African Studies,
University of London, 1949–74.

His many books include *The Arabs in History* (1950, 6th edition
1993), *The Emergence of Modern Turkey* (1961, 2nd edition
1968), *Istanbul and the Civilization of the Ottoman Empire*
(1963), *The Assassins* (1967), *The Muslim Discovery of Europe*
(1982, reissued 1994), *The Political Language of Islam* (1988),
Race and Slavery in the Middle East (1990), *Cultures In Conflict:
Christians, Muslims and Jews in the Age of Discovery* (1995)
and *The Middle East: 2000 Years of History from the Rise of
Christianity to the Present Day* (1995). His books have been
translated into more than twenty languages, including Arabic,
Persian, Turkish, Malay and Indonesian.

Semites and Anti-Semites

AN INQUIRY INTO CONFLICT AND PREJUDICE

Bernard Lewis

PHOENIX GIANT

A PHOENIX GIANT PAPERBACK

First published in Great Britain by George Weidenfeld and Nicolson Ltd in 1986
This paperback edition published in 1997 by Phoenix,
a division of Orion Books Ltd, Orion House, 5 Upper St Martin's Lane,
London WC2H 9EA

A CIP catalogue record for this book is available from the
British Library.

ISBN 0 75380 033 0

Printed and bound in Great Britain by
Butler & Tanner Ltd, Frome and London

Contents

Acknowledgments

MY THANKS are due first and foremost to my research assistant, Corinne Blake, whose skill, scholarship, and energy enormously lightened the task of writing this book, and whose critical acumen saved me from falling into a number of pitfalls. She is in no way responsible for those other pitfalls into which I tumbled with my eyes open and by my own choice. I would also like to express my appreciation to Mary Alice McCormick, whose meticulous care and unfailing good temper survived the many changes in my typescript from first draft to final copy. I am indebted for comments, criticisms and suggestions of various kinds to Priscilla Barnum, Theodore Draper, Grace Edelman, David Eisenberg, Zvi Elpeleg, Yuval Ginbar, Judy Gross, Cathleen Kaveny, Itamar Rabinovitch, Shimon Shamir, Elliott Shore, Frank H. Stewart, and some others who made helpful comments but prefer not to be named. I offer them my gratitude for those of their suggestions which I accepted, and my apologies for those which I resisted. My thanks are due to the editors of *Survey* and of *Encounter*, in which earlier versions of some paragraphs in chapter 9 were published. Finally, I must record my debt to my colleagues at Princeton University, who in their various ways have deepened my understanding of the problems discussed in this book.

Preface to the new edition

The Middle East has undergone the impact of a series of major changes—global, regional, and local—in the years that have passed since this book was first published. These have transformed but not resolved the issues with which it deals. I have therefore added an afterword to examine the interaction of conflict and prejudice in this new phase.

Once again, it is my pleasant duty to acknowledge my indebtedness to friends and colleagues who helped in various ways. I am especially indebted to Asher Susser and Esther Webman for their prompt replies to my many enquiries. I must add that they are in no way responsible for either my opinions or my errors.

Introduction

O N OCTOBER 3, 1980, unknown terrorists placed a bomb in a synagogue in the rue Copernic in Paris. Planned to explode as the worshippers were leaving, it in fact blew up a little early and therefore did much less than the intended damage. Four were killed, two of them non-Jewish passers-by, and ten were injured. The prime minister of France, Raymond Barre, appeared on television a few hours later to express his compassion for the victims and his outrage at the perpetrators. Appalled by what had happened, he exclaimed: "They aimed at the Jews, and they hit innocent Frenchmen." Barre's meaning was clear: that the deed was done by Arabs, determined to strike at Jews because of their quarrel with Israel, and that they had killed and maimed Frenchmen who happened to be nearby, but who were not Jews and had no connection with the Arab–Israeli conflict. That, however, was not exactly what he said, and his listeners, particularly his Jewish listeners, did not miss the implication that those citizens of Paris at prayer in the synagogue were somehow neither French nor innocent. What made Barre's spontaneous outburst more significant is that, as far as is known, he is in not an anti-Semite, and his anger was directed not against the Jews—for whom he was expressing his sympathy—but against those who had struck at them. Many French Jews, while encouraged by the widespread revulsion and anger expressed by their compatriots, asked themselves why their prime minister, in a spontaneous response to an emotional situation, should have spoken in this way. And the uncertainty remains, whether the perpetrators were indeed Arabs, or French anti-Semites.

On September 21, 1982, after the first reports of the massacre of Palestinians at Sabra and Shatila, a group of teachers at one of the major French high schools, the Lycée Voltaire in Paris, declaring themselves to be "outraged by the massacres in the Palestinian camps in Beirut," stopped all courses between 10 A.M. and midday. They drafted two letters, one to the president of the French Republic, demanding the breaking of diplomatic and economic relations with the state of Israel and the official recognition of the PLO; the other to the Israel Embassy in Paris, demanding the immediate and unconditional withdrawal of Israeli troops from Beirut and Lebanon. These two letters, with appropriate explanations, were read to the students of the school assembled in the main courtyard.[1] There is no evidence that the teachers of this or other schools had ever been moved to such action by events in Poland or Uganda, Central America or Afghanistan, South Africa or Southeast Asia, or for that matter in the Middle East where the massacre at Sabra and Shatila, with all its horror, lacked neither precedents nor parallels.

Like Barre's remarks about a bomb in a synagogue, the response of the Western media to Sabra and Shatila raises profound and disquieting questions, more than can be answered by reference only to the Israeli invasion of Lebanon in June 1982 and the destruction that followed, however appalling this may have been.

There are similar ambiguities in some other European responses to these events. In Italy, for example, the boycotting by airport workers of the Israeli airline El-Al, the distribution of badges with the shield of David and swastika intertwined, and the use of the slogan Nazisrael might perhaps be ascribed to moral indignation at the excesses of the Israelis or of their Lebanese Christian allies. This explanation could hardly however be extended to cover such other protests as the explosion of bombs in synagogues in Milan and in Rome—the latter resulting in the death of a two-year-old boy and the wounding of thirty-four other persons, or such lesser events as the cancellation, by Milan hotel, of a scheduled bar mitzva reception, at the demand of the labor unions. Nor were Italian Jews greatly reassured by the words of comfort offered to them by Luciano Lama, the Italian trade union leader, after the explosion of the bomb in Rome; "Jewish friends, do not shut yourselves in upon yourselves, do not isolate yourselves, do not turn the old ghetto into a new ghetto."

The action of the Paris schoolmasters and of some others were clearly inspired by hostile feelings toward Israel, possibly, though not certainly, also toward Jews. The same may be true of some of the media. In the era which began with the rise of Hitler but did not end with his fall, it is almost axiomatic that "Jews are news." Even the most minor skirmishes on the borders between Israel and her neighbors are extensively reported and discussed, while the great war between Iraq and Iran, already the fourth and soon to be the third bloodiest war of this century, passes almost unnoticed. Only toward the end of the fourth year of the war, when both sides began to attack neutral shipping, did the world press begin to give it some sporadic attention.

What is significant about the media response to the events in Sabra and Shatila is not that they received so much attention; that is normal where Israelis or other Jews are involved. Nor is it particularly significant that this attention seems so disproportionate when compared with the treatment of other crimes in other places. The Israelis—rightly—are judged by standards different from those applied to authoritarian governments, which in any case do not permit foreign news services to monitor their activities. The condemnation of the Israeli role was well founded, and many Israelis, and finally the Israeli authorities, joined in it. What is significant, and in need of explanation, is neither the attention nor the condemnation, but rather the way in which the news from Sabra and Shatila was handled and presented. Characteristic features were the suspension of critical judgment by journalists who normally exercise a salutary skepticism;[2] unhesitating acceptance and publication of what soon proved to be self-evident propaganda from obviously partisan sources; the use of violent and tendentious language in presenting straight news. Particularly striking, and revealing, was the frequent use of language evocative of the Nazis in discussing this massacre and, more generally, the Israeli invasion of Lebanon. Such words as "blitzkrieg," "lebensraum," "genocide," and "final solution" were freely used to reinforce the comparison, sometimes stated and often implied, between the Israelis in Lebanon and the Nazis in conquered and occupied Europe. Most reports concentrated their whole attack on the Israelis who, as was known from the start, had not actually participated in the massacre and whose negligence or complicity had not yet been established, and almost failed to mention the Lebanese Christian militias who actually did the deed. The careless reader or viewer could easily have got the impression that this was a massacre unique in the modern history of the Middle East, and that it was perpetrated directly by the Israelis. Neither was true.

Even the media themselves, sharply criticized for some professional lapses in this matter, seem to have become unhappy about the
treatment of the Sabra and Shatila affair. The publication of the
report of the Israeli commission presided over by Chief Justice
Kahan gave them an opportunity to reconsider and then to close the
case as suddenly and as irrationally as they had begun it. Clearly,
powerful and complex social and psychological forces are at work in
determining the attitudes and actions of journalists, and of the public
whose deeper feelings and desires they seem to have diagnosed with
middling accuracy.

The comparisons—both explicit and implied—between Israelis
and Nazis reflect a significant change in Western attitudes to both.
On June 19, 1969, at a press conference in the Hague, Maḥmūd
Riyāḍ, the Egyptian foreign minister, likened Israeli conduct in the
occupied areas to that of the Nazis during the German occupation of
Holland. At that time, memories were still too fresh for such a statement to pass unchallenged, and the minister found himself constrained by his angry audience to withdraw his remarks. Since then
a new generation has grown up, and the knowledge of what Nazi
behavior really meant has passed, for many, from memory to history.
Like the similar comparisons that were sometimes made in the late
sixties between British and American city policemen and the Nazi
Gestapo, parallels drawn between the Israelis and the Nazis have a
double character. If the Israelis were no better than the Nazis, then
it follows that the Nazis were no worse than the Israelis. This proposi-
tion, though palpably false, even by the most hostile account of Israeli
activities, brought welcome relief to many who had long borne a
burden of guilt for the role which they, their families, their nations,
or their churches had played in Hitler's crimes against the Jews,
whether by participation or complicity, acquiescence or indifference. This feeling was naturally strongest among the heirs and compatriots of the Nazis, the Fascists, and the collaborators. But it also
evoked a powerful response in the English-speaking countries,
where many had chafed under the restraints imposed upon them by
the revulsion against anti-Semitism in the immediate post-Hitler era.
Reports of Israeli misdeeds brought relief and opportunity.

Another difficult and painful question arises from the bomb explosion at the synagogue in the rue Copernic, and from terrorist attacks,

by Arabs or by European anti-Semites, on Jewish synagogues, sports clubs, and, on August 9, 1982, on a Jewish restaurant in Paris, where an explosion left six dead and twenty-two wounded. By now, Jews who go to pray or to congregate with other Jews in the cities of Western Europe have become accustomed to the grim sight of armed police or troops or sometimes even tanks and armored cars stationed to protect them from both their anti-Zionist and anti-Semitic enemies. Even in America there have been attacks on synagogues and on Jews, though these have been few and relatively innocuous, compared with Europe—acts of hooliganism rather than of terrorism.

Arab spokesmen in the West are careful to insist that their quarrel is with the Israeli state and Zionist ideology, not with the Jews as such nor with the Jewish religion. This argument is not strengthened by attacks on Jewish religious buildings or communal centers in Europe. It is fatally undermined by the seething hatred commonly expressed in Arabic books, newspapers, magazines, and even school textbooks in many parts of the Arab world. This hatred is not directed only against Israel and Zionism; it embraces the Jews and Judaism, which are condemned and vilified through the three thousand years of their history in book after book, article after article, speech after speech. The tone of much of this writing is set in a book published in Alexandria in 1950, in which the author, after observing that Jews remain Jews even if they embrace Christianity or Islam, reaches this conclusion: "The Jews and Zionism are like an evil tree. Its root is in New York, its branches all over the world, its leaves the Jews—all of them, old and young, male and female, without exception, are its thorny leaves and poisoned thorns, and the poison is swift and deadly."[3] At that time, such attacks were still comparatively rare. In the years that followed they became commonplace. Even such subjects as biblical history or Hebrew literature, in what are intended to be scholarly publications, become the vehicles of anti-Jewish polemic. In the present atmosphere in most Arab countries, it is virtually impossible to say anything which might arouse sympathy for the Jews, past as well as present. A striking example of this is the absence, amid the vast literature devoted to Jews, Judaism, and Jewish history, of any compassionate or even accurate account of the destruction of the Jews in Hitler's Europe. Where these writers mention the Holocaust at all, their practice, with few exceptions, is rather to deny or minimize, to excuse, extenuate, or even justify what happened. Some writers cite it as proof of the hateful character of the Jews, and of the well-deserved retribution which their misdeeds brought upon them.

In Egypt, which has a peace treaty and diplomatic relations with Israel, the film *Sophie's Choice* was banned because "it plays on the same themes as do the Zionists in depicting the chastisement of the Jews." The report of the Israeli commission on Sabra and Shatila was published *in extenso* in the mass circulation Egyptian weekly *al-Muṣawwar* (February 18, 1983), with a prefatory note saying that in view of the extreme importance of this document, the editors were giving it to their readers in full. They did not in fact give it in full. There were more than twenty small cuts, by which the editors or translators deftly removed every reference to the role of the Lebanese Christians who actually perpetrated the massacre and every sentence or allusion in defense or even in extenuation of Israeli behavior.

To all this, and much else besides, a common answer, given by or on behalf of Arabs, is that they cannot be anti-Semitic, since they themselves are Semites. The logic of this would seem to be that while an edition of Hitler's *Mein Kampf* published in Berlin or in Buenos Aires in German or Spanish is anti-Semitic, an Arabic version of the same text published in Cairo or Beirut cannot be anti-Semitic, because Arabic and Hebrew are cognate languages.[4] It is not a compelling argument.

In the Middle East, in the Soviet bloc, in the West, and now also in the previously unconcerned Third World, there has in recent years been an increasing wave of publicly expressed and sometimes violent hostility which is variously directed against Israel, Zionism, and the Jews. Those who express this hostility in a Western or Soviet context usually try to distinguish between two things; on the one hand, criticism of a state and its policies or opposition to an ideology and its consequences, which are perfectly legitimate; on the other hand, prejudice against a people or—in the West—a religion, which for the most part they do not admit and indeed sometimes denounce. The targets of this hostility and of the violence that may be associated with it often have difficulty in distinguishing between the two types. Jews tend to dismiss the attempt to make such a differentiation as so much hypocrisy, and to treat them all as one and the same—hatred of the Jews, commonly known as anti-Semitism. A commonly expressed view would run something like this: they hate Jews, and whether they bomb them or abuse them as Israelis, Zionists, or simply as Jews, makes no difference.

It is not, of course, as simple as that, and it can make a great deal of difference, though the difference between hostility to Jews and opposition to Israel or Zionism is not always easy to determine with any precision or certainty. Even the terms are difficult to define, and are used with multiple and changing meanings. What is Israel, what is Zionism, and who, for that matter, are the Jews?

Of the three, Israel is easiest. It is the name of a state which was established on May 14, 1948, and since then has conducted itself, as do other states, in the pursuit of its own interests and the application of policies designed to serve those interests. These policies may be good or bad, effective or ineffective, compatible or incompatible with the interests of other states, and opposition to them is not in itself a sign of prejudice any more than is opposition to the activities of other states in the world that are involved in conflicts. A clash of national or state interests may generate prejudice or be affected by it. It is not in itself evidence of prejudice.

To define Zionism is altogether a more difficult task. Originally, the term denoted a certain analysis of the Jewish predicament and a prescription for its cure. This was, briefly, that Jews were persecuted because they were strangers everywhere and had no home of their own. The answer was to create a Jewish national home which would eventually develop into a Jewish state. This would provide shelter for those Jews who needed it, encouragement and if need be help for those who continued to live elsewhere. It would also create a center where Jews, without fear of either persecution or suspicion, could develop their own Jewish culture and way of life. Above all, it would be one place in the world where Jews could live as Jews, not dependent on the sufferance or tolerance or goodwill of others, but as masters in their own home. Some argued that this Jewish national home might be built anywhere in the world, where there was empty land and a willing government, and attempts were made in Uganda, Australia, Sinai, South America, and, under Soviet auspices, in the remote Siberian province of Birobidzhan, on the border of Mongolia. Most of these never got beyond the stage of discussion; none of them achieved any results. There was only one place to which Jews felt they had an historic claim, and which had an emotional appeal powerful enough to evoke the necessary effort and endurance. That was the ancient land of Israel.

There were many, including Jews, who rejected this diagnosis and prescription. Some, especially among the religious Jews, saw in Zionism an impiety, an intrusion of alien secular nationalist notions into the Jewish religious community, and a blasphemous attempt to force the hand of God, from whom alone would come redemption. Other opponents saw in Zionism both a danger to the position of Jews in the countries of which they were or hoped to become citizens, and a source of conflict with the Arabs of Palestine and, beyond them, with the Arab and Islamic worlds. This consideration was particularly important with those governments, corporations, and other institutions and individuals who for political, strategic, commercial, or career reasons wished to remain on good terms with the Arab and Islamic worlds.

Those who, for whatever reason, opposed the idea of a Jewish state in Palestine made every effort to prevent its establishment. With the growth of the Jewish national home in Palestine, especially after the triumph of militant anti-Semitism on the continent of Europe in the nineteen thirties and early forties, and again with the birth of the Jewish state in 1948, the terms of debate changed. In particular, the content and purpose of opposition to the Jewish state changed. To prevent the birth of such a state was one thing; to terminate it, after it was born, another. Some who favored contraception balked at abortion; some who would tolerate infanticide stopped short of murder. Even in the Soviet Union, few were willing to go that far. The critics and opponents of Israel denounced its policies and sought ways of reducing its territories, but with one exception, they no longer spoke of dismantling the Jewish state or driving its inhabitants into the sea.

The one exception was the Arab world and its more faithful adherents. It remained the clearly expressed aim of the Palestinian organizations and of the Arab governments behind them to eliminate the Jewish state and establish an Arab Palestinian state in its place. In the political usage of the Arabs and of their committed supporters elsewhere, the word "Zionism" now acquired a second meaning. As used by many Arab writers and spokesmen, a Zionist was one who did not share their belief that Israel must be destroyed in order to achieve justice in the Middle East. By this definition, even as consistent a critic of Israeli policies as Charles de Gaulle could be called a Zionist; so too could the rulers of the Soviet Union, where even at the moments of greatest hostility the elimination of the state of Israel has never been public Soviet policy. And of course, by this definition, the term "Zionist" embraces almost all Jews, including most of those who had previously been indifferent or even hostile to Zionism. Only those Jews actively opposed not merely to the policies, but even to the existence of Israel are exempted.

In a third and still wider definition, there are no exemptions. In some Soviet, Arab, and latterly also other Islamic polemical writings, "Zionist" simply means "Jew," and therefore anti-Zionist means anti-Jew. A good example of this occurs in one of the writings of the Ayatollah Khomeini. A comparison of the Persian text with a French translation shows that the word Jew in the first is replaced by the word "Sioniste" in the latter.[5]

What then, is a Jew? Many answers can be found to this question, among the Jews, their enemies, and their friends. Only one answer can be considered as authoritative. According to rabbinic law, a Jew is one who is born to a Jewish mother or converted to the Jewish religion. Whatever his failures of faith and of practice, he remains a Jew. According to rabbinic law, he remains legally a Jew even after conversion to another religion. On this point Israeli law departs from rabbinic law, and considers that the apostate has ceased to be Jewish. Clearly, this is not a purely religious definition, since Jewishness can be acquired by inheritance. Equally clearly, it is not a racial defini-tion; for the racist, fathers are no less important than mothers, and racial identity cannot be acquired by conversion or forfeited by apostasy. This definition, adapted from ancient rabbinic texts, is now part of the law of the state of Israel. In this matter Judaism in effect adopts an intermediate position between the Christian doctrine that all human beings, including the children of Christians, are born sin-ners and become Christians only by baptism, and the Muslim doc-trine that all human beings are born Muslims but some are made Christians, Jews, or pagans by their parents.

For the Nazis, their disciples, and their dupes, the Jews are a race, and they and their descendants remain Jews, whatever language they speak and whatever religion they profess. Jewishness is thus essentially different from such forms of identity as religion and na-tionality, which can be adopted or relinquished at will. According to rabbinic law, there is no such thing as a half Jew or a quarter Jew. One is either a Jew or not a Jew. A child of a Jewish mother and a Gentile father is a Jew; the child of a Gentile mother and a Jewish father is not a Jew. For the Nazis, a Jew converted to Christianity is still a "full Jew" [*Volljude*]. One Jewish parent produces a half Jew; one Jewish grandparent a quarter Jew. Between these two definitions, those of the Jewish rabbis and of the Jews' bitterest enemies, a whole range of other definitions have been offered, using ethnic, cultural, and even social and economic criteria, as well as religion and race.

As the definitions adopted for Israelis, Zionists, or Jews vary, so too does the nature of the hostility directed against them. There is great confusion on this subject, whether among Jews, Jew haters, or the vast majority of mankind who belong to neither of these two categories. Broadly speaking, this hostility is of three types.

The first of these is opposition to Israel, possibly also to the Zionist movement and ideology which created and in some measure maintain it. Zionism is an ideology, Israel a state ruled by a government. Men of good faith may reasonably oppose or reject that ideology or criticize the policies of that government without necessarily being inspired by prejudice. It is unreasonable and unfair to assume that opposition to Zionism or criticism of Israeli policies and actions is, as such and in the absence of other evidence, an expression of anti-Semitic prejudice. The Arab–Israeli conflict is a political one—a clash between states and peoples over real issues, not a matter of prejudice and persecution. It is not necessary to assume that Arab hostility to Israel is a result of anti-Semitism; there are other adequate reasons by which it can be explained.

A second type, more difficult to define, is what one might call common, conventional, in a sense even "normal" prejudice, sometimes giving rise to "normal" persecution. Parallels to it might be found in the suspicion and resentment which are often directed against neighbors of another tribe, another race, another faith, or from another place, or the attitudes which majorities sometimes adopt toward minorities. There are many examples all over the world of minority groups, often of alien origin, which play some specific economic role, and arouse hostility, even persecution, in consequence. Such are the Lebanese in West Africa, the Indians in East Africa, and the Chinese in Southeast Asia. Hostility to Jews is often stimulated or aggravated by similar causes, and it will be argued that the attitude to Jews in the multidenominational and polyethnic societies of premodern Islam was of this character, before it was transformed by the introduction of anti-Semitic notions and writings from Europe.

The third type is anti-Semitism. Hatred of the Jews has many parallels, and yet is unique—in its persistence and its extent, its potency and virulence, its terrible Final Solution. Another case that is sometimes compared with the Holocaust in Hitler's Europe, the fate of the Armenians in Turkey, is of a different order. A remark attributed to Adolf Hitler "Who after all today is speaking about the destruction of the Armenians?" is often quoted to prove the similarity of the two cases. In fact it suggests the opposite. The remark is reported to have been made by Hitler in a secret speech delivered to the German military commanders on August 22, 1939, on the eve of the invasion of Poland. The speech had nothing whatever to do with the physical extermination of the Jews, which, though begun after the invasion, was not adopted as a policy by the Nazi leadership until the Wannsee conference in January 1942. It referred to the imminent conquest and colonization of Poland, and was part of Hitler's orders to his military commanders to use the utmost ferocity in dealing not only with the Polish armed forces but with the Polish civil population.[6] The suffering of the Armenians was an appalling human tragedy, and Armenians are still marked by its memory, as Jews are by that of the Holocaust. But unlike the persecution of the Jews, it was limited both in time and in place—to the Ottoman Empire and even there only to the last two decades of Ottoman history. More important, it was a struggle, however unequal, about real issues; it was never associated with either the demonic beliefs or the almost physical hatred which inspired and directed anti-Semitism in Europe and sometimes elsewhere.

A much closer parallel to the persecution of the Jews may be found in the enslavement and maltreatment of the black peoples of Africa, by their brown and white neighbors in Asia, North Africa, Europe, and ultimately the Americas. Like that of the Jews, their suffering extended over many countries and continents, and has endured for many centuries, including segregation, violence, and deprivation of rights. Like anti-Semitism, hostility to blacks is often expressed in a deep, visceral hatred, and seeks to justify itself with pseudoscience and pseudophilosophy. Blacks in America, like Jews in anti-Semitic Europe, were cut off from normal contact with other human beings, and isolated, in fact or in law, in crowded and insalubrious special quarters, for which Americans have, appropriately, borrowed the European Jewish word ghetto. Though there have been no massacres in America of either blacks or Jews, there have been outbreaks of racial violence, and, in the South, many blacks long lived in fear of the lynch mob. But despite these important resemblances, there is one crucial difference, and that is the desire of the anti-Semite to eliminate, to destroy, and in the final stage physically to exterminate his victim. The black hater may be as passionate in his hatred, as sadistic in his cruelty, as the Jew hater, but his purpose is to dominate and humiliate, to use and exploit; certainly not to destroy. On the contrary, he regards the black man as a valuable possession whom he would buy and sell like a commodity, breed and rear like cattle or work animals for his use. The Jew in contrast was not seen as a potentially useful animal, to be domesticated and put to work, but as a pest to be destroyed. There is much brutality and ruthlessness in the history of white–black relations, but there are no pogroms, and there are no extermination camps. This is the essential difference between the two most appalling and widespread manifestations of racism in the nineteenth and twentieth centuries.

The term anti-Semitism is often used to denote "normal" prejudice directed against Jews, and even to describe political or ideological opposition to Israel or to Zionism. This is misleading. In what follows it will be limited to the third category—the special and peculiar hatred of the Jews, which derives its unique power from the historical relationship between Judaism and Christianity, and the role assigned by Christians to the Jews in their writings and beliefs, more especially popular beliefs, concerning the genesis of their faith.

There are clear and obvious differences, moral as well as political, between the three types of hostility. But Israel is a Jewish state, and Zionism defines a Jewish problem and solution. Inevitably, the three interact and may even merge. It is often difficult to determine the motives and purposes of those involved. It would be palpably unjust, even absurd, to assert that all critics or opponents of Zionism or Israel are moved by anti-Semitism; it would be equally mistaken to deny that anti-Zionism can on occasion provide a cloak of respectability for a prejudice which, at the present time, and in the free world, is not normally admitted in public by anyone with political ambitions or cultural pretensions.

In its extreme form, the anti-Semitic view of history portrays the Jew as a satanic force, as the root of virtually all evil in the world, from the earliest time to the present day. In this view, he is engaged in an eternal and universal conspiracy, to infiltrate, corrupt, and ultimately rule the gentile world. For this he uses a variety of methods, all of them sinister. In medieval times, Jews were accused of poisoning wells, spreading the plague, and practicing ritual murder; in more modern times with inventing both capitalism and communism, and using the one or the other or both together to dominate the world. More recently, they have been blamed for the enslavement of black Africa and even accused—by some feminists—of introducing patriarchy and male domination through the worship of Jehovah and the dethronement of the great Mother Goddess of the ancients.[7] Since it is manifestly impossible to maintain these and similar propositions on any rational basis of evidence, the anti-Semite resorts to another characteristic device—the invention of facts and the fabrication of evidence to support them.

The most famous of all these forgeries is undoubtedly the so-called *Protocols of the Elders of Zion*. Concocted by the Russian czars' disinformation service, this book has served as the basis for worldwide anti-Semitic propaganda. It was successively used by the czarist police, the Whites in the Russian civil war, the German and other Nazis, and certain Arab governments and organizations, in their anti-Jewish propaganda. Careful and documented exposures of its fraudulent origin have relegated it, in the free world, to the lunatic fringes, but have done little to diminish its effectiveness elsewhere. Because of its enormous impact, and the actions taken by those who believed in it, it has been accurately described as "a warrant for genocide."[8]

For most Jews, that genocide was the most shattering event in their history; for the older generation of Israelis and many Jews elsewhere, it is the central experience of their personal lives, and their thoughts and actions are dominated by the knowledge that what has happened once can happen again, and by the determination that it must not. No understanding of the Jews and of Israel, of Zionism or anti-Semitism, is possible without reference to the fate of the Jews in Nazi Europe.

CHAPTER ONE

The Holocaust and After

IN THE YEARS 1939 TO 1945, between five and six million human beings, one million of them children, were rounded up, herded into camps, and put to death in a variety of ways, simply because they were Jews. In the earlier stages they were lined up and mowed down by machine gun fire, to fall neatly into the ditches which they had just been forced to dig. Later, a new technology of murder was devised by which far greater numbers could be tidily and expeditiously put to death, while their salvageable remains —hair, teeth, and animal fats—were preserved and stored by their frugal murderers for future use.[1]

This operation was conceived and planned by the Nazi rulers of Germany, and in large measure executed by Germans. They were not alone in this, however. The successful completion of the task depended on many others besides the Germans themselves—on the active collaboration of significant numbers of people in the countries influenced or conquered by Germany, the complicity of many more, and the indifference of vast masses, not only in German-occupied Europe but extending to neutral lands and even, in a certain sense, to the governments and peoples of the Western alliance.

The five or six million Jews who died in the German death camps were only a fraction of the tens of millions who lost their lives in Hitler's war. But they were unique in certain important respects. Germans succeeded, before their final defeat and surrender, in exterminating almost all of the Jews in occupied countries, amounting to about one-third of all the Jews in the world. There can be no doubt that they would have slaughtered the Jews of any other countries that might have fallen into their hands. No other group, not even the Russians, suffered comparable losses, nor were any the targets of

comparable ferocity. Indeed, with the solitary exception of the Gypsies, no other group was designated for systematic and total extermination.

The reason for their destruction was not that they were opponents or enemies of Germany—indeed, the earliest victims of Nazi
persecution were the Jews of Germany, proud, loyal, and patriotic
German citizens. It was not, as in some areas occupied by Germany,
to clear living space for German settlement, since the Jews were too
scattered and in Eastern Europe too impoverished to offer any pros-
pects for such a policy. Some Jews were indeed engaged in resistance
against the German occupation, but, among Jews as among others,
these were a small, militant minority among the general civil population who asked only to be left alone. They were not removed because
their removal was essential to the German war effort. On the contrary, the attack on the Jews obstructed the German war effort, by
diverting transport, personnel, and resources urgently needed elsewhere and—in a broader perspective—by depriving the German
war effort of manpower and of skills that might otherwise have
served it to good purpose. They were chosen for death simply because they were Jews—not even by their own definition of Jewishness, their own acceptance and assertion of identity, but in accordance with a definition devised by their persecutors. This included not
only Jews who knew themselves to be such, but substantial numbers
of Christians, agnostics, and others whose Jewishness might consist of
no more than partial Jewish descent. Jewishness, for the Nazis, was
not a religious or cultural quality; it did not consist in belonging to
a community or a people. It was an attribute of race, inherited and
immutable, and so potent that even one grandparent out of four
belonging to this race transmitted an indelible taint which put its
inheritor beyond the pale of humanity.

The doctrine in accordance of which the rulers of Nazi Germany
diagnosed this problem and devised what they called its final solution
was known as anti-Semitism. At the present day, when anti-Semitism
has become a term of abuse, of condemnation, which few, even
among anti-Semites, will apply to themselves, it is well to recall that
the term was originally invented and used by the adherents of the
doctrine, not by its opponents. For those who believed in it, anti-
Semitism was seen as a kind of antisepsis, its purpose being to identify, isolate, neutralize, and eventually eliminate a dangerous poison

which if left unchecked would spread and infect the whole of what was variously defined as European, Christian, Western, or Aryan civilization.

For the Nazis, though not for all anti-Semites, the key word is Aryan. In the demon-ridden nightmare of Nazi ideology, two demiurgic figures are engaged in a cosmic struggle for the domination of the world. They are the Aryan and the Semite, replacing the good and evil principles of more conventional cosmologies. The Aryan, who achieves his finest embodiment in the German race, represents beauty, creativity, and above all strength. He alone is capable of creating cultures and building civilizations, which some lesser breeds may help to preserve and transmit. The Semite is incapable of creation or even conservation. He can only destroy, and he is engaged in a constant effort, using his own and other inferior races, to penetrate and undermine Aryan society, to defile and mongrelize the glorious Aryan race. Even the detested presence of African colonial troops in the French occupation forces in Western Germany after World War I was attributed by Hitler to this evil Jewish purpose: "It was and is the Jews who bring the Negro to the Rhine, always with the same concealed thought and the clear goal of destroying, by the bastardization which would necessarily set in, the white race which they hate."[2]

According to Nazi doctrine Jews were alien and hostile intruders in Europe because they belonged to another race, different from that to which most Europeans belonged, inferior, and therefore hostile. While most Europeans belonged to the Aryan race, Jews were part of the Semitic race, and in this lay the main difference. In principle, therefore, other nations and peoples belonging to the same Semitic race should have been seen by the Nazis as equally inferior and contemptible, if not equally dangerous. Indeed, Hitler in *Mein Kampf* speaks with contempt of Asian and African nationalist movements, and commends the use of brutal severity in suppressing them. The early Nazi theoretical literature accords a certain secondary status to Far Eastern peoples, as imitators and conservers of the culture which the Aryans alone are capable of creating, but dismisses Arabs and other Semites as inferiors incapable of creative cultural effort. According to a standard Nazi textbook of *World History on a Racial Basis*, every original element in Arabic culture is borrowed from Aryan peoples; even the *Thousand and One Nights* are not an original Arab production but are based on copies of Persian and Indian, and therefore Aryan, works.[3] In a Nazi essay on Islam, Jengiz Khan, the Mongol conqueror and destroyer of the Caliphate, is praised as one who tried to save the Middle East from its Semitic oppressors.[4] One of the major Nazi theorists, Alfred Rosenberg, in his authoritative *Myth of the Twentieth Century* even warns the white races to be on their guard "against the united hatred of colored races and mongrels led in the fanatical spirit of Muhammad."[5]

In the event, however, these theoretical formulations proved to have little real effect. Apart from the Jews, only one people, the Gypsies, despite their impeccably Aryan origins, were singled out for destruction, and only one other race, the blacks, subjected to unremitting hatred and contempt. The Arabs, in contrast, though classed as Semites in the Nazi literature, were accorded a very different treatment by the rulers of the Nazi state. Despite some initial reluctance and continuing uncertainty, due more to political than to ideological considerations, the Nazis decided that the Arabs might be useful to them, and made some effort both to win Arab sympathy for Nazi ideas and to mobilize Arab support for German purposes.

In the first of these enterprises, they achieved some, but limited, results. In the second, however, despite presumed racial incompatibilities and despite an evident lack of commitment, they were remarkably successful. As the major challengers to the British and French empires, the Germans had an obvious attraction for the unwilling subjects of those empires in the Middle East and elsewhere. As the leading exponents and practitioners of hostility to the Jews, they could count on ready and sympathetic attention from those who felt themselves threatened by the growth of the Jewish National Home in Palestine. That they themselves were contributing very largely to the growth of that Jewish National Home, by driving their own Jews into exile, does not seem to have weighed very much with their Arab listeners.

If the German government was unwilling to make specific promises on future Arab political aims, they were in contrast unambiguously forthcoming on the Jewish question. German promises to the Arab leaders to eliminate the Jewish National Home were obviously heartfelt and sincere, and no doubt compensated for their cautious agueness in other matters.

Active hostility to Jews from those who, for one reason or another, had become Hitler's allies or sympathizers was to be expected. More surprising, and more wounding, were the negative reactions among many of those who themselves had been Hitler's victims or his opponents in arms. These reactions ranged from murderous violence to cold insensitivity. This latter term may reasonably be applied to some senior British and American officials who—as the contemporary record reveals—during the war received the news from Germany about massive slaughter first with scepticism and then with unconcern. After the armistice they saw the wretched survivors of the death camps primarily as a political embarrassment.

Even more devastating was the reception given to some of these survivors when they attempted to return to their former homes. By August 1945 about 80,000 Jews had reached Poland, out of the 3 million who had lived there in 1939. Of these some 13,000 were serving in the Polish Army, the remainder were survivors of the camps and refugees who had managed to escape into the Soviet Union or elsewhere during the German occupation. Hitler and the German forces had gone, but anti-Semitism—neither new nor alien in Poland—remained, and found justification in the presence of a number of Jews in the new administration which was being set up under Soviet auspices. The first serious anti-Jewish outbreak occurred in Cracow on August 11, 1945. It was followed by others all over Poland, in which some hundreds of returning Jews were murdered by mobs. The worst occurred in the city of Kielce in June 1946, in which dozens of returning Jews were killed by their neighbors.[6] The civil authorities did little to halt these murderous outbreaks; the ecclesiastical authorities refused to denounce the hatreds which had caused them. The attitude of the people, the church, and the authorities to these events quickly persuaded the returning Jews that the thousand-year-long history of the Jews in Poland had come to an end and that only by going elsewhere could they hope to rebuild their shattered lives. For most of them, elsewhere meant a place where their survival would not be dependent either on the goodwill of their neighbors or the protection of some alien authority.

In general, however, in the civilized world, there was a revulsion against anti-Semitism, as the full horror of the Nazi genocide became known. The liberation of the German camps by the advancing Allied armies, followed by the trial of the German war criminals at Nuremberg, produced a worldwide reaction. It gave rise to feelings of compassion for Jewish suffering and, as a consequence, of sympathy for Jewish purposes. This also affected great numbers, both of individuals and of institutions, that were uneasily conscious of their own, at best, equivocal roles in the Nazi Holocaust—the failure of all but a chosen few to resist or even protest the Nazi crimes against the Jews; the willingness of far too many to accept and even assist in the commission of these crimes; the refusal of others, beyond the Nazi reach, to discommode themselves either to prevent the crime or to succor its victims.

In this new atmosphere anti-Semitism was seen as an obscenity, something to which even anti-Semites would not admit openly. In the English-speaking countries, notably in the United States, the genteel but effective forms of discrimination which had quietly limited Jewish advancement were largely, if sometimes unwillingly, abandoned under the pressure of a public opinion which was no longer prepared to accept such discrimination and which saw in a restricted fraternity the first step on the road to Auschwitz. Even the anti-Semitic repartee which had previously been commonplace was now taboo except among trusted intimates.

In England, where the barriers against Jews had been fewer, the ban on anti-Jewish remarks was less strict. A few were still heard from time to time even in public. A famous example was the off-the-cuff remark by Ernest Bevin, the British Foreign Secretary, at a press conference, when he was becoming impatient with Zionist insistence on a hearing for their claims to a Jewish state: "If the Jews, with all their sufferings, want to get too much at the head of the queue, you have the danger of another anti-Semitic reaction through it all." This was too much for the raw nerves of the survivors, and Dr. Chaim Weizmann was expressing the general Jewish response when he asked: "Is it getting too much at the head of the queue if, after the slaughter of 6,000,000 Jews, the remnant . . . implore the shelter of a Jewish homeland?"[7]

The last three years of the British Mandate in Palestine, from 1945 to 1948, produced a tragic confrontation between the Jews in Palestine and their sympathizers, and the government and soldiers of that one country which for a whole year had stood alone against Hitler's Europe and had formed the nucleus of the alliance which ultimately defeated and destroyed him. In essence, this was not a matter of prejudice or hostility, but a clash of interests and purposes.

Before long it amounted to an armed conflict between the Jewish community in Palestine, determined to establish a Jewish state, and the British government, determined to prevent it, in the ultimately vain hope of winning Arab support, or at least acquiescence, for British imperial purposes.

Inevitably, the armed conflict in Palestine produced an anti-Zionist and in some measure an anti-Jewish reaction, first among British officials and soldiers serving in Palestine, then among the British public generally. The former had, since the early years of the Mandate, tended to develop Arab sympathies. The latter were particularly outraged by the terrorist tactics adopted by some of the Jewish organizations. In the 1940s, it should be recalled, terrorism had not yet entered on its new and still current phase, in which the objective is media coverage and the method is to strike at those, preferably unarmed and innocent bystanders, whose sudden and dramatic death would be most conducive to this end. The terrorism of that generation, of both the mufti's men and the Jewish Irgun in Palestine, and of others in Aden, Greece, India, and elsewhere, was directed not at the media but at the adversary and was intended to weaken and frighten him by striking at the institutions, personnel, and symbols of his power. Even this could deeply shock and outrage public opinion. On July 30, 1947, in fulfillment of a threat to exact vengeance for the hanging of three Irgun men in the Acre jail on the previous day, two British sergeants who had been captured by the Irgun were hanged, their bodies taken to a nearby wood, hung between two trees, and booby trapped. When British troops found them and cut down the first body, the mine exploded. It blew the corpse to pieces, and wounded the British officer who cut it down. The same evening British soldiers and policemen roamed through Tel Aviv breaking the windows of shops and vehicles and assaulting passers-by. The following day when the story of the hangings and the booby trap appeared on the front pages of the English newspapers, with banner headlines and photographs, a wave of anger followed and there were anti-Jewish demonstrations in London, Manchester, Liverpool, and other cities. In the circumstances, and by the standards of the time, the response was mild. Some windows were broken in Jewish shops and synagogues; there were many cases of willful damage and a few of suspected arson. There were no cases of bodily injury to Jews.

The failure of the British policy in Palestine, and the general reprobation of that policy in a world still shocked by the recent revelations of Nazi crimes, brought a change in the atmosphere. After the termination of the British Mandate in May 1948, public manifestations of anti-Jewish sentiment, in England as in the rest of the Western world, ceased to be socially or politically acceptable. If anything, there was a move to the opposite extreme, and even reasonable criticism of Jewish action was muted, either out of compassion or fear of being charged with anti-Semitism. Even the peoples of continental Europe, who had always had a stronger stomach than the British or the Americans in these matters, developed a new squeamishness. Overt anti-Semitism was generally condemned. In Germany it was legally forbidden. In most of the countries of continental Europe the Jewish communities were reduced by the Nazi genocide to a small fraction of what they had once been. The one exception was France, where the remnants of the old Franco-Jewish community were suddenly reinforced by a large-scale immigration of Jewish refugees from elsewhere, especially from Arab North Africa. With Britain, which had never known the Nazi yoke and where the Jewish community therefore had suffered no more than the normal hazards of war, these constituted the two largest Jewish communities in Europe west of the Soviet Union.

In addition to the revulsion from Nazi atrocities there was another development in postwar Europe which helped to divert the pressure from the Jews. This was the change taking place in much of Western Europe in the significance of the term race. Before the war, apart from a few small groups of seamen who had settled in seaports, blacks were almost unknown in Europe. Of the few who were seen around, most were students, or sometimes doctors and other professionals who had elected to stay after completing their studies. The racial difference between whites and blacks was in general only perceived as an issue by that small minority of Europeans with direct experience or knowledge of Africa or the West Indies. The only occasion when significant numbers of Africans were present in a European country, and their presence gave rise to tensions with the local white population, was when French African colonial troops formed part of the French occupation force in Germany after World War I and helped to fuel the racism of the young Adolf Hitler. But more commonly the term "race" had been used to denote the different groups among Europeans, of the type that today would be described as ethnic. The word race was for example normally and even officially used in Britain to denote the four elements—English, Scottish, Welsh, and Irish—that together composed the British nation. With the rise of Nazism and the growing influence of Nazi phraseology, even among anti-Nazis, the term race came to be used almost exclusively to denote the difference between the so-called Aryan and Semitic races—basically a new and pseudoscientific way of saying gentiles and Jews. It was not until the postwar period, with the worldwide acceptance of American usage, that the word race came to be used in a more strictly anthropological sense. It came to denote, above all else, the difference between whites and blacks.

The first non-Arab government after the fall of Hitler to initiate an official hate campaign—albeit slightly disguised—against Jews was that of the Soviet Union.[8] Almost from the time of the great October Revolution, the Soviet regime in dealing with its Jewish citizens had been locked in a dilemma of its own making. In almost all Western countries, apart from those with explicitly anti-Semitic regimes, the Jews were considered as a religious minority, sharing the same nationality as the majority. In English, both British and American, and in French, the word nationality is much the same as citizenship, denoting the state to which one owes allegiance and the label on one's passport. Men and women of American or British or French nationality might be of different religions; this is not relevant to their nationality, i.e., their citizenship, and is not recorded on their passports or other identity documents. The Soviet Union, as an atheist, Marxist state, did not recognize religion as a category, nor enter it on any official documents. It did however recognize Jews as a distinct entity, and classified them as an ethnic nationality—in Russian, *natsional'nost'* Soviet passports and other official documents have two rubrics where Western passports have only one. One of them indicates the bearer's *grazhdanstvo*, or citizenship; the second his *natsional'nost'*, or ethnic nationality. The first, for all who owe allegiance to the Soviet Union, is called Soviet; the second may be Russian, Ukrainian, Armenian, or any of the other ethnic groups, great or small, within the Soviet Union. For those born to Jewish parents, whatever their religious belief or unbelief, their *natsional'-nost'* is Jewish, and this is inscribed in all documents, at school, work, play, in the forces, even on a reader's ticket for the library. Ethnic nationality, unlike religion, cannot be changed by an act of conversion, and a Soviet Jew recorded as such on his papers must remain so for the rest of his life—unless he manages, as some have done, to disappear and reappear in another part of the country, with forged papers.

In the early days of the Soviet regime, Jews were no worse off than other nationalities and very much better off than they had been under the czars. They were even allowed the privilege, accorded to other nationalities, of developing their own culture in their own language, deemed to be Yiddish. True, the Jewish religion was discouraged, but so were all others. Zionism was proscribed and suppressed, but so were all ideologies besides communism and all allegiances other than that owed to the Soviet state. They lived for the most part in poverty and fear, but so did most of their Soviet compatriots except for the small ruling groups—and in these Jews were well represented.

The first sign of a serious deterioration in the relative position of the Jews came with the gradual withdrawal and final disappearance of their cultural rights and privileges. They were still classed as Jews by nationality, but were systematically cut off from the sustenance of their Jewish roots. Yet even while they were being Russified in language and culture, they could not become Russians except by fraud, with all the moral and personal dangers that this involved.

The position became far worse after the German–Soviet agreement of August 1939, and the virtual alliance between the two dictators which followed it. The whole tone of the Soviet media toward Nazi Germany changed dramatically. Anti-Semitism suddenly became tolerable and even respectable, and Jews were looked at now —also officially—in a different way. After the outbreak of war in 1939, when the Soviets joined with the Germans to partition Poland, Soviet authorities in the annexed Polish territories began immediate action against Zionist organizations and leaders. Two Jewish socialist leaders, unconnected with Zionism, and suspected of insufficient enthusiasm for the Soviet cause, were summarily executed. Similar repressions of Jews, Judaism, and Zionism followed in other East European territories annexed by the Soviet Union during the phase of collaboration with Nazi Germany—in the three Baltic republics which were wholly absorbed, and in Bessarabia, forcedly taken from Rumania with Nazi acquiescence. The purpose of these actions does not appear to have been to oppress the Jews as such but merely to dejudaize them, cut them off from any Jewish connections or affinities, and place them in the same uncomfortable limbo as the Jews of Russia herself.

This phase came to an end in June 1941 when Hitler launched a devastating attack against the Soviet Union. Nazi Germany was now the enemy, and Nazism, in all its aspects, odious. Soviet Jews played their full part in the defense of the Soviet Union against the invaders and Stalin even permitted some limited revival of specifically Jewish activity. A "Jewish Anti-Fascist Committee" was formed in Moscow, with a number of Jewish writers and actors—some of them rehabilitated for the occasion. The purpose was to appeal to Jews in Britain and above all in the United States and thus help to mobilize public opinion in favor of the Soviet Union and ultimately in favor of a second front in the West.

Like so many others before and after him, Stalin greatly overestimated the effectiveness of Jewish influence, but it certainly served some purpose. This relatively benign attitude continued for a while after the end of hostilities. Soviet authorities turned a blind eye to Jewish emigration from Eastern Europe and the Soviet government for once agreed with the United States and gave its blessing to the creation of the State of Israel. Russia even permitted the satellite government of Czechoslovakia to supply the arms which saved the infant state from death in its cradle. It is difficult to believe that Stalin, who killed countless millions in his own concentration camps, was moved by compassion for the plight of Hitler's surviving victims. A much more likely explanation is that he saw in Jewish migration to Palestine and the struggle for a Jewish state a useful way of weakening and eventually eliminating the power of Britain, then still his principal Western rival in the Middle East.

By the beginning of 1949, however, it was becoming clear that Soviet recognition of Israel was not aiding Soviet policy as expected. Stalin felt free to resume and extend the anti-Jewish attitudes which were first discernible during the interlude of friendship with Hitler. Before and during the war this was tacit and on a small scale, and consisted principally in limiting or barring Jewish access to positions

of trust and power. Many Jews still remained in the upper reaches
of the communist hierarchy, but fewer and fewer were permitted to
set foot on the lower rungs of the ladder.

In January 1949 Stalin inaugurated the first of what was to be a
long series of anti-Jewish campaigns. In all of these Stalin and his
successors were careful—at least at the higher levels—not to identify
the adversary simply as the Jews, or even as the Jewish ethnic nationality *(natsional'nost')*. They preferred to use transparent synonyms,
and, in case anyone failed to get the point, took care to emphasize
in various ways the Jewish origins of the persons under attack. The
traditional Russian practice of citing people by name and patronymic
was useful in this regard. For those who had changed their names or
who—as was common among senior communists—made use of a
pseudonym, the old and identifiably Jewish name was usually added
in brackets—that is, where the name was cited in a negative context.
Thus if G. A. Fulanov received some honor or decoration, he was the
good Russian G. A. Fulanov. If, on the other hand, he was accused
of some crime, he became Grigori Aaronovich Fulanov (formerly
Finkelstein). A famous example was that old enemy of Stalin, Leon
Trotsky, now cited as "Lev Davidovich Trotsky (formerly Bron-
stein)."

The first postwar attack on the Jews began with the campaign
against "cosmopolitanism" in the Soviet press. Launched in *Pravda*
in January 1949, the campaign against cosmopolitanism was at first
concerned with theatrical and other artistic matters. The word was
used as a term of abuse for those writers, artists, and critics who
showed undue awareness of Western writing, art, and criticism. Its
meaning was soon changed, widening to include political and ideological activities and offenses, and at the same time narrowed, to
become a virtual synonym for Jews.

The "rootless cosmopolitan," as he was usually called, was contrasted with the true patriot or even with the "indigenous population." He was "an alien without a motherland" and "incapable of
understanding true Russian patriotism."[9] That such charges accorded ill with communist internationalism did not trouble the increasingly chauvinistic leaders of the Russian state. The attack on
Jewish culture had begun as far back as 1938, and by 1940 all Yiddish
schools had been closed, as had the Yiddish sections in the Belorus-
sian and Ukrainian academies of sciences. All teaching and research

in Jewish subjects was brought to an end. At the same time Jews were progressively excluded from any branch of governmental or party apparatus concerned with defense and foreign affairs. In January 1948 Shlomo Mikhoels, the director of the Yiddish language state theater and chairman of the wartime Jewish Anti-Fascist Committee was killed in a traffic accident later revealed to have been officially arranged.[10] Before long such subterfuges were no longer thought to be necessary, and in August 1952 more than twenty prominent Jewish cultural figures were executed as "spies and bourgeois nationalists."

From Russia the campaign against cosmopolitanism was extended to the Soviet-dominated states in Eastern Europe. In November 1952 a purge and show trial in Czechoslovakia ended with the confession and execution of Rudolf Slansky, a lifelong Stalinist and secretary-general of the Czechoslovak Communist Party. In the course of the trial, he and his fellow accused confessed that they had been Zionists, bourgeois Jewish nationalists, traitors, and spies throughout their careers.

This was followed by the "Doctors' Plot" in January 1953, when a group of doctors, most of them Jews, was accused of plotting to murder Stalin and other Soviet leaders in the interests of American intelligence and "the international Jewish bourgeoisie." The power behind both the Doctors' Plot and the Slansky plot, according to the accusers, was the American Jewish Joint Distribution Committee, a well-known charitable organization concerned with social relief and rehabilitation. The Soviet, Soviet-controlled, and Soviet-influenced media gave immense publicity to these two events, and found occasion to stress their Jewish character. Of the fourteen accused in the Czechoslovak trial, eleven were Jews; of the nine doctors, seven were Jews. While both plots were said to have been organized by American intelligence, the organizing agency was described as Jewish, and the ideological impetus as "Zionism and Jewish bourgeois nationalism."

The charges against the Slansky group and the doctors were duly echoed by communist and fellow traveling writers in the West, in an obedient chorus of denunciation. The organizers where possible made a special point of mobilizing Jewish communists for this work.[11]

Various reasons have been adduced for Stalin's drive against the

Jews in his last years. One was disappointment with the return on his support for the Jewish state at the moment of its creation. Another, perhaps more important, was concern at the electrifying impact of the emergence and early victories of Israel on Soviet Jews. The Jews, even more browbeaten and dispirited than the rest of Stalin's subjects, responded to the birth and successes of Israel with messianic joy; in particular, the arrival of the first Israeli ambassador to Moscow was greeted by crowds of Jews with unrestrained enthusiasm. To the Soviet authorities, who tolerate no links between any section of Soviet population and any authority beyond Soviet control, this was a danger signal.

Another motive was certainly the usefulness of anti-Semitism in the troubled Soviet domains in Europe. In these countries, anti-Semitism had long been a powerful factor in social, economic, and public life. In Eastern Europe, unlike Western Europe, the post-Hitler era did not bring a decline in anti-Semitism through compassion for the victims, but rather an increase, directed principally against those survivors who attempted to come home. What made matters far worse, was that so many of these survivors had come in the wake of the Soviet armies, and some played a prominent role in the first governments set up under Soviet auspices. At some stage Stalin seems to have decided that it was better to have anti-Semitism working for Soviet power than against it. Thereupon, Soviet propaganda in Eastern Europe made great efforts to identify its enemies as Jews and thus harness the widespread and deeply felt feelings of hostility to Soviet advantage.

Finally, in the system of capricious and arbitrary autocratic rule established by Stalin, the personal feelings and motivations of the dictator cannot be discounted. Among many signs of growing paranoia in Stalin's last years, he was greatly concerned with imagined dangers from world Jewry. Such themes would have been familiar to him from the czarist empire in which he was born and received his education.

The death of Stalin in March 1953 brought a temporary respite, if only from the more extreme forms of anti-Jewish activity. The doctors were released, and the whole case against them ascribed to a "machination." Rudolf Slansky and his fellow accused had already been executed and could no longer benefit from this change of policy. They were, however, accorded the communist form of recompense in an afterlife by being "rehabilitated." Khrushchev's famous secret speech in February 1956, denouncing the evils of the Stalin era, raised new hopes among the Jews as among other elements in the Soviet population.

For the Jews at least these hopes were of brief duration. Khrushchev soon showed that while he did not share Stalin's paranoiac fantasies, his view of the Jewish role in the Soviet realms was not vastly different from that of his predecessor. His off-the-cuff remark, during a visit to Poland, that "there are too many Abramoviches around here" was heard and understood by both the Abramoviches and their gentile neighbors. By this time few but hard-core communist Jews had remained in Poland; most of the others had left. Now even the communists realized that their time had come, and as unobtrusively as possible took their departure. The communist rulers of Poland undertook a very thorough and far-reaching campaign against "Zionism and bourgeois Jewish nationalism," from which they hoped to gain a double advantage, by ingratiating themselves at once with their Russian masters and their Polish subjects. Khrushchev, outstanding among Soviet leaders for his frankness, explained his own views on Jewish matters to a group of French socialists who interviewed him in May 1956:

If now the Jews wanted to occupy the top jobs in *our* republics, they would obviously be looked upon unfavorably by the indigenous peoples. The latter would ill receive these claims, especially at a time when they consider themselves no less intelligent and no less able than the Jews. Or, for instance, in the Ukraine if a Jew is appointed to an important job and he surrounds himself with Jewish fellow workers, it is understandable that there may be hostility towards the Jews.[12]

In the early sixties the Soviet authorities launched a new campaign against the Jews, this time on two fronts, the religious and the economic. The attack on Judaism was part of a general campaign against religion, which for some reason the Soviet authorities again decided to regard as a threat. But the polemics against the Jewish religion were markedly different from those directed against the other two large religious groups in the Soviet Union, Christianity and Islam. The diatribes against Judaism differ not only in their violence and crudity of language but also in the projection of present problems into past events, for example in the treatment of the biblical Joshua

as a Zionist expropriator and King David as an aggressive expansionist as well as a philanderer, and also in the use of anti-Semitic stereotypes such as conspiracy, greed, and the desire to dominate. The
selectivity of Soviet anti-religious propaganda is graphically illustrated in a cartoon in the *Bakinskii rabochii* of June 4, 1985, published in the predominantly Muslim republic of Azerbaijan. A book,
marked with a shield of David, drips liquid into two bottles labelled
poison and venom. Two villainous-looking characters are in the fore-
ground, one explaining to the other: "These poisons act first of all on
the brain." Both are pointing at the book with the Jewish emblem.
Other books, in the background, bear a cross and a seated Buddha.
There is no crescent.

Far more serious, for its victims, was the drive against what the
authorities called "economic crimes." Embezzlement, theft, bribery,
currency speculation, and corruption in general have long plagued
the Soviet Union. From time to time the Soviet authorities launch
campaigns against such crimes, mobilizing the whole apparatus of
state, party, press, and security forces for the purpose. A major campaign of this kind was conducted between 1961 and 1964, in which
Jews were singled out as the main victims. While tens of thousands
of men and women were accused and punished, media attention was
focused on those who were Jewish, with appropriate use of anti-
Semitic stereotypes both in the description and in the accompanying
cartoons. Thus, of eighty-four persons sentenced to death for economic crimes in 1962, forty-five were Jews, i.e., 54 percent. In the
Ukrainian Republic the proportion was seventeen out of twenty-one,
or 81 percent.[13]

It was in connection with these campaigns that Trofim K. Kichko
published his famous book *Judaism without Embellishment,* attacking the Jewish religion and those who professed it throughout the
ages. This was so crudely anti-Semitic in content, language, and illus-
trations that even communist parties in the free world joined in its
condemnation. The ideological commission of the Communist Party
of the Soviet Union responded by condemning and withdrawing the
book and dismissing Kichko from the party. A few years later he was
rehabilitated. In January 1968 he was granted the certificate of honor
of the Supreme Soviet of the Ukraine, and published a new book,
Judaism and Zionism, which appeared in Kiev in the same year. In
Kichko's perception of history, the Jewish religion teaches "thievery,

betrayal, and perfidy" and a "poisonous hatred for all other peoples."
The true objective of the Jewish religion, in his judgment, is the
fulfillment of God's promise that "the whole world belongs to the
Jews." The practical aim of Zionism is to create a "world Jewish
power" in Palestine for this purpose.

Kichko's second book, which was given mass circulation, was part
of a new wave of anti-Zionist propaganda, launched in July 1967, in
the wake of the Six Day War, which affected all the countries in the
Soviet bloc. In Poland it led to the dismissal of even communist Jews
(few others remained) from their jobs, and the more or less forced
departure of almost all of the surviving Jewish remnant.[14]

It was not only in the Soviet Union that the dramatic events of
June 1967 brought a radical change of attitudes. In the past even
well-wishers had been accustomed to see the Jews primarily as victims, usually helpless, and as candidates for succor, where this could
be provided without endangering important national or commercial
interests. By his swift and smashing victories over vastly greater and
more powerful enemies, the Jew had defaulted on his stereotype as
the frightened victim, to be destroyed, abandoned, pitied, or rescued
at the discretion of those more fortunate than he, as circumstances
might indicate. For many, this was a profoundly disturbing change.
In Europe, in America, and in the Middle East, among the Jews and
Arabs themselves, this sudden and total transformation of the relationship between the Jews and their adversaries started changes of
attitude which have continued to the present day. To understand
them it is necessary to look more closely at the peoples and ideologies
involved, as well as the policies and perceptions that influenced the
course of events.

CHAPTER TWO

Semites

THE NAME SEMITE comes from Shem, the eldest of the three sons of Noah. In the Greek and Latin versions of the Bible, Shem becomes Sem, since neither Greek nor Latin has any way of representing the initial sound of the Hebrew name. The Bible tells us that everyone on earth was drowned except for Noah and his family and that all mankind are descended from his three sons, Shem, Ham, and Japheth. The lines of descent from the three of them, described in the tenth chapter of Genesis, represent a kind of mythologized ethnology, enumerating the peoples of antiquity whose names were known at the time when this chapter was written, and setting forth the relationships between them. Many of the names listed in this chapter are otherwise unknown to historical scholarship, and efforts to identify them have so far been without avail. Some, with varying accuracy, have been conventionally adopted or assigned as the appellations of other peoples. Madai and Javan may well be the Medes and the Ionian Greeks. It is however highly improbable that Togarmah represents the Turks. Some, in contrast, are readily recognizable as the names of peoples and countries well known from other sources of ancient history. Such for example are Canaan, Mizraim (Egypt), and Cush (Ethiopia).

In later times the idea was widely adopted by Christians, and to a lesser extent by Muslims and Jews, that the three sons of Noah represented the eponymous ancestors of three major racial or linguistic groups. According to this interpretation, Ham was the ancestor of the dark-skinned peoples of Africa, Shem of the Hebrews and their various cognates, and Japheth the ancestor of the Medes, Persians, Greeks, and other peoples who, many centuries later, came to be known as Aryans. The total implausibility of such a theory, in the face of the historical, linguistic, archaeological, and ethnographical evidence, did not prevent its survival until the nineteenth century among scholars, and for very much longer among nonscholars.

While Shem and his sons are of biblical antiquity, the Semite is of much more recent origin, dating from eighteenth-century Europe. The notion that some languages may be related to other languages was by no means new. Already in ancient times Jewish scholars were aware of the kinship between Hebrew and Aramaic; in medieval times they were able to perceive and even make use of the similarities between Hebrew and Arabic in their studies of grammar and lexicography. But it was not until the development of comparative philology in eighteenth-century Europe that the notion of families of cognate languages emerged and developed. For a long time the only ancient languages and texts known to European scholarship were the Greek and Latin classics on the one hand and the Hebrew and Aramaic texts preserved by the Jews on the other. The latter were supplemented by an increasing interest in Arabic and in the languages used by the Eastern Christians, with whom the Church of Rome had been gradually extending its contacts. The extension of European activities in the Middle East and above all in India brought new cultures and literatures within range of the exploring minds of European scholarship, and with the discovery and decipherment of the Zoroastrian and Hindu scriptures, written in the ancient languages of Persia and India, a new dimension was added to the study of language.

It was at this time that the two protagonists, the Semite and the Aryan, came into existence. Both of them are myths, and part of the same mythology. Both originated in the same way, and suffered the same misuse, mostly indeed at the same hands. Both names have their origin in scholarship and refer to language. Both date from the great development of comparative philology in the late eighteenth and early nineteenth centuries. By that time, European scholars had recognized two major groups of languages in which most of the civilizations west of China are expressed. One, the larger, consists of Sanskrit and its derivatives in India; the successive phases of the Persian language; Latin and Greek; and most of the languages of modern Europe, Slavonic, Germanic, Romance, and Celtic alike. German philologists called this family of languages "Indo-Germanic," combining the names of its easternmost and westernmost components. Philologists in France and Britain preferred the name "Indo-European," allegedly because both the Celtic and Romance languages could advance some claim to the westernmost position. There is no doubt about the easternmost subfamily, which consists of the languages of Iran and the Sanskritic languages of India. To these the name Aryan or Indo-Aryan is commonly applied. This word, which occurs in both old Persian and Sanskrit, has the meaning of noble—a common enough way for peoples to designate themselves. The name Iran, in the ancient form Eryana, means the land of the Aryans. The Sanskrit form Arya was used from early times to designate the worshippers of the Brahmanic gods. Its extension to cover all the Indo-European languages was a misuse of terms. Its transformation from a linguistic to an ethnic and ultimately even racial designation was an error of scholarship that was to have profound social, political and moral consequences.

As far back as 1704 the German philosopher and polymath Gottfried Wilhelm von Leibniz had identified a group of cognate languages which included Hebrew, old Punic, i.e., Carthaginian, Chaldaean, Syriac, and Ethiopic. To this group he gave the name "Arabic," after its most widely used and widely spoken member.[1] To call a group by the name of one of its members could easily give rise to confusion, and Leibniz's nomenclature was not generally accepted. It was not until 1781 that this group was given the name which it has retained ever since. In that year, August Ludwig Schlözer contributed an essay on this subject to a comprehensive German work on biblical and Oriental literature. According to Schlözer, "from the Mediterranean Sea to the Euphrates and from Mesopotamia down to Arabia, as is known, only one language reigned. The Syrians, Babylonians, Hebrews and Arabs were one people. Even the Phoenicians who were Hamites spoke this language, which I might call the Semitic."[2] Schlözer goes on to discuss other languages of the area, and tries to fit them, not very successfully, into the framework provided by Genesis 10.

The idea that Semitic languages derived from one original language (by German philologists sometimes called *Ursemitisch* or proto-Semitic) and that the peoples speaking these languages were descended from one people exercised considerable influence and caused some confusion. By 1855 the French scholar Ernest Renan, one of the pioneers of Semitic philology, wrote complaining:

We can now see what an unhappy idea Eichhorn [sic; should be Schlözer *apud* Eichhorn] had when he gave the name of Semitic to the family of Syro-Arab languages. This name, which usage obliges us to retain, has been and will long remain the cause of a multitude of confusions. I repeat again that the name Semite here [Renan is referring to his pioneer study on Semitic philology] has only a purely conventional meaning: it designates the peoples who have spoken Hebrew, Syriac, Arabic or some neighboring dialect, and in no sense the people who are listed in the tenth chapter of Genesis as the descendants of Shem, who are, or at least half of them, of Aryan origin.[3]

Renan was of course right in pointing to the dangers of taking "the generations of the sons of Noah" as a basis for philological classification. He might have gone further. The descendants of Ham, conventionally the ancestor of the Africans, include, in addition to Egypt and Ethiopia, Canaanites and Phoenicians, who lived in the Syro-Palestinian area and spoke a language very similar to Hebrew.

The confusion between race and language goes back a long way, and was compounded by the rapidly changing content of the word "race" in European and later in American usage. Serious scholars have pointed out—repeatedly and ineffectually—that "Semitic" is a linguistic and cultural classification, denoting certain languages and in some contexts the literatures and civilizations expressed in those languages. As a kind of shorthand, it was sometimes retained to designate the speakers of those languages. At one time it might thus have had a connotation of race, when that word itself was used to designate national and cultural entities. It has nothing whatever to do with race in the anthropological sense that is now common usage. A glance at the present-day speakers of Arabic, from Khartoum to Aleppo and from Mauritania to Mosul, or even of Hebrew speakers in the modern state of Israel, will suffice to show the enormous diversity of racial types.

The philologists—or some of them—continued their unavailing and sometimes rather equivocal protests against this misuse of their work. Thus, the great German Semitist, Theodor Nöldeke, in an essay called "Some Characteristics of the Semitic Race," published in about 1872, remarked:

Similarly, in drawing the character of the Semites, the historian must guard against taking the Jews of Europe as pure representatives of the race. These have maintained many features of their primitive type with remarkable tenacity, but they have become Europeans all the same; and, moreover, many pecularities by which they are marked are not so much of old Semitic origin as the result of the special history of the Jews, and in particular of continued oppression, and of that long isolation from other peoples, which was partly their own choice and partly imposed upon them.[4]

Nöldeke, it may be noted, was a professor at the University of Strassburg, a city which contained one of the oldest and most important Jewish communities in western Europe. One wonders how much comfort they derived from his observations.

Since the days of Schlözer and even Renan, the list of Semitic languages known to scholarship has lengthened considerably. Many scholars now go further and perceive a link between the Semitic languages and another group called Hamitic, a term coined by analogy with Semitic, and applied to a group of languages spoken by the indigenous inhabitants of the Horn of Africa and some other African regions. Because of some remote and ancient connections between these two groups of languages, they are considered to form one group, called Hamito-Semitic, on the analogy of Indo-European.

Of the many Semitic languages that have been spoken and written in the course of the millennia, very few are still used on any scale at the present day, and of these only two, Hebrew and Arabic, receive much attention outside the countries where they are used. At the present time as in antiquity, the Semitic languages are virtually confined to a limited area, in southwest Asia and northern Africa. Isolated transplants have survived in two regions outside this zone. One of them is the Mediterranean island of Malta, where the local language, Maltese, is based on a dialect of North African colloquial Arabic. It is incidentally the only Semitic language spoken by a Christian European people. On the other side of the North African language zone are the Semitic languages of Ethiopia.

These last are the only Semitic languages spoken exclusively by dark-skinned Africans. The speakers of both Arabic and Hebrew range in racial type from fair-skinned white to brown and occasionally even black. At the present day, Hebrew is spoken as mother tongue only in the Republic of Israel, but it is also studied and used by Jews everywhere as a religious and sometimes also cultural language; as the medium of the Old Testament, it has for many centuries occupied an important though now somewhat diminished position in the Western curriculum of classical and scriptural studies.

Arabic is spoken as mother tongue in the wide belt known as the Arab lands, bounded by the borders of Turkey and Iran in the east and by the Mediterranean and Atlantic Oceans in the north and west and extending from Iraq to Morocco, and also by significant minorities in the neighboring lands in both Asia and Africa. In addition, it is the language of prayer and of law, of the scriptures and the classics, for the hundreds of millions of non-Arab Muslims throughout the world, and its growing strategic and economic importance have won recognition for its historical and cultural significance in both the Soviet and Western worlds.

While the spoken forms of Arabic vary as much from country to country as do Spanish, Portuguese, and Italian, the written language is the same all over the Arab world. With the rapid spread of literacy Arabic is acquiring additional strength as a unifying factor. Arabic was brought to all these countries, outside Arabia, in the seventh and eighth centuries—by Middle Eastern standards, only yesterday. But in the course of fourteen centuries it has almost completely replaced the many languages that were previously used in these countries. Coptic and Syriac, once in general use in Egypt and Syria, survive only as the liturgical languages of the Eastern Christians. Kurdish and Berber are still the languages of important minorities, the one in Iraq, the other in North Africa. But both consist of many dialects, without a standard language, and neither has a written literature. The more ancient languages of the area—those of the Assyrians and Babylonians in what is now Iraq, of the Canaanites and Phoenicians in Syria-Palestine, of the ancient Egyptians in Egypt—have all long since disappeared and been forgotten. Only the efforts of modern scholarship made possible the uncovering of their monuments, the decipherment of their scripts, and the elucidation of their literatures and languages.

In recent years a new doctrine has been developed in the Arab countries which has come to dominate the teaching of history in schools and the popular projection of the past in the media. It has even had some effect on scholarly writing. According to this view, the great Arab expansion after the advent of Islam in the seventh century, which took them out of their home in the Arabian Peninsula into the countries of the Fertile Crescent and then eastward across Iran to Central Asia and westward across Egypt to North Africa and Spain, was not, as had previously been believed, a religious or imperial expansion. It was a war of liberation, in which the free Arabs living in Arabia rescued their brethren who were the oppressed subjects of Persian and Roman imperialism. To justify this interpretation, it is necessary to maintain that all the inhabitants of these countries before the advent of Islam were in fact Arabs, even if known by other names. There was of course considerable Arab settlement in the borderlands of Iraq, Syria, Palestine, and even Egypt in pre-Islamic times, but the vast majority of the inhabitants of these countries belonged to other ethnic groups and spoke other languages. Modern Arabic historiography has extended the Arab name and identity to all or nearly all the ancient Semitic peoples in the Fertile Crescent.

One of these ancient peoples presented problems—the one that is still in existence, bearing the same name, using the same language, and, most troublesome of all, professing the same religion. Had the Israelites accompanied the Canaanites and Phoenicians and Assyrians and Babylonians into extinction, no doubt they too could have been claimed as Arab ancestors. But they did not. Their return in the past century, to claim the land of their forebears and dispute it with its Arab inhabitants, made their adoption even more difficult. There have been various responses to this difficulty. For some—especially those influenced by European anti-Semitism—the ancient Israelites and modern Jews are all the same, all bad, and therefore quite distinct from Arabs. For others, the biblical Israelites and their achievements were indeed authentically Arab, and are therefore unrelated to the modern Jews. Some limit this denial to European Jews, and make use of the theory that the Jews of Europe are not of Israelite descent at all but are the offspring of a tribe of Central Asian Turks converted to Judaism, called the Khazars. This theory, first put forward by an Austrian anthropologist in the early years of this century, is supported by no evidence whatsoever. It has long since been abandoned by all serious scholars in the field, including those in Arab countries, where the Khazar theory is little used except in occasional political polemics.

The rewriting of the past is usually undertaken to achieve specific political aims. By depicting the great Arab Islamic expansion in the seventh century as a war of liberation rather than of conquest, the Arabs can free themselves of the charge, even in the distant past, of imperialism—the most heinous crime in the current political calendar. By establishing a direct link with the ancient inhabitants of their countries, they can strengthen national pride, and moreover foster that sense of identity with the homeland through the ages which is the basis of Western-style patriotism. At a time when the interests of the Arab states are taking precedence over pan-Arab aspirations, this is an important factor. Finally, in bypassing the biblical Israelites and claiming kinship with the Canaanites, the pre-Israelite inhabitants of Palestine, it is possible to assert a historical claim antedating the biblical promise and possession put forward by the Jews. This line of argument is accompanied by the common practice in Arab countries, in textbooks, museums, and exhibitions, of minimizing the Jewish role in ancient history or, more frequently, presenting it in very negative terms. A few complaisant Westerners have been willing to join in these procedures. All this is of little relevance to the realities of the Arab–Israeli conflict, or even to the merits of the rival claims. The Arab case in Palestine would not be strengthened by showing that the ancient Canaanites were Arabs; it is not weakened by showing they were not.

In terms of scholarship, as distinct from politics, there is no evidence whatsoever for the assertion that the Canaanites were Arabs. Clearly, in Palestine as elsewhere in the Middle East, the modern inhabitants include among their ancestors those who lived in the country in antiquity. Equally obviously, the demographic mix was greatly modified over the centuries by migration, deportation, immigration, and settlement. This was particularly true in Palestine, where the population was transformed by such events as the Jewish rebellion against Rome and its suppression, the Arab conquest, the coming and going of the Crusaders, the devastation and resettlement of the coastlands by the Mamluk and Turkish regimes, and, from the late nineteenth century, by extensive migrations both within and from outside the region.

Through invasion and deportation, and successive changes of rule and of culture, the face of the Palestinian population changed several times. No doubt, the original inhabitants were never entirely obliterated, but in the course of time they were successively Judaized, Christianized, and Islamized. Their language was transformed into Hebrew, then to Aramaic, then to Arabic.

The problem of Semitic origins goes back to a time for which no written records are available, and in which therefore little can be said with any certainty. The discussion of the problem has been further complicated and confused by the changing meanings of the vocabulary in which it is discussed. As the word race is used at the present time, the Semites were never a race. The earliest accounts and pictures show them to have been of diverse racial origins and types. It is however accepted by most scholars that the Semites were originally an ethnic group, with some degree of racial homogeneity, and speaking one language, from which all the Semitic languages are by various routes descended. There is no agreement concerning the "original home" of the Semites, which various scholars have put in Arabia, in Syria, in Mesopotamia, and even in Armenia and North Africa. For the whole of the period for which written evidence is available, there is no doubt at all that the home of the Semites was Arabia, more particularly the north Arabian desert. It was from there that in successive waves of migration they spread into the neighboring countries of the Fertile Crescent and even, crossing the Red Sea, into the Horn of Africa.

By no means all the ancient civilizations of the Middle East were expressed in Semitic languages. The Sumerians, who founded the first civilization in Mesopotamia, spoke a language which was neither Semitic nor Indo-European, but of an entirely different family. The language of the hieroglyphs, the vehicle of the marvelous civilization of ancient Egypt, may possibly have some remote affinities with Semitic and Hamitic languages, but it is not of the Semitic family. There were important Indo-European groups, such as the Medes and Persians, the Hittites, and other lesser elements. The Philistines, a sea people who came from the Mediterranean islands and for a while colonized—and named—the coast of Palestine until they were finally conquered by the Hebrew kings, spoke a language known only from a few words preserved in the Hebrew Bible. These suffice to show that whatever it may have been, it was not Semitic. But for the last few thousand years, the dominant languages of the Fertile Crescent have belonged to the Semitic family and the civilizations expressed in these languages exercised an enormous influence far beyond their own borders.

Until the nineteenth century, the Christian world knew no more of the ancient history of the Middle East than could be learned from scattered information in the Hebrew Bible and the Greek classics. Jewish scholars, who read the Bible but not the classics, were corre-

spondingly worse informed. Muslim scholarship, familiar with neither the one nor the other, was dependent on such memories as had
filtered into Islamic literature, and knew even less. In the course of
the nineteenth and twentieth centuries exploration and excavation,
philological and historical scholarship added several millennia to the
political and cultural record of the Middle East, and transformed the
perceptions held by Middle Eastern peoples of their own role in the
world. This record reveals a pattern of migration and settlement, by
which successive waves of Semites came out of the Arabian desert
and created new states and civilizations.

The earliest such movement of which there is historical mention
took place in the third millennium before Christ. It brought the
peoples who came to be known as Babylonians and Assyrians into the
Mesopotamian river valley, where they encountered and ultimately
dominated the older civilization of the Sumerians. The oldest surviving documents in a Semitic language are early Babylonian inscriptions, written in the cuneiform writing, or wedge script, which was
invented by the Sumerians and used in a number of ancient languages of the region. Though the Babylonians and Assyrians created
a rich and interesting culture, they are remembered chiefly as ruthless conquerors. The names of such of their rulers as Sennacherib and
Nebuchadnezzar have been immortalized by the Bible. Their long
history entered its final stage toward the end of the sixth century B.C.,
when Mesopotamia was conquered by the founder of the new Persian Empire, Cyrus the Mede, and the independent political existence of the Assyrians and Babylonians was brought to an end. Thereafter they disappeared from view and fell into an oblivion from
which they were rescued by Western scholarship in the nineteenth
and repossessed by Iraqi patriotism in the twentieth.

The second major Semitic culture to appear on the stage of history is commonly known by the name of Canaanite. In the Bible the
name Canaan is in general limited to the area now occupied by
Israel, Jordan, and Lebanon, and the adjective Canaanite applied to
the different but closely related peoples that inhabited it. Such were
the Moabites, the Edomites, the Ammonites, and, most important,
the Phoenicians, a seafaring and trading people who lived on the
coast and who came to be widely known in the Mediterranean world.
Phoenician inscriptions have been found as far north as central Turkey, and as far west as Tunisia, where the famous ancient city of

Carthage was founded by Phoenician settlers. The Carthaginian or Punic language is a form of Phoenician. Archaeological discoveries have shown that languages of the same family as Canaanite were spoken in central and northern Syria, at least as far back as the middle of the second millennium B.C. It was among the Canaanite peoples that one of the most momentous inventions in human history is first attested—the alphabet. This represented an immense advance on the hieroglyphic writing of the Egyptians and the syllabic wedge script of the Sumerians and Assyro-Babylonians. The Canaanite alphabet served as the basis of the Hebrew, Greek, Latin, and probably most or all other alphabetical scripts in the world.

Linguistically, the Hebrew language of the Old Testament is of the Canaanite family. A comparison of biblical Hebrew with Phoenician, Moabite, and other inscriptions suggests that the languages of the Hebrews and their neighbors were closely related and probably mutually intelligible—an impression confirmed by various stories and allusions in the Old Testament, in which Israelites and their neighbors communicate without difficulty. This contrasts with other passages in which biblical authors indicate their inability to cope with more distant languages such as Egyptian, Assyrian, and even Aramaic.[5] Significantly, the word Hebrew, as the name of a language, does not occur in the Old Testament, where the language spoken by the Israelites is either called "Jewish" or "the language of Canaan" (Isaiah 19:18). Whether the Hebrews were already speaking a Canaanite language when they arrived in Palestine or, like so many ancient conquerors, adopted the language of the people they conquered, has been much disputed. The migration of the Hebrews seems to have begun about 1200 B.C., when the invasion of the sea peoples weakened both the Hittite and Egyptian Empires, which between them controlled the Syro-Palestinian lands, and allowed the entry of the Hebrews and some other related tribes. Under the judges and later the kings, they created a political power which for brief periods attained considerable strength and territorial expansion. This political power ended with the conquest first of the Kingdom of Israel by the Assyrians, then of the Kingdom of Judah by the Babylonians, and the departure of a large part of its people into Babylonian captivity. The Syro-Palestinian lands, like the Assyrian and Babylonian lands, finally lost their independence when they became part of the Persian Empire of Cyrus towards the end of the sixth century B.C.

The Hebrews, like the other Semitic peoples, used writing and produced religious, poetic, historical, and some other books. But their fate was entirely different. Alone among the peoples of the region, they retained their memory, their language, and their religion. Thanks to this, their ancient literature was not buried and forgotten like the rest, but was preserved and understood, eventually to become, through its adoption as the Jewish and later the Christian canon, part of the heritage of mankind.

By the beginning of the Christian era all these ancient Semitic languages, both the Assyro-Babylonian and the Canaanite families, were dead. Even Hebrew was no longer the everyday spoken language of the Jews in Palestine and elsewhere, surviving only as the language of scripture and hence, also, of religion, worship, and law. In the whole of the Fertile Crescent, the older Semitic languages had been replaced by another language of the same family, known as Aramaic. The name Aram is attested at least as far back as 2000 B.C., and appears more and more frequently from about 1400 B.C. The breakdown of the Assyrian Empire and the weakening of other political structures opened the way to a new invasion of the Fertile Crescent by Aramaic speaking tribes. The political achievement of the Aramaeans was minimal, and the states they established were of no great strength or duration. Their importance lies in their cultural achievement, especially in the triumph of their language which, in various dialects, became the common language of the Fertile Crescent, and the diplomatic and commercial language far beyond that.

During the great age of the Persian empire, from the sixth to the fourth century B.C., most of the Fertile Crescent, that is, the north Semitic world, was temporarily united in the Persian imperial system. A single administrative language was needed, and Aramaic met this need. The language was carried east and west by returning exiles, as well as by Aramaic-speaking colonies in Anatolia, Persia, Arabia, and Egypt. For the Jews in Mesopotamia and Palestine it became a semisacred second language after Hebrew. Much of the Talmudic and other rabbinic literature is written in one or another form of Aramaic. In the form of Syriac, it served as the vehicle of an important religious literature among the Christians of the eastern churches. It remained the main spoken language of the Fertile Crescent, for Christians, Jews, and others, until it was gradually superseded by Arabic. Today Aramaic survives only in a few places—in three Christian villages in a remote valley thirty miles north of Damascus, and in a few isolated Christian and Jewish communities in the area where Turkey, Iraq, and Iran meet. Most of these have now emigrated to more congenial surroundings.

The major Semitic civilizations of antiquity all appeared in the Fertile Crescent and its desert borderlands, and are expressed in languages belonging to the northeast and northwest Semitic groups. There were, however, others, belonging to another subgroup of the Semitic family, sometimes known as south Semitic or southwest Semitic. These first appeared in two important cultures which evolved at the southern end of the Red Sea, one on the Arabian, the other on the African side. In the course of the first millennium B.C., a number of states were founded in the southwestern corner of the Arabian Peninsula, in the area now occupied by the Republics of North and South Yemen. They left behind a considerable number of inscriptions, which record their beliefs and activities, and attest to the relatively high culture which they attained. They are written in a language known to scholarship as South Arabian. Its speakers, however, did not call it that, nor did they refer to themselves as Arabs, rather using a number of local, tribal, territorial, and dynastic names. Their language, though akin to Arabic, is not an Arabic dialect but a distinct language. The long history of South Arabian civilization drew to an end when the country was conquered first by the Ethiopians, then by the Persians, and finally by the Muslim Arabs coming from further north. Under their rule, the old languages died out except for a few local dialects, and were replaced by Arabic.

The Ethiopian armies who crossed the Red Sea to invade South Arabia were in a sense returning to their ancestral homeland. At an early and unknown date, not later than the first half of the second millennium B.C., numbers of South Arabians crossed the Red Sea and founded outposts and trading stations in Africa. It is possible that other Semitic-speaking populations were already established in that area. By the sixth century B.C., South Arabian influence in Ethiopia is attested by inscriptions. These show that by the fifth century B.C. an Ethiopian state with a relatively high level of material culture was already in existence. By the third century A.D., the Ethiopian kingdom of Axum had become a regional great power, advancing in all directions, notably northward into Nubia and eastward across the Red Sea into Yemen. It was at about this time that Christianity was brought to Ethiopia, and became the religion of the state. Ever since then, Ethiopia has been a predominantly Christian country, and for this reason isolated from its neighbors and thus also from the other Semitic-speaking peoples. Though at the present time there is a very large Muslim population in Ethiopia, the dominant religion remains Christianity. The old Ethiopic language is dead, surviving only as a medium for classical studies and religious liturgy, but several of the living languages of Ethiopia, and notably the state language, Amharic, are of the south Semitic family.

The last Semitic migration, the first to be extensively recorded in historical writings, and incomparably the most extensive and—in world historical terms—the most significant of all of them was that of the Arabs. The Arabs are by a long way the last of the Semitic peoples to appear with a speaking role on the stage of history. Though the name "Arab" is mentioned occasionally in ancient writings, in the Talmud, in inscriptions, and in Greek texts, as referring to the residual inhabitants of the peninsula, the oldest surviving monument in the Arabic language is an inscription of five lines, in Nabatean writing, dated A.D. 328. It is not until the sixth and seventh centuries that we have Arabic texts in any numbers and of any significance. But although Arabic is the youngest of the Semitic languages in terms of historical records, nevertheless linguistically and structurally it is the most archaic of all of them and thus probably the nearest to the ancestral Semitic language. Since northern Arabia was the reservoir from which the successive waves of migration came, this is not surprising.

Muhammad, who for Muslims was the last and greatest of the Prophets, was an Arab. The book he brought, the Qur'ān, is in Arabic. The empire which his followers created, extending from the Pyrenees to the borders of India and China, was ruled by Arabs. It had Arabic as its language of scripture and prayer, of culture and education, of government and commerce. In the Fertile Crescent, Egypt and North Africa, in part through the immigration of Arabs from the peninsula, in part by the Arabization of the existing population, Arabic came to be not only the official but also the most widely used language. Most of the previous languages either disappeared or survived only in a very attenuated form. Some countries like Persia, Central Asia, and later Turkey, were Islamized but not Arabized; that is, they adopted the Islamic religion but retained their own

languages. In these countries, Arabic still had a profound impact, as
the language of the Holy Book and Holy Law. These languages were
modified and sometimes completely transformed under Arabic influence, and drew on Arabic for the greater part of their abstract and
theoretical vocabulary. In most of the languages spoken by Muslims
in Asia and Africa, Arabic is as important as Latin and Greek combined in the languages of Christendom. Persian and Turkish in Asia
and Swahili and Hausa in East and West Africa are not Semitic languages, and are structurally quite different from Arabic and the rest
of the Semitic family. They use, however, a very large vocabulary of
Arabic and therefore Semitic words. By any standard, Arabic must
rank as one of the great historic vehicles of civilization, comparable
with Latin and Greek in the West and with Chinese in the Far East.

At the present day Arabic is by far the most widely spoken and
written of all the Semitic languages. By the nineteenth century, it
was, apart from Ethiopia, the only Semitic language that was spoken
by any numbers. With the revival of Hebrew among the Jewish
settlers in Palestine during the last hundred years, there was a second.

Hebrew had never been completely dead. It had been cherished
by Jews everywhere as the language of scripture and prayer and also,
along with Aramaic, as the language of law. It was also extensively
used as a literary language, and right through the Middle Ages and
into modern times many Jews wrote poetry, essays, history, and other
narratives in the Hebrew language. Used extensively in correspondence, even in private and commercial correspondence, it could
serve as a medium of conversation between educated Jews of different countries and with different mother tongues. It was not, however, a living, spoken language. It was no one's first language, and
was only exceptionally known by women. The language of childhood,
of the home, and of the family was not Hebrew. Usually, it was the
language of the country or a language brought from some previous
country of habitation. Often this language was spoken in a specific
Jewish dialect. Such dialects might have a large loan vocabulary of
Hebrew words, and be written in the Hebrew script. They were not
Hebrew, and apart from the dialects of the Jews of the Arabic-speak-
ing countries and of Ethiopia, they were not even Semitic.

The first children for nearly two thousand years to grow up speaking Hebrew from infancy were born and educated in Palestine in the

late Ottoman era, among the founders of the new Zionist settlements in Palestine. This extraordinary and probably unique phenomenon followed from a deliberate decision by their parents. It was made possible by practical necessity—by the need for a common language to unite these settlers. They had come from many countries, speaking many languages. Only Hebrew was familiar to all of them; more important, only Hebrew was acceptable to all of them. The rebirth of Hebrew, and the emergence of modern Hebrew as a lively, literary idiom, dates back to the eighteenth century, and to the impact of the European enlightenment on the German and East European Jews. Its development as a spoken language was inseparable from the growth of the Jewish settlement in Palestine. From 1948 it was the first official language (the second is Arabic) of the state of Israel; the second language of the immigrants and the mother tongue of the Israeli-born. It is also the second language of the Arab and other non-Jewish citizens of Israel, who have of necessity acquired a knowledge—for some a mastery—of the official and dominant language of the country.

So strange a sequence of events as the survival of Hebrew, alone among the languages of antiquity, and its rebirth in the twentieth century as a living and developing language can only be understood against the background of modern Jewish history.

CHAPTER THREE

Jews

IN THE SECOND HALF of the nineteenth century, when the Hebrew revival was well under way and when political Zionism was born, there were about seven and three quarter million people in the world known as Jews. They were scattered over a wide area, in many continents and in conditions of great diversity. Among them several distinct and different groups may be discerned. Two of these groups were, by most of the criteria of the countries and societies within which they lived, nations. The remainder were religious minorities, with varying degrees of acceptance and assimilation among the nations to which they belonged and of which—though this was not always agreed—they formed a part.

The larger and more active of these two groups was the Yiddish-speaking Jewish community of Eastern Europe. The vast majority of these Jews lived in lands which had formerly formed part of the Polish-Lithuanian realm. Jews had been migrating to these lands since the high Middle Ages, some from southeastern Europe and the Black Sea area, the great majority from Western Europe and especially from the Rhineland. The ferocious massacres and repressions of Jews in western Europe at the time of the Crusades on the one hand, and the tolerant and even, at times, beneficent policies of medieval Polish rulers on the other, led to a great movement of Jews across Europe from France and Germany to Poland and Lithuania. They brought with them their own distinctive idiom, a medieval west German dialect which in Eastern Europe evolved into a subtle and expressive language. Cut off from the German-speaking lands and surrounded by Slavic speakers, it borrowed a good many Slavic words and expressions. Spoken only by Jews, it was enriched by many words, expressions, and even modes of thought from the Bible, the

Talmud, and other Judaic literature. Written exclusively in the Hebrew script, it became the vehicle of a rich and varied literature. Scholars have sometimes called it Judeo-German. Those who spoke it, and their neighbors, called it Yiddish, a word which in Yiddish means Jewish. Among the Jews of Eastern Europe the two languages, Hebrew and Yiddish, were brought into a remarkable symbiosis. Hebrew, often referred to as *lashon qodesh,* the tongue of holiness, was the language of scripture, of worship, of all serious literature. But it was not only read and recited; it was also used actively and widely written, both in correspondence and in works of literature. Yiddish, in contrast, was the language of conversation, and therefore of family, personal, social, and communal life. At first it was of lowly status —a common image was that Hebrew was a princess and Yiddish her servant—but, like the vernaculars of Western Europe, it gained in status and dignity through the quality of literary works which enriched it. And just as Yiddish was given cultural and historical depth by its absorption of the Hebrew literary heritage, so too Hebrew was given vitality and flexibility by the common Yiddish speech of those who wrote it.

The year 1648 brought the beginning of a series of disasters for the Jews in Poland, far worse than anything their ancestors had encountered in medieval Western Europe. In Poland, the Jews were by this time far more numerous than they had ever been in the West; they were also more exposed. In the West, there had always been some—feudal lords, church dignitaries, or others—who for whatever reason had tried to protect their Jewish subjects and who were sometimes able to prevent or at least to halt the massacres. In Poland, where the central government was impotent and where the Polish Catholic population suffered along with the Jews, there was no one to help or interpose.

The attack came from the Ukrainian Cossacks, who had already launched a series of unsuccessful rebellions against their Polish overlords. In the Ukraine, Polish Catholic noblemen and gentry owned the land worked by Orthodox Ukrainian peasants, while the Polish state increasingly tried to establish the power of the central authority and eliminate the cherished autonomy of the Ukrainian Cossacks. The heightened religious feelings and tensions in Western Europe (this was the time of the Thirty Years' War in Germany) also affected Eastern Europe, where the conflict was not between Catholic and

Protestant, as in the West, but between Catholic and Orthodox. The
political domination and economic exploitation of the Ukraine by the
Poles was the more resented because of the religious difference.

As so often in their history, the Jews were caught in the middle
between these two great forces. As stewards, bailiffs, and toll collec-
tors for the Polish gentry, as the licensees of mills and inns, it was
they, rather than the Poles, who were in daily contact with the
peasantry, and through whom the Polish yoke was immediately felt.
In 1648 the Polish Diet abolished the special status of the Cossacks,
including the right to elect their own hetman or chief, and instead
subjected them to the absolute authority of a commission of Polish
magnates. In 1648 the Cossacks elected a new hetman by acclama-
tion, and at once began their rebellion against the Polish state.

His name was Bohdan Khmelnitsky. For the Ukrainians, he is a
national hero, and his campaigns a war of liberation. A Soviet military
decoration is named after him; so too is an avenue in Moscow,
through which one passes on the way to the only surviving synagogue
in that city. For the Jews, he was the perpetrator of the most appalling atrocities committed against them between the fall of Jerusalem
to Rome and the rise of Hitler in Germany. For ten years the Cossacks and their allies, the Muslim Tatars from Crimea, ravaged far
and wide, doing immense slaughter. Some Jews, relatively fortunate,
fell into the hands of the Tatars, who, following their own customs,
were content to take them alive and sell them into slavery. Some,
sent to the slave markets of Istanbul, were ransomed by their Jewish
co-religionists. The great majority, however, were not so fortunate,
and tens of thousands were butchered in the Cossack fury. Only
those willing to accept baptism into the Orthodox Church were
spared. They were very few. In the general confusion, Poland was
invaded from both east and west. From the east, the Russians followed the Ukrainians and invaded much of Belorussia and Lithuania,
where Jewish residents were massacred or expelled. From the west,
Poland was invaded by the Swedes. This time it was the invaders who
accorded humane treatment to the Jews, and the Poles who, accusing
them of complicity with the hated Protestants, exacted a heavy price
in blood when the invaders departed.

The loss of life among the Jews in Poland between 1648 and 1658
has been estimated at at least 100,000. The devastation of innumerable town and village communities is beyond calculation. The whole

course of East European Jewish history was dominated by the memory of this experience.

One of the consequences of the Khmelnitsky rebellion was a major step forward in the rising power of Russia, soon to dominate Eastern Europe. The rulers of Russia, like their Byzantine predecessors and their Cossack henchmen, were in general not well disposed towards Jews. On December 4, 1762, the Empress Catherine II of Russia, known as Catherine the Great, published a decree inviting foreigners to come to Russia and offering them the right of free movement and settlement in her imperial domains. The empress was one of the great enlightened despots of the eighteenth century, a friend and admirer of Voltaire and Diderot, and her invitation, calling upon foreigners from the West to come and join in the modernization of Russia, is full of the spirit of liberal enlightenment. This open and generous invitation was, however, limited by two words—*krome zhidov,* except Jews.[1]

On the evidence of her diaries, Catherine had nothing against the Jews, but on the contrary regarded them as a useful and productive element that would have helped the economic development of her domains. But even she, the ruthless despot, did not dare fly in the face of the deeply rooted prejudices of her subjects, and instead felt obliged to give way when her advisers quoted the decree of her "sainted predecessor" the Empress Elizabeth: "I do not wish to receive any profit or advantage from the enemies of Jesus Christ."[2]

But in the late eighteenth and early nineteenth centuries, with the partition of Poland and the annexation by Russia of the greater part of the former Polish territories, the czars acquired by conquest and annexation the Jewish subjects they had refused to admit by any other means. Along with the territories which they coveted and took, the czars now found themselves rulers of millions of new subjects, including many who were unwelcome to them and to whom they were unwelcome. The earlier solution, of massacre and expulsion, was no longer feasible. For one thing, the numbers were too great and the economic loss would have been too serious; for another, this was now the Age of the Enlightenment, in which such behavior was not acceptable to those whose esteem was valued. After a period of uncertainty and disagreement among the Russians themselves as to the appropriate status to be accorded to their new Jewish subjects, a solution was found in an imperial statute of 1804 establishing what

came to be known as the Pale of Settlement. This accorded Jews
rights of residence, and some other political rights, in an area consisting of thirteen provinces *(gubernia)*. The Pale consisted of the territories of Russian Poland, Lithuania, Belorussia, and the Ukraine,
together with the three provinces in the Black Sea area captured
from the Turks at the end of the eighteenth century, and designated
New Russia. They were not permitted to live in Russia proper, and
even in the Pale of Settlement they were forbidden to lease lands or
keep inns in the villages.

The Jewish community living in these areas conformed in general
to the pattern of minorities in Eastern Europe: a common culture
and way of life, a common religion, a putative common descent, and
a common language, Yiddish, exclusive to them. They had their own
literature, schools, and even, in the rabbinical seminaries, their own
centers of higher education. The Jewish communal bodies had nothing like the autonomy which they had enjoyed in the old Polish state,
but still had some responsibilities, notably for the collection and
payment of state taxes. The Pale of Settlement even, in a sense,
provided the Jews with a common territory. They did not form the
majority in that area, except perhaps for a few parts, but this was less
of an anomaly than might at first appear in regions of very mixed
population. They had no political existence and no legal nationhood,
but this was true of all but a few of their neighbors. Like the Poles,
the Ukrainians, the Balts, and many others among the innumerable
subject peoples of the Russian Empire, the Jews formed an ethnic
and cultural, but not a legal nationality. In addition to the Jews in the
Russian Pale of Settlement, there were similar groups of Yiddish-
speaking Jews beyond the Russian western border, in the former
Polish territories which had been annexed by Prussia and by Austria-
Hungary, as well as in Rumania. By about 1880 the Jews in this area
are estimated to have been between five and six million, perhaps
about three quarters of the entire Jewish population of the world at
that time.

To the south of the vast Russian Empire there was a second and
quite different Jewish community, living in the lands of Islam in the
Middle East and North Africa, and more especially in the Ottoman
Empire. Under the sultans as under the czars, the Jews conformed
to the prevailing pattern, here a very different one. In the Ottoman
lands the non-Muslim subjects of the state were organized in religio-

political communities called *millet*. [3] Of these, the Jews ranked third in numbers and in importance after the Greeks and Armenians. The Turks and Arabs were not classed as *millets* but, along with the Kurds and other predominantly Muslim peoples, were part of the sovereign Muslim *millet*.

In the Islamic lands, religion was the prime determinant of identity, far more important than ethnic origin or language. In the early nineteenth century, for example, the term Greek in Ottoman usage denoted, in the first instance, membership of the Greek Orthodox Church rather than of any ethnic or linguistic group, and included Orthodox Christians speaking Rumanian, Albanian, Bulgarian, Serbian, and Arabic as well as Greek. The Jewish *millet* was also multilingual, including speakers of Arabic, Spanish, Greek, Kurdish, Aramaic, Turkish, and other languages. The Ottoman Empire, like Poland in earlier times, had played host to great numbers of Jewish refugees fleeing from persecution in the West. Many Jews came to the Ottoman lands in the late fifteenth and early sixteenth centuries, mostly from southern Europe and, above all, from Spain. Like their coreligionists from further north, they brought with them the language of their country of origin, and a form of Spanish has remained in use among the Jews of Turkey and other former Ottoman territories to the present day.

The origins of Judeo-Spanish in many ways parallel that of Judeo-German in Eastern Europe. With an archaic form of Spanish as base, it absorbed a considerable vocabulary from the local languages, in this case principally Turkish and Greek, as well as a Hebraic and Talmudic component. Like Yiddish, it was written in the Hebrew script, and, used alongside Hebrew, served as the medium of a Jewish literature. The development of Ladino, as this language is sometimes called, did not however parallel that of Yiddish. For one thing, the numbers were much smaller, and unlike the Yiddish speakers in Poland and the adjoining countries they did not secure the general adoption of their language by their Jewish compatriots. Judeo-Spanish was commonly used in Turkey and in some of the Balkan countries under Turkish rule. But Greek Jews still spoke Greek, Jews in Arab countries still spoke Arabic, and isolated minorities continued to speak Kurdish, Aramaic, and other languages.

In most respects, the relations of the Ladino-speaking Jews with their non-Jewish neighbors were far better than in Eastern Europe.

The Jews of the Ottoman Empire never had to face anything like the Khmelnitsky massacres. They were, however, profoundly affected by one of its indirect consequences. In 1648, the year when the Khmelnitsky massacres began, a young Jew in Izmir, a student of the cabala called Shabtay Sevi, proclaimed himself to be the awaited Messiah. According to certain cabalistic writings, this was to be the year of the resurrection, and perhaps also of the redemption. The coming of the first miserable refugees from Poland, bringing terrible stories of rapine, sacrilege, and murder, seemed to portend the time of troubles which would precede the coming of Messiah and the establishment of God's kingdom on earth. There had been many false Messiahs during the centuries of the Jewish exile. None was so well heralded, nor so widely accepted as Shabtay Sevi. All over the Ottoman Empire, he was received with delirious acclaim in Jewish communities, and even as far away as Hamburg, Amsterdam, and London, staid Jewish businessmen sold their homes and possessions and prepared themselves for the journey to Jerusalem redeemed.

This strange episode in Jewish history came to a grotesque end when the Messiah of Izmir, arrested and imprisoned by the Turkish authorities on a charge of sedition, saved himself by becoming a convert to Islam, and spent the rest of his days as a pensioner of the sultan. Some of his most devout followers, seeing even this as part of his mission, followed him into the dominant faith, and founded the strange crypto-Jewish Muslim sect of the *dönme*. The remainder were left to face the realities of failure and humiliation.[4]

The Shabtay Sevi affair had a tremendous impact. It left a double legacy, on the one hand, discouragement verging on despair among the Jews; on the other, a reinforcement of rabbinical authority among the Jews in the Ottoman Empire. This was sanctioned and upheld by the state, which conferred on the Jewish communal leadership extensive coercive powers over their people.

Most of the Jews of the Islamic world lived under the rule or suzerainty of the Ottomans. There were however some communities beyond the Ottoman frontier, notably in Iran and Central Asia in the east and in Morocco in the west. There are no reliable statistics for any of these countries, but the number of Jews under Muslim rule in the Middle East and North Africa toward the end of the nineteenth century is estimated roughly at one million.

Some time in the Middle Ages two place names in the Hebrew

Bible, of uncertain meaning, were conventionally applied to Germany and Spain. The former was called Ashkenaz, the latter Sepharad, and in course of time the terms Ashkenazi and Sephardi were applied, respectively, to Jews of German and Iberian origin. There is no difference of doctrine, and almost no differences of law between the two, which diverge only in relatively minor points of synagogue ritual and liturgy. After the destruction at the end of the fifteenth century of what had once been the great and flourishing Jewish communities of Spain and Portugal, most of the surviving Jews in these countries fled to other Mediterranean lands, and notably to the Muslim lands in North Africa and the Middle East. There they joined the indigenous Jews in these countries, and the term Sephardi was used, inaccurately but almost universally, to denote these Jewish communities of the Muslim lands, although only a small proportion of them had originated in Spain. Small numbers of Spanish and Portuguese Jews also settled in France, Holland, North Germany, England, and the New World, but the overwhelming majority of Jews in these countries were of Ashkenazic origin.

Between them, the two great Jewries of the East, the Ashkenazic Jews of the Russian Empire and the Sephardic Jews of the Ottoman Empire, comprised the overwhelming majority of the Jewish people as a whole. Although the largest, they were also the least fortunate sections of the Jewish people. The Russian Jews were held back by oppression, the Ottoman Jews by the generally unfavorable circumstances in which they found themselves.

The Yiddish-speaking Jewry in Eastern Europe was unhappy with its status and was seeking without much success to better it. The Jewish *millet* of the Ottoman Lands in contrast was on the whole well satisfied with its status, but saw it gradually being eroded and crumbling away. The remaining and much smaller part of the Jewish people consisted of more or less assimilated religious minorities struggling with varying success to become part of the nations within which they lived. The further west, the smaller were the communities, and the greater the degree of assimilation. The largest of these communities were in the two Germanic empires of Central Europe, Germany and Austria-Hungary. Both had mixed communities, consisting of assimilated Western Jews in their western provinces, and unassimiliated or half assimilated ex-Polish Jews in the annexed eastern provinces. There were other much smaller groups in Western

Europe—France, Holland, Italy, and England—and there were new but growing communities in the United States and other countries of European settlement overseas. These Jewish minorities were barely distinguishable in language, culture, and way of life from their compatriots of the majority religion. The differences were diminishing with the parallel processes of emancipation and secularization. To the innocent optimists of the early decades of this century, it seemed that there would be no halt or hindrance to the continuation and completion of this process. They were to learn otherwise.

In the countries of Western Europe and the Americas, Jewish population figures are necessarily estimates, since the census in these countries, by tradition, does not include a question about religion. Such estimates are, however, scientifically grounded in various demographic methods. In the vast Russian Empire, official figures of Jewish population are available from 1897, when the first full census was completed. There are some fairly good estimates for the immediately preceding period. There are of course reliable figures for both Germany and Austria. In all these countries, the quality of statistics improves rapidly in the late nineteenth and early twentieth centuries, with the exception of those territories—especially in the Middle East and North Africa—to which modern administrative procedures had not yet been introduced.

A study of Jewish demography in the late nineteenth and early twentieth centuries reveals a number of interesting facts and trends. The most striking is the rapid increase in population. According to accepted estimates, the Jewish world population in about 1800 stood at some two and a half million. By 1840, it had risen to about four and a half million, by 1888 to seven and three quarter million, by 1900 to ten and a half million, and by 1939 to about seventeen million.[5]

In the eighteenth and nineteenth centuries, there was a major shift from Islam to Christendom. During the Middle Ages, the main centers of Jewish habitation and activity were in the Muslim lands— in the Near East, North Africa, and Spain. The proportions began to change after the end of the Middle Ages, and by about the beginning of the eighteenth century, European Jews are estimated to have reached numerical equality with their coreligionists in the lands of Islam. By 1800 they were more than half, and by the end of the nineteenth century an overwhelming majority of the total. Thereafter the massacre of the European Jews by Nazi Germany increased the relative importance of the Jews of the Orient.

These changes were due in part to the general decline of the Islamic world and the rise of the Christian world—phenomena which were shared in both cases by the Jewish communities living among followers of the majority religions. Jews were also affected by the rapid increase in the European birthrate during the nineteenth century, indeed to a greater extent than their Christian neighbors. From about 1800 the Jews became a predominantly European people.

Parallel with the shift from Islam to Christendom there was, within the Christian world, a shift in the opposite direction, from western to eastern Europe. By 1800, East European Jews are believed to have formed less than half of the whole. By 1825, this had risen to two thirds, by 1880 to three quarters. Thereafter the proportion of East European Jews in world Jewry began to decline, dropping about half in 1925. This latter change was due to the migrations of East European Jews, which began approximately in 1880, and which carried them in great numbers first into the adjoining central European territories, and then beyond them, especially to the English-speaking world, England, the British Empire, and the United States, and also to Latin America. The position of the Jews varied enormously, in their material and cultural condition, the measure of tolerance enjoyed or intolerance suffered, and the degree of integration into the life of the countries in which they lived.

In Central and Western Europe and in the overseas countries, the Jews in general enjoyed a high degree of tolerance during the nineteenth century. They had most though not all civic and political rights; such restrictions as they still suffered were irritating rather than onerous. They still had to face some hostility from their neighbors, but this was not serious by comparison either with earlier or subsequent periods in the history of continental Europe. The Jews of these countries had no spoken language of their own, other than that of the country. Hebrew, which they cherished, survived only as the language of sacred and liturgical texts. It was known only to rabbis and other learned men; the rest of the Jewish community knew at most only enough Hebrew to read their prayers without understanding them. Politically, too, the Jews of the West were identified with the countries of which they were citizens, as far as they were permitted, and sometimes more than that.

Nationalism was in the air in nineteenth-century Europe, and

Jews were affected in different ways. In the West, they became fervent patriots of the countries in which were more or less equal citizens. In the two Easts, European and Islamic, the situation was more complex and more difficult. Theoretically, the change from religious to national identities and loyalties should have improved their position, by transforming them from a barely tolerated religious minority to an integral part of the nation. In fact, with few exceptions, their position went from bad to worse. The old religiously expressed intolerance was modernized and magnified; the old restraints were weakened or removed. In a time of rapid social change and heightened ethnic awareness, the Jews were still seen, by followers of the majority religions, as unbelievers. In addition, they were now depicted as aliens to the nation, and exposed to different kinds of hostility, ranging from violent persecution in some countries to petty but wounding snobbery in others. The capacity of Jews to confront a hostile world was also changing and diminishing. For the traditional believing Jew, to suffer for his religion was a voluntary trial which he could endure with dignity, fortitude, and confidence. For the aspiring citizen of a modernizing state, it was a degradation and an affront against which he had no inner defense of self-respect.

If the new nationalism confronted Jews with new problems, to some it also suggested a new solution. If the nation—an entity defined by descent, culture, and aspiration—was the only natural and rightful basis of statehood, then the Jews were also a nation, and must have their own state. This was a very different notion from the old belief, cherished through the millennia, of a divine promise of an end to the dispersion, an ingathering of the exiles, and a rebuilding of Jerusalem.

The first modern precursor of this new idea, which in time came to be known as Zionism, was a Bosnian rabbi called Yehuda Alkalay, who in 1843 produced a scheme for a man-made Jewish restoration in Palestine, without waiting for the Messiah. The problem was posed for him and his contemporaries, in an acute form, by the anti-Jewish troubles and repression in Damascus in 1840; the model for a solution was provided by the Serbian and Greek national revivals and the establishment of an independent Serbia and Greece, after centuries of Ottoman domination.[6] There were other such examples of national liberation in nineteenth-century Europe, and in 1862 a rabbi in Posen, in Prussian Poland, exhorted his coreligionists to "take to heart the examples of the Italians, Poles, and Hungarians." [7] By now these ideas had gone beyond the rabbinical circles which had hitherto almost exclusively provided Jewish intellectual leadership. In the same year Moses Hess, an emancipated radical German Jew, published his *Rome and Jerusalem*, the first of a long series of socialist Zionist utopias. In the course of the nineteenth century, the idea of a Jewish national restoration in Palestine became widely known. It aroused the attention of Jews in many lands; it even attracted the attention of Christian observers as diverse as Napoleon, Lord Palmerston, Lord Shaftesbury, and the novelist George Eliot.

The term Zionist and the political movement called by that name were both born in Austria-Hungary, where assimilated modern Jews and unassimilated traditional Jews lived side by side, encountering both modern and traditional antagonisms. The founder of the Zionist organization was Theodor Herzl, a Hungarian-born Jew working as a journalist in Vienna; the history of the Zionist movement is conventionally dated from the publication of his booklet, *The Jewish State*, in 1896.

Herzl had until then been an assimilated Western Jew—ignorant of Hebrew and even of Judaism, unconcerned with Jewish affairs. He achieved his personal moment of truth when, as the Paris correspondent of a Vienna daily newspaper, he attended the trial on charges of treason of Captain Alfred Dreyfus. An Alsatian Jew who was a career officer attached to the French General Staff, Dreyfus was charged with selling military secrets to Germany. Found guilty by a court-martial in 1894, he was sentenced to life imprisonment in a fortress. A long series of judicial struggles followed, which ended only in 1906, when Dreyfus was declared innocent and restored to his rank. During these years, when the bitter struggle between the pro-Dreyfus and anti-Dreyfus factions dominated public life in France, French anti-Semitism revealed itself as a vicious and powerful force. The strength of anti-Jewish feeling, and the willingness of high dignitaries in the church, the state, and the army to condone the condemnation of an innocent man and the fabrication of evidence for this purpose, came as a profound shock. This was all the greater, in that this first rampant outbreak of militant anti-Semitism occurred in France—the home of the great Revolution, of the liberal principles of liberty, equality, and fraternity, the first country which had given full equality to all its citizens irrespective of creed. There had been earlier attacks on the newly emancipated Jews of Western Europe, but they had for the most part been confined to journalism and pamphleteering, and could be dismissed as of little importance. Even the sometimes hostile portrayal of Jewish characters by the great nineteenth-century novelists was no doubt unpleasant for Jews in society, but did not seem to pose a serious threat. The campaign against Dreyfus, the vehemence with which it was expressed, and the support which it mustered, made some Jews in France and other Western countries wonder how fragile their recently gained rights really were.

For the majority, the answer was to persevere in the path of emancipation and assimilation. During the eighteenth and nineteenth centuries—earlier in Holland and England—Jews in Western countries had made immense progress and were gaining steadily in civil and ultimately political rights. The Dreyfus Affair—which ended happily—revealed the depths of feeling against the Jews. It also revealed the strength and numbers of those who were willing to do battle to protect their Jewish compatriots. To many, probably most, who considered the matter, it seemed reasonable to assume that even the Dreyfus Affair was no more than a temporary setback, a brief revival of old feelings and prejudices which had no place in the modern age.

There were others, still a small minority in Western Europe, who took another view, and accepted Theodor Herzl's argument that assimilation and emancipation could not work. The Jews, he said, were a nation. Their problem was neither economic nor religious, but national, i.e., political. It could be solved only by the Jews acquiring a territory over which they would exercise sovereignty and in which they would form a state.

If the response to Theodor Herzl and his movement in Western Europe was limited and sometimes indeed very negative, the situation was very different in Eastern Europe, where his diagnosis and prescription were seen as having far greater relevance. If, with few exceptions, the Jews of the West were too confident, the Jews of Islam too remote and isolated to respond to Herzl's appeal, those of Eastern Europe found his arguments familiar as well as cogent.

The position of east European Jews was vastly different from that of their coreligionists in the West. The parallel processes of emancipation and assimilation, which had transformed the Western communities, had barely begun in Eastern Europe and were soon reversed.

The position of the Jews of Poland after the partition of that country among Prussia, Russia, and Austria varied greatly. In both Prussian and Austrian Poland, Jews gained greatly from inclusion in a modern or modernizing state with some respect for human rights and the rule of law. In Prussian Poland, where the state was more modern, the nation homogeneous, and the Jewish minority relatively small, the process of Germanization was rapid. In Austria, where a less modern state ruled over a multinational population, and the Jews were more numerous, the process of modernization was slower, but by no means imperceptible. But by far the greater part of the Polish Jews passed under Russian rule, and their situation was much worsened by this change.

As a result of the successive partitions of Poland, the largest Jewish community in Europe came under the rule of that state which had hitherto shown the least tolerance towards Jews. From time to time during the nineteenth century there were attempts at liberalizing reforms, but these were of limited effect, and during the last decades of czarist rule the position of the Jews in the Russian Empire became steadily worse. The defeat of Russia by Japan and the unsuccessful revolution of 1905 subjected Russian society and the czarist state to grave strains. The rulers responded by trying, with some success, to divert popular anger against the Jews, who were accused of being both revolutionaries and Japanese sympathizers. Anti-Semitism now became a part of Russian official policy, and was actively promoted at both the bureaucratic and popular levels. A particularly active part was played by the armed gangs, with local police and clerical support, known as the Black Hundreds. These served as the spearhead of active and violent anti-Semitism, fomenting and organizing pogroms. Ruling over greater numbers of Jews than could be disposed of with premodern techniques of persecution, the Russian government resorted instead to active discrimination and oppression. Jews were deprived of most of the ordinary rights of citizens; they were not allowed to penetrate east of the Pale into the older Russian lands, nor to go, without special permission, to St. Petersburg, Moscow, or other Russian cities. Some Jews, privileged through wealth, were given the right of residence in these places. The impoverished majority were excluded.

Within the Pale of Settlement, Jews suffered at the hands both of their Russian masters and their Polish neighbors. The old Polish tolerance, which had made Poland a haven of refuge for the harassed Jews of Western Europe, was now gone, and relations between Jews and Poles worsened in the harsh conditions of Russian government. Ruled by the Orthodox Russians and deprived of any institutional political structure of their own, the Poles found the citadel of their nationhood in the Catholic Church. Ousted from their previous position of dominance by the new Russian nobility and administration, they were pushed down in the social and economic scale, and compelled to compete for a livelihood with their own former Jewish henchmen. Though Jews had fought for Poland in 1794 and in the unsuccessful risings against Russia in 1830 and 1860, they were rebuffed by the Poles, who for the most part refused to recognize them as part of the Polish nation.

When the Jews had sought to fight alongside the Poles, they were first rejected, and then accepted only in separate Jewish formations attached to the militia and not to the regular army. The Russians proceeded differently. Jews were drafted into the army, but—with the exception of the very few who had managed to acquire medical or other professional qualifications—were confined to the lowest ranks. A ukase (a Russian imperial decree) of 1827 instituted a special arrangement for Jewish boys. A specified number were to be conscripted at the age of twelve or less and were to serve for twenty-five years, this period to date from when they reached the age of eighteen. This practice was reminiscent of the famous *devshirme*, the Ottoman levy of Christian boys from among the subject populations in the Balkan Peninsula. The sultans abandoned this practice in the early seventeenth century; the czars adopted it in the nineteenth.

Russian hostility to the Jews was still of the old-fashioned religious and not the new-fashioned racial kind. Professing Jews were almost totally excluded from the officer corps, the civil service, the universities, the professions. But baptism opened almost all doors, and the Jewish convert to the Russian Orthodox Church could rise to high and important positions. Some few availed themselves of this opportunity. One such was the Orientalist Daniel Chwolson (1819–1911). Born in a village called Eyshishok, in Lithuania, he went to university in Breslau, in Germany, since Russian universities were closed to him. After his return to Russia, he was baptized into the Orthodox

Church and this made possible his appointment in 1855 as a professor at the newly established Faculty of Oriental Languages in the University of St. Petersburg. Legend has it that Chwolson was once asked if he had become a Christian out of sincere conviction, to which he replied: "Yes, I was convinced it was better to be a professor in St. Petersburg than a *melamed* (Hebrew schoolteacher) in Eyshishok."[8]

In general, however, there were remarkably few such converts. If the Russian and Polish Jews were subject to far harsher conditions than their coreligionists elsewhere, they were also better equipped to resist and survive them. The Polish Jews had retained a strong communal organization dating back to the days of the old Polish monarchy and to the high degree of autonomy which they had enjoyed under Polish rule. This communal organization, though badly shaken and much diminished, nevertheless remained strong enough to give some backbone to Jewish life. The Jews also had their own educational system, from primary schools to rabbinical seminaries, almost entirely under their own control. Though this education was in a sense medieval, it nevertheless preserved a living intellectual tradition, based on the Talmudic and related rabbinic literature. The curriculum of the Jewish schools did not equip their products for modern life in the nineteenth century, still less in the twentieth. It did, however, give them a rigorous intellectual discipline, and a strong sense of their own historical and cultural identity. It also gave them a cultural standard which was certainly no worse and in many ways better than that of the peoples among whom they lived.

The situation of Jews in Russia changed decisively for the worse after March 13, 1881, when revolutionaries threw a bomb which killed the Czar Alexander II, just at the moment when he was about to install some form of constitutional government. The new czar, Alexander III, and his advisers believed that the problems of Russia would only be solved by autocracy and repression. Konstantin Pobedonostsev, the chief procurator of the Holy Synod and the czar's most influential adviser, set forth his own program for solving the problem posed to Russia by its vast Jewish population. One third would become Christians, one third emigrate, one third perish.

Orthodoxy, Russification, and autocracy were the dominant features of Russian government in this period. All this made life uncomfortable for the Jews. The old rules against them were more strictly enforced, and new ones were now devised. The Pale of Settlement had already been reduced, and severer restrictions imposed on movements of Jews outside it. Now still further restrictions were imposed on residence, travel, and livelihood even within the Pale. Beginning Easter 1881, a new and ominous dimension was added to the persecution of Jews in Russia—the pogrom. The attack on the Jews in Russia was no longer primarily official, bureaucratic, and to that extent regulated. It was popular and violent and threatened not just their livelihood but their lives.

Massacre was no new experience for the Jews of Europe, but it was not a recent one. In the West, the ages of humanism and the Enlightenment had virtually put an end to the excesses of the Middle Ages, and even in Eastern Europe, despite severe repression and occasional outbreaks, there had been no large-scale massacres of Jews since the seventeenth century. The Russian pogroms beginning in 1881 came therefore as a shock not only to the Jews, but to the public opinion of the civilized world, which at that time still showed concern and could still command respect. Meetings of protest in London, Paris, and elsewhere were attended by prominent members of the churches, parliaments, universities, and other figures of public life. These no doubt helped to limit though not to end the pogroms, which continued into the twentieth century.

Pogrom is a Russian word meaning massacre. It passed from Russian into the English language at about this time, with the specialized meaning of a massacre of Jews. There were many such massacres, the most famous of which occurred in the city of Kishinev, in the province of Bessarabia, in the spring of 1903. There can be no doubt that the czarist police at the very least tolerated, and frequently instigated these attacks on the Jews.

In the circumstances, it was hardly surprising that the Jews of Eastern Europe should have given some attention to Zionism, as well as to other proposed solutions of a problem that daily grew more acute and more dangerous. Before very long it was the Jews of Eastern Europe, and East European Jews settled in the West, who provided the mainstay of the Zionist movement founded by Theodor Herzl. Indeed, in a very real sense, Jewish nationalism and the State of Israel, its ultimate result, were the creation of the Yiddish-speaking Jewry of Eastern Europe. Its romanticism, its socialism, its populism, its linkage of religion and national identity are all familiar features of East European political thought and life.

Zionism has many sources. Some of these are traditionally and authentically Jewish, notably the Jewish religion itself, with its recurring stress on Zion, Jerusalem, and the Holy Land, and on the interwoven themes of bondage and liberation, of exile and return. These occupy a central position in the Jewish religious tradition, and a worshipper is reminded of them daily and throughout the year in the liturgy of the synagogue.

Another source was Hassidism, a movement of religious revival and messianic hope which arose among Polish Jews in the late seventeenth century, in part as a response to the shock of the Khmelnitsky massacres, and which affected large parts of East European Jewry. This movement, which gave new warmth and vitality to the rabbinic Judaism of that time, was an important, perhaps a necessary prerequisite to the growth and spread of the Zionist movement. Certainly, a large proportion of the pioneers of Zionism were men of Hassidic background. Hassidic Jews, or rather Jews of Hassidic origin, figured even more prominently in the Hebrew revival, which provided an essential cultural background for a movement of Jewish national liberation. The origins of the Hebrew revival have been traced back to Germany of the Enlightenment and even to Renaissance Italy, where for the first time Jews, emerging from their ghettos, were affected by the intellectual movements agitating their Christian compatriots, and tried to bring these ideas to their fellow Jews in a new Hebrew secular literature. The Hebrew revival first became a major factor in nineteenth-century Russia, where there were Jews in sufficient numbers, with a high enough level of literacy in Hebrew, to produce the writers, printers, publishers, distributors, and readers of Hebrew novels, poems, essays, and magazines. By 1880 Hebrew, though still not a spoken language, had undergone a considerable process of modernization, and was extensively used to discuss the problems of modern Jewish life as well as the more conventional topics of religion and law.

Linked with these new trends was the Jewish tradition of Messianism—the belief in a Redeemer who would rescue the Jews from captivity and exile and restore them to their promised homeland. There had in the past been many aspirants to this role, some better known than others. The failure and apostasy of Shabtay Sevi, the last of these messiahs, brought disillusionment and despair. After this time, the Jews—now exposed to new, external influences—began to look elsewhere for the realization of their messianic hopes, and to turn from religious to secular redemption.

There was plenty for the redeemer to do. Throughout Eastern Europe Jews were the victims of poverty, repression, permanent discrimination, and occasional persecution. Some Jews were attracted by ideas and ideologies current among the Eastern European peoples amid whom they lived. Some of these ideologies seemed to offer solutions, which the gradual growth of secular knowledge among the Jews made accessible and even attractive. Socialism, populism, and even anarchism all made their contributions to the emergence of yet one more brand of East European ethnic nationalism. There were some who believed that the Jews should fight for freedom shoulder to shoulder with their gentile neighbors, defining their cause and their objectives sometimes in national, sometimes in class terms. Others—the Zionists—saw the basic cause of their troubles in the universal minority status of Jews, and believed with Herzl that only in a Jewish country, ruled eventually by a Jewish state, would they be able to achieve true emancipation.

Many East European Jews found a more personal solution to their problems by emigrating. Between 1870 and 1900 more than half a million East European Jews migrated westward. Between 1900 and 1914 the figure exceeded about a million and a half. Altogether about one third of East European Jews are estimated to have left their homes for the West. Of the remainder, the overwhelming majority stayed where they were, most of them engaged in a precarious personal struggle for survival. Some—few but important—sought a political end to their troubles through participation in Russian and other revolutionary movements.

Another group, insignificant in numbers but far-reaching in effect, found another way. In 1882, fourteen years before the publication of Herzl's *Jewish State,* a group of Jewish students formed an organization called Lovers of Zion. Their aim was emigration—not to Western lands of opportunity but to a remote Ottoman province known in Christendom but not—at that time—to its inhabitants as Palestine. The settlements which they and their successors founded, in the teeth of immense difficulties and obstacles, formed the nucleus of what eventually became the State of Israel.

Between 1917, when the British government published the Balfour Declaration giving its blessing to the idea of a Jewish national home in Palestine, and 1933, when Adolf Hitler came to power in Germany, the development of the Jewish National Home under the British Mandatory Government in Palestine was steady but slow. The great majority of the new Jewish immigrants came from Eastern Europe, and their motives for going to Palestine, rather than elsewhere, were predominantly ideological. They were coming to build a Jewish national home. To this end they built farms and villages, roads and cities, and created a new structure of Jewish life.

Between the two world wars the Jews of Europe suffered two major disasters. The second and the greater began with the triumph of Adolf Hitler in Germany in 1933. The first, following the collapse of czardom, was in Eastern Europe. The ravages of revolution, civil war, and intervention, with the resulting disruption and famine, decimated the population in general. The Jews were at a disadvantage, being attacked as Poles by the Russians, as Russians by the Poles, and as Jews by both. The Ukraine was once again the scene of appalling massacres, reminiscent of the days of Bohdan Khmelnitsky. Between 1917 and 1920 at least 75,000 Jews were slaughtered in the Ukraine, as well as smaller numbers in some of the newly independent nations of Eastern Europe.

Gradually, with the ending of warfare and the consolidation of the new regimes, the situation of the Jews as of others began to improve. The early years of the new Soviet regime in Russia were a time of appalling hardship, but Jews were no worse off than others. In the emergent national states of Eastern Europe, the Baltic Republics, Poland and Rumania, Jews were very far from enjoying either security or equal rights, but the endemic anti-Semitism of these countries was somewhat restrained by a regard for outside opinion. In Germany and Austria, where the limits on Jewish advancement set by the old imperial regimes were to a large extent removed by the new republics, the Jews were able to enter many places that were previously closed to them. In Western Europe and the Americas they seemed to be well on the way towards complete acceptance and integration as a religious minority no different from any other.

In all these countries there were from time to time signs and portents, which were picked up and interpreted by the Zionists and ignored by most others. The new Polish republic, reconstituted from the lands which had previously been partitioned among Poland's three neighbors, had inherited some three million Jews, of whom at least one third were living in destitution. The new Polish rulers were first interested in restoring their own national life, which they identified with Polish Catholicism. They had little interest in the needs of their Jewish and other non-Catholic or non-Polish minorities. The Jews found themselves subject to all kinds of restrictions—in access to education, to professions, even to handicrafts, and many of them sought a solution to their problems in emigration. Similar problems made life difficult for Jews in Rumania and other East European countries.

At the beginning of 1933 Adolf Hitler, whom many had been prepared to write off as a crank from the lunatic fringe, was elected chancellor of the German Reich. Even then, few besides his own followers and disciples believed that he would really carry out the appalling promises of his writings and speeches. Instead, it was widely assumed that the responsibilities of power would bring a wiser and calmer approach to Jewish as well as to other problems.

They did not. The war against the Jews was among the very first tasks which he attacked on his accession to power. German Jews were deprived of all rights and subjected to humiliation and persecution. Before very long, the same and then far worse treatment was extended to the Jews of other countries—to Austria and Czechoslovakia as these were brought under the control of the German government and ultimately to almost the whole of continental Europe.

In 1914 the Jewish population of the area which subsequently became Mandatory Palestine was estimated at 90,000. During the war years it was somewhat reduced, but began to increase again under the British Mandate, reaching 181,000 at the beginning of 1933. Thereafter it rose rapidly, reaching 446,000 by the outbreak of war and close on 600,000 at the time of the establishment of the Jewish state in May 1948. Between 1945 and 1948 the major immigration came from Europe—the human debris left by the destruction of Hitler's empire. A second wave, which began before the establishment of the state and continued after it, came from the Arab countries.

Like the white Anglo-Saxon Protestants in the United States, the

East European pioneers and their descendants in Israel have ceased to form the majority of the population. Again like their American counterparts, the founding fathers of Israel and their descendants have struggled to retain their primacy. This rests on two important elements. One, the more practical, is their continued predominance in the interlocking system of personal, family, and institutional loyalties, which constitutes the Israeli establishment. The other is through the stamp which they imposed on the very nature of the Israeli state and society. The first modern Jewish settlement in Palestine was the creation of East European pioneers. Subsequent immigrants from Central Europe and later from the countries of Asia and Africa were constrained with greater or lesser willingness to assimilate to the pattern established by these pioneers. In recent years, there has been increasing resistance to this process of assimilation.

Since the establishment of the state, there has been only a trickle of immigration from Europe and the Americas. For a while a wave of anti-Semitism brought some immigration from South America; a temporary relaxation in the laws preventing the departure of Soviet citizens allowed some thousands of Russian Jews to settle in Israel. In addition to these, there has been a small movement of individuals and families from Western Europe and English-speaking countries. By far the most important immigration, however, since the establishment of the state, came from the Arab and other Islamic countries of the Middle East and North Africa. They and their descendants now form a majority of the total Jewish population of Israel, and they have begun, perceptibly, to penetrate the upper reaches of the political and military establishment. With their higher birthrate, their majority is likely to grow. With increasing opportunity, they are likely to play a greater role.

In recent years there have been serious tensions between the two major components of the Jewish population, which are sometimes presented as a clash between Ashkenazic and Sephardic Jews. This is a misnomer. These are terms relating to the ritual of the synagogue and are in any case used loosely and inaccurately. Some, borrowing the vocabulary of fashionable politics, speak of a clash between Euro-American and Afro-Asian Jews, but that too is irrelevant. What is occurring now in Israel is a confrontation between the Jews of Christendom and the Jews of Islam, both groups bringing with them certain attitudes, habits, and cultural traditions from their countries and societies of origin. They have now come together in an intense symbiosis. The results which they achieve will be significant not only for the Jews of both communities and for Israel, which is obvious, but even in a sense for Islam and Christendom themselves.

CHAPTER FOUR

Anti-Semites

THE TERM ANTI-SEMITISM was first used in 1879, and seems to have been invented by one Wilhelm Marr, a minor Jew-baiting journalist with no other claim to memory.[1] Significantly, it first appeared as a political program in Vienna, the capital of the sprawling and variegated Hapsburg monarchy, which was also the birthplace of Zionism and of many other nationalist movements, and the meeting place of traditional Eastern and secular Western Jews.

Though the name anti-Semitism was new, the special hatred of the Jews which it designated was very old, going back to the rise of Christianity. From the time when the Roman Emperor Constantine embraced the new faith and Christians obtained control of the apparatus of the state, there were few periods during which some Jews were not being persecuted in one or other part of the Christian world. Hostility to Jews was sometimes restrained, sometimes violent, sometimes epidemic, always endemic. But though hatred of the Jew was old, the term anti-Semitism did indeed denote a significant change—not the initiation but rather the culmination of a major shift in the way this hatred was felt, perceived, and expressed. In medieval times hostility to the Jew, whatever its underlying social or psychological motivations, was defined primarily in religious terms. From the fifteenth century onward this was no longer true, and Jew hatred was redefined, becoming at first partly, and then, at least in theory, wholly racial.

The earlier hostility was basically and indeed profoundly religious. It was concerned with the rejection by the Jew of the Christian redeemer and message, and was documented by the account in the Gospels of the Jewish role in the life and death of Christ. The Jew was denounced and at times persecuted as a Christ killer and as a denier of God's truths. While this hatred might be stimulated and directed by the roles which Jews were compelled to play in medieval Christian society, their persecutors did not normally condemn them for being different in race and language. Conversion to Christianity, if sincere, was considered to confer full equality and acceptance. This seems to have been true in practice as well as in theory, in Eastern as well as in Western Europe. Indeed, it is said that in the medieval Duchy of Lithuania, Jews who adopted Christianity were accorded the status of noblemen, because of their kinship to the Mother of God.

This religious hostility acquired racial overtones when Jews were compelled, under penalty of death or exile, to adopt Christianity. A voluntary conversion may be accepted as sincere. A forced conversion inevitably arouses the suspicion, above all among the enforcers, that it may be insincere. This is particularly true where the converts are very numerous, where they tend to intermarry with the families of other converts, and where they continue to play the same role in society that brought them envy and hatred as Jews. There had been occasional forced conversions throughout the Middle Ages, but these were mostly minor and episodic. The only full-scale expulsion of Jews from a whole country was from England in 1290, but the numbers were few, and there seems to have been little or no aftereffect among the English.

A very different situation arose in Spain, where Jews were present in great numbers, and had been very prominent in the social, cultural, economic, and occasionally even the political life of the country. Their position had been profoundly affected, both for good and for evil, by the eight-centuries-long struggle between Islam and Christendom for the domination of the peninsula. While Muslims and Christians lived side by side, both were obliged, even in the intervals of warfare, to show some tolerance to one another, and Jews benefitted from this in both Christian and Muslim Spain. But as the final Christian victory grew nearer, there was less and less willingness to tolerate any presence that would flaw the unity of Catholic Spain. In 1492, with the defeat and conquest of the Emirate of Granada, the last Muslim state on Spanish soil, the reconquest and rechristianization of Spain was complete. In the same year an edict of expulsion was pronounced against Jews, followed some years later by a similar decree against Muslims. Followers of both religions were given the choice of exile, conversion, or death.

From this time onward no professing Jew or Muslim remained in Spain or—a few years later—in Portugal. Great numbers departed in exile, but many preferred to stay, and went through a form of baptism in order to qualify. Not surprisingly, they were regarded with some suspicion by their neighbors, and there can be no doubt that there were great numbers of crypto-Muslims and crypto-Jews masquerading as Catholics. The former were commonly known as Morisco, in allusion to their presumed homeland in Africa. The latter, who had no homeland other than Spain, were called Marrano, a Spanish word meaning hog. A more polite designation for both groups was *nuevos Cristianos*, new Christians, in contrast to the *viejos Cristianos*, the old Christians, free from "any taint of Moorish or Jewish blood."

Even before the expulsions, the absence or presence of such a taint had become an obsession, affecting the crown, the church, and much of Spanish society. The *converso* or convert was suspect to all three. The king needed loyalty against the ancient Moorish enemy. The Holy Office of the Inquisition was determined to extirpate heresy and unbelief—and where were these more likely to occur than among the *conversos* and their descendants? And the general population, delighted with the expulsion of unwelcome neighbors and competitors, were appalled to find that many of them were still around, lightly disguised as Christians. As far back as 1449, the first statute of purity of blood (*estatuto de limpieza de sangre*) was promulgated in Toledo. It declared *conversos* unworthy to hold positions of public or private trust in the city and dominions of Toledo. A series of other statutes to defend the purity of blood followed in the fifteenth century and after, by which Moriscos and Marranos were barred from various offices and orders and, incidentally, from the Inquisition itself, in which *conversos* had at an earlier stage been very active. In 1628 or shortly after, a Spanish inquisitor called Juan Escobar de Corro explained what was involved: "By *converso* we commonly understand any person descended from Jews or Saracens, be it in the most distant degree. . . . Similarly a New Christian is thus designated not because he has recently been converted to the Christian faith but rather because he is a descendant of those who first adopted the correct religion."[2]

Several of the monastic orders adopted rules barring *conversos* and their descendants from membership. At first, the Papacy was opposed to such rules, insisting on the equality of all baptized Christians, but in 1495, a Spanish Pope, Alexander VI, formally ratified a statute passed by a Spanish order barring all *conversos* from membership. Thereafter, most such statutes were approved or at least tolerated by the popes. Thus, for example, in 1515 the archbishop of Seville, a former grand inquisitor, barred second generation descendants of "heretics" from holding any ecclesiastical office or benefice in the cathedral of that city. This statute was approved by the Pope, and subsequently extended to include the grandchildren and later the great-grandchildren of heretics. In 1530, the bishop of Cordova adopted a similar set of rules but went further, banning even the admission of New Christian choirboys. Describing the descendants of Jews and *conversos* as "a trouble-making tribe *(generación)*, friends of novelties and dissensions, ambitious, presumptuous, restless, and such that wherever this tribe is found there is little peace,"[3] the decree bars the admission of such persons as prejudicial to the interests of the Church. The statute prescribed a procedure to establish the purity of a candidate's blood. He must swear a solemn oath that he is not of Jewish or Moorish descent, and must give the names of his parents and grandparents with the places of their birth. An investigator was to be sent to these places, and only after he had established that there were no New Christians among the candidate's ancestors could he be admitted.

In its origins, the concern with "purity of blood" is religious, not racial. It begins with the suspicion that the *converso* is a false and insincere Christian, and that he imparts these qualities to his descendants. The notion of purity of blood was not new, but in the past, in medieval Christian Europe, it had had a social rather than a racial connotation, being concerned more with aristocratic than with ethnic superiority. But the special circumstances of fifteenth and sixteenth century Spain—the old confrontation with the Moors, the new encounter with blacks and Indians in Africa and the Americas, and the presence in Spain of New Christians in such great numbers and in such active roles, brought in time an unmistakably racial content to the hostility directed against these groups.

But even while the Spanish Inquisition was completing its allotted task, to seek out and destroy the hidden remnants of Spanish Judaism and Islam, further north a new spirit was moving, and a new and radical idea was put forward—that religion was a private affair and no concern of the state, and that followers of all religions were equally entitled to the rights of citizenship. As a result of the terrible religious and quasi-religious wars which devastated France, Germany, the Netherlands, and Britain in the sixteenth and seventeenth centuries, a kind of war-weary tolerance, or perhaps rather lassitude, began to appear. The once universal religious fanaticism was by no means dead, but increasing numbers of people, both rulers and philosophers, began to seek for ways in which Catholics and Protestants of various denominations could live side by side in peace, instead of waging perpetual war.

One of the most influential was the English philosopher John Locke, whose *Letter Concerning Toleration* was published in both Latin and English in 1689. Many of the ideas expressed in it were already current among philosophers in Britain and on the Continent. In one respect, however, Locke went far beyond his predecessors, and that is in his conclusion that "neither Pagan nor Mahometan, nor Jew, ought to be excluded from the civil rights of the commonwealth because of his religion."[4] There were no "Mahometans" in Western Europe and few who dared avow themselves pagans. There were however Jews, who gradually became aware of the new mood and the opportunities which it offered them.

The first European country to give civil emancipation to its Jews was Holland. It was followed within a short time by England, which granted extensive though by no means equal rights to Jews both at home and in the English colonies beyond the seas. The ideas of Locke and other English libertarians spread both to the American colonies and to France, where they contributed significantly to the ideologies of both the American and French revolutions. Though neither revolution immediately accorded full equality to Jewish citizens, both took the first significant steps which ultimately led in that direction. In Germany, too, the eighteenth-century enlightenment brought a change in attitudes, though it was not until Germany was conquered by Napoleon's armies that the new revolutionary doctrines gave some measure of civil rights to the German Jews. Imposed by French bayonets, these were a cause of fierce controversy in the years that followed the French departure.

Even in revolutionary France, the path of freedom did not run

smooth.[5] The famous Declaration of the Rights of Man, passed by the
French National Assembly at the end of August 1789, had significant
gaps. For one thing, it did not apply to the black slave population of
the French West Indies, whose fate became a subject of passionate
debate. Their emancipation did not come until later. For Jews—
present and visible in France—things went somewhat faster. In January 1790, after some argument, the status of "active citizens" was
extended to the old established Sephardic community of Bordeaux.
But the far more numerous Jews of Alsace-Lorraine, living among a
rather more hostile population, were excluded and it was not until
the end of September 1791 that the National Assembly passed a
general law enfranchising all Jews.

Several of the interventions in the debate express in vivid terms
the point of view of the eighteenth-century Enlightenment and its
philosophers. Thus, for example, a Protestant spokesman, pleading
for his own people, added a word for the Jews as well:

I ask of you gentlemen, for the French Protestants, for all the non-Catholics
of the Kingdom, that which you ask for yourselves, liberty, equality of rights;
I ask them for this people torn from Asia, always wandering, always proscribed, always persecuted for more than eighteen centuries, which would
adopt our manners and customs, if by our laws that people were incorporated with us, and to which we have no right to reproach its morals, because
they are the fruit of our own barbarism and of the humiliation to which we
have unjustly condemned them.[6]

And Robespierre himself adjured the Chamber:

The vices of the Jews derive from the degradation in which you have
plunged them; they will be good when they can find some advantage in
being good.[7]

Such statements in defense of the Jews and their rights did not
begin with the French Revolution. They were part of a tradition
which dates back to the late seventeenth century and which continued into the twentieth—a tradition which has been called philo-
Semitism, which defended the Jews against their detractors, attributed their faults to persecution, and pleaded for their admission
to equal rights and full citizenship. This was a new phenomenon,
without precedent in the history of Christendom. It had a powerful
effect on the Jews who, in this new atmosphere and thanks to new
laws, began to emerge, at first warily, then more confidently, from

their seclusion—from the physical ghettoes in which their rulers and neighbors had for so long confined them, from the ghettoes of the mind in which they had enclosed themselves.

But this new situation brought new enemies, or at least new forms of enmity. One kind came from the very circles that had been most helpful to Jewish emancipation—from some of the deists and liberal philosophers of the Enlightenment. For many of these, the Church was the main enemy of humanity, and the Bible—the Jewish Bible —was the instrument of the Church. Voltaire's famous phrase, "Ecrasez l'infâme," expressed succinctly what the deists thought of the Church, and what they wished to do to it. But in eighteenth-century Europe, even in the Protestant democracies, to attack the Church, or to question the Bible, was still hazardous if not impossible. It was safer and easier to tackle the enemy from the rear—to criticize and ridicule the Old, not the New Testament; to attack not Christianity but Judaism, the source from which Christianity sprang and of which it still retained many features. If, for Christians, the crime of the Jews was that they had killed Christ, for the new anti-Christians it was rather that they had nurtured him. This line of thought continued into the nineteenth century, when a favorite accusation levied against the Catholic Church by its enemies in Germany was that it was "penetrated through and through with Semitism." This reached new heights in Hitler's time.

One of the most vehement critics of the Jews, in these terms, was the great Voltaire, whose hostility to both Judaism and the Jews— allegedly due to some personal difficulties with individual Jews— finds frequent expression in his writings. Indeed, the question has been asked whether Voltaire was anti-Jewish because he was anti-clerical, or anti-Christian because he was anti-Jewish. An acute observer, the Prince de Ligne, after spending eight days as Voltaire's guest at Ferney and hearing his views at length, remarked: "The only reason why M. de Voltaire gave vent to such outbursts against Jesus Christ is that He was born among a nation whom he detested."[8]

Voltaire himself remarked, in one of his notebooks, in his own English: "When I see Christians cursing Jews, methinks I see children beating their fathers. Jewish religion is the mother of Christianity, and grand mother of the mahometism."[9] There are other indications in Voltaire's writings of a cast of thought which can fairly be described as racist, as when he remarks, quite wrongly, that in ancient

Rome "the Jews were regarded in the same way as we regard Negroes, as an inferior species of men."[10] In another place, ironically, in his *Traité de Métaphysique,* his philosophical narrator observes that white men "seem to me superior to Negroes, just as Negroes are superior to monkeys and monkeys to oysters."[11]

Some clue to Voltaire's antiblack racism may be found in a detail from his biography. The philosopher was engaged in a number of financial enterprises, some of them rather questionable. The most relevant was a large-scale investment in a slave trading enterprise out of the French port of Nantes, which according to contemporary witnesses made him "one of the twenty wealthiest *(les mieux rentés)* persons in the kingdom."[12]

It was indeed against the blacks, and in defense of the enormously profitable slave trade, that the new form of racism first made its appearance. It was not until some time later that it was applied to the Jews. Both the American and French revolutions, despite their passionate love of liberty, had neglected to extend it to their black slaves, the one in the southern states, the other in the West Indies. This contradiction did not pass unnoticed, and before long the slave dealers and plantation owners found themselves on the defensive against the growing barrage of criticism, dating back to before the revolutions, in three of the major West European colonial powers— England, France, and Holland—and later also in the United States. For ordinary individuals, simple greed may suffice to justify their actions. For a society, however, formally at least committed to a religion or an ideology, some theoretical justification is required, for themselves as well as for others, to justify so fearsome an action as the enslavement of a whole race. When the Israelites, in accordance with the universal practice of the ancient world, enslaved the Canaanites whom they had conquered, they felt the need to legitimize this in terms of their own religious ethic, and found an answer in the story of the curse of Ham—Noah's son, who committed an offense against his father and was punished by a curse of servitude falling upon him and his descendants. In the biblical story, it is only on one line of his descendants, Canaan, that the curse in fact fell. When the Muslim Arabs, advancing into tropical Africa from the Middle East and North Africa, initiated the great flow of black slaves into the outside world, they too felt the need to justify this action. The first answer was that the blacks were idolators and therefore liable to Holy War and en-

slavement; and when—with the spread of Islam among the blacks—
this no longer sufficed, some of them adapted the story of the curse
of Ham and, transferring it from the Canaanites to the Africans,
amended the curse of servitude to a double curse of servitude and
blackness.

Some of these ancient and medieval stories found their way,
through Spain and Portugal and the Atlantic islands, to the slave
plantations of the New World. But by the end of the eighteenth
century—after the American and French Revolutions—the curse of
Ham and similar arguments were no longer sufficient. A substitute,
or rather a supplement, was found in the new science of anthropology, which had made impressive progress in this period. Scientists
were now beginning to classify human beings according to their
color, the size and shape of their bodies, the shape and measure-
ments of their skulls. From the anthropologists, this new knowledge
affected such major intellectual figures as Johann Gottfried Herder
(1744–1803) and Immanuel Kant (1724–1804), both of whom gave
great importance to ethnic and even racial factors in culture and
history.

Herder and Kant, like the early anthropologists, were still men of
the Enlightenment. Attached to their own races, they were nevertheless ready to respect some others, and did not develop a doctrine
of racial superiority. But some of the writers of the late eighteenth
and early nineteenth centuries introduced a new idea, which was to
have far-reaching and devastating consequences. Men had always
known that those who were unlike them in race or other collective
features were different, foreign, and probably hostile. They were
now taught that the other was not only different but inferior, and
therefore genetically doomed to a subordinate role to which he must
be kept. Specifically, according to this doctrine, the blacks were not
only uncivilized—a condition which could be ascribed to environmental and historical factors. They were also, unlike the white sav-
ages who roamed the forests of northern Europe in antiquity, incapable of becoming civilized, and therefore—and this was the crux—
best suited to a life of useful servitude. A similar argument, for similar reasons, may be found in some medieval Islamic philosophers,
with the difference that by them it was applied to the fair-skinned
northerners as well as to the black southerners, both of whom
differed from the light brown ideal of the Middle East and had

therefore, in this perception, been created by God to serve them.

The application of this new kind of racism to Jews seems to date from the early years of the nineteenth century, and was encouraged by the German struggle against Napoleonic rule and French revolutionary ideas. In a pamphlet published in 1803 and entitled "Against the Jews: A Word of Warning to All Christian Fellow Citizens . . . ," the writer argues: "That the Jews are a very special race cannot be denied by historians or anthropologists, the formerly held but generally valid assertion that God punished the Jews with a particularly bad smell, and with several hereditary diseases, illnesses and other loathsome defects, cannot be thoroughly proved, but, on the other hand, cannot be disproved, even with due regard to all teleological considerations."[13] In this sample, the characteristic mixture of medieval bigotry and modern pseudoscience is unusually transparent. In the course of the nineteenth century, it became much more sophisticated.

The doctrine that races were unequal and could indeed be situated in a hierarchy from the highest to the lowest was not entirely new. It is already to be found in Aristotle and other ancient Greek writers, and reappears in the Islamic philosophers of the Middle Ages. For the ancient Greeks, the medieval Muslims, and the modern philosophers, it served the same purpose—to justify slavery. While even Herder and Kant at times betray their own principles, the former in his remarks against Negroes, the latter in his references to Jews, there were others who preferred the view expressed by the great German scientist and humanist Alexander von Humboldt: "In maintaining the unity of the human species, we reject, by a necessary consequence, the appalling distinction of superior and inferior races. . . . All are equally fit for freedom." Quoting his brother, Wilhelm von Humboldt, he sought to "envisage mankind in its entirety, without distinction of religion, nation, or race, as a great family of brothers, as a single body, marching towards one and the same end, the free development of its moral powers."[14]

Doctrines of racial inequality, though by no means absent, are a comparatively minor theme in anti-Jewish literature until well past the middle of the nineteenth century. Even the Count de Gobineau, whose *Essay on the Inequality of Races,* published in 1853–55, became a classic of modern racism, was not really concerned with Jews. Instead, the attack on the Jews concentrated on two new accusations, both of them consequences of the emancipation of the Jews in Western Europe and their entry into European society. One of them was that the Jew resisted assimilation; the other was that he practiced it too effectively.

The first was a modernized restatement of a charge familiar since antiquity, and paradigmatically formulated by the classic Jew hater, Haman, who said to King Ahasuerus: "There is a certain people scattered abroad and dispersed among the people in all the provinces of thy kingdom; and their laws are diverse from all peoples; neither keep they the king's laws: therefore it is not for the king's profit to suffer them." (Esther 3:8). In a milder form, the same complaint is made by a number of Greek and Roman authors, who could not understand why the Jews persisted in worshipping and obeying their own peculiar God, at once exclusive and universal, and would not be content to let Him and His rites take their place in the mutually tolerant polytheism of the Hellenistic and Roman worlds.

The kings and prelates of medieval Christendom had a better understanding of the Jewish position, and insisted even more strongly than the Jews, if for somewhat different reasons, on their separateness. The Fourth Lateran Council, convened by Pope Innocent III in 1215, decreed that Jews must wear a specific badge or mark on their outer garments, to distinguish them from Christians. This innovation, which was no doubt inspired by an earlier Islamic practice, spread very rapidly, and the "badge of infamy," usually yellow, was enforced in many parts of Europe. The ghetto system began even earlier. Sporadic attempts were made by local authorities in Europe to segregate Jews in various places, and in 1179 the Third Lateran Council resolved that Christians "who will presume to live with them [Jews] be excommunicated."[15] With the growth of hostility, what began as Jewish neighborhoods became a form of enforced segregation. The word ghetto seems to have been first used in Venice, where in 1516 Jews were restricted to an area of the city called the Ghetto, a local word meaning gun foundry. The practice —and the name—spread rapidly to other Italian cities and then to other parts of Europe, and came to denote the walled quarters, with barred gates, to which Jews were legally confined, and from which they were only allowed to emerge at limited times and by special permission.

The post-Christian and sometimes anti-Christian deists and liber-

als saw no reason to maintain such distinctions, which they regarded
as part of the old order that they were committed to overthrow. For
them, Jewish separateness was an evil, above all for the Jews themselves, who were its principal victims. Some even gave this a quasi-
racial content, agreeing to the list of evil qualities ascribed to the
Jews, and attributing them not only to the environmental effects of
persecution and repression, but to the genetic effects of excessive
inbreeding. The Emperor Napoleon is a good example of the mixed
and sometimes confused perceptions and intentions of the revolutionaries and their successors towards the Jews. Napoleon never singled out his Jewish subjects for oppression, and seems to have meant
well toward them. As early as 1798, at the time of his expedition to
Egypt, he even issued a proclamation to the Jews, inviting them to
enlist in his forces and help reconquer their promised land.[16]

Not surprisingly, nothing came of this, but the Jewish question
continued to engage his occasional attention. As with others of his
time, Napoleon's pronouncements on the Jewish question seem to
combine the remnants of medieval ecclesiastical bigotry with the
beginnings of the new pseudoscience. The Jews, for Napoleon, were
a race, and vitiated by bad blood: "Good is done slowly, and a mass
of vitiated blood can only be improved with time." Napoleon's solution was extensive intermarriage: "When, in every three marriages,
there will be one between Jew and Frenchman, the blood of the Jews
will cease to have a particular character."[17] It will be noted that for
the emperor, the intermarriage which he desired was to be between
Jews and Frenchmen, not between Jews and Christians, and the
difference between them was blood not creed.

The Count Stanislas de Clermont-Tonnerre was expressing a
common view when he urged the French National Assembly in December 1789 "to refuse everything to the Jews as a nation, to grant
everything to Jews as individuals." It was a common view among the
philo-Semites that Jewish separateness was an anomaly and was the
cause of all the many Jewish defects, the existence of which they
readily admitted. The solution was to end that anomaly, for the Jews
to emerge from their ghettoes, become part of the general population in every way—in other words, to cease to be Jews in any mean-
ingful sense. Lessing, perhaps the greatest of European philo-
Semites, subtly ridicules this attitude. In one of his plays a vulgar and
loud-mouthed anti-Semitic servant, suddenly discovering that his

revered master is a Jew, tries to atone for his previous hostile remarks by observing, in defense of the Jews, that "there are Jews who are not at all Jewish."[18] Some Jews responded to this kind of defense, and the implied invitation, with eager enthusiasm; others with outrage. Both kinds of responses can still be found among Jews to the present day.

While those Jews who insisted on remaining in the ghetto aroused one kind of indignation, their brothers who accepted the invitation to come out soon found themselves confronted by another, far more serious and dangerous kind of resentment. Before long Jews began to appear in increasing numbers in the high schools, in the universities, and finally—when they were admitted—in the professions. As in the Middle Ages, they encountered fewest obstacles in the worlds of trade and finance. But while in the Middle Ages they had—with few exceptions—been mere hucksters or usurers, in nineteenth-century Europe the most successful among them became bankers and brokers, financiers and entrepreneurs. Very few, of course, ever reached such heights, but there were enough to provide raw material for new stereotypes. Nineteenth- and to some extent twentieth-century fiction, in English, French, and German, offers some interesting Jewish characters, reflecting the reaction of Christian Europe, sometimes positive, more often negative, to this new element that was penetrating into its midst. Such, for example, is the portrayal of the Jew, by Trollope in England and Balzac in France, as the greedy upstart, the ambitious and acquisitive parvenu who corrupts and dominates through his skill in acquiring wealth and using it to serve his ends. The figure of the corrupting parvenu is by no means exclusively, or even predominantly, Jewish, but there were always some writers who shared the perception expressed by T. S. Eliot in two famous lines:

> The rat is underneath the piles.
> The jew is underneath the lot.[19]

From the Middle Ages to the present time, the Jews have had defenders as well as accusers in Christendom.[20] If some Popes imposed the ghetto and the yellow badge, others tried to alleviate the Jewish burden. Notable among them was Innocent IV, who denounced the blood libel as a lie and defended the Talmud against its traducers. The same causes were taken up by other Christian scholars, such as the sixteenth-century German canonist and Hebraist Johannes Reuchlin, and more recent scholars like Theodor Nöldeke and Franz Delitsch in Germany and Pavel Konstantinovich Kokovstov in Russia, who used their scholarly authority to refute charges of ritual murder. A noteworthy example was the "Declaration of the Notables," a condemnation of anti-Semitism published in Germany in 1880, and signed by such eminent scholars and scientists as Johann Gustav Droysen, Theodor Mommsen, Rudolf Virchow, and Ernst Werner von Siemens.[21] There is also a literary philo-Semitism. Lessing in Germany, Gorki and Andreyev in Russia, Emile Zola and Anatole France in France, wrote and spoke in defense of the Jews in general as well as of individual Jews under attack. In England, Byron, Browning and George Eliot, in their writings, showed deep sympathy for Jewish sorrows and aspirations, and even Shakespeare, while presenting his Jew, Shylock, in terms obviously affected by traditional anti-Semitic stereotypes, nevertheless gave him some noble lines expressing the Jew's complaint against his persecutors and his appeal to their common humanity.

By the mid-nineteenth century anti-Semitism was underpinned by a new theoretical and polemical literature, portraying the Jew as an evil and dangerous intruder in European society, whose penetration and depredations must be stopped if that society was to survive. By now, the difference and the danger are defined, usually though not exclusively, in racial rather than religious terms. As anthropology had provided the pretext for the earlier wave of antiblack racism, so now philology provided a theory and a vocabulary for anti-Jewish racism. The peoples of Europe were Aryans; the Jews were Semites. As such, they were alien, inferior, and noxious.

For the new anti-Semites, the issue was not religion. Indeed Wilhelm Marr, the inventor of the term anti-Semitism, rejected religious polemics as "stupid" and said that he himself would defend the Jews against religious persecution. For him, the problem lay not in religion, which could be changed and was in any case unimportant, but in the ultimate reality, which was race. In his booklet *The Victory of Judaism over Germanism*, he even pays a kind of tribute to the Jews, whose "racial qualities" had enabled them to resist all their persecutors and maintain their struggle for eighteen centuries against the Western world. They had finally won their victory and had conquered and subjugated this Western world.[22] While the philo-

Semites in their discussion of the Jews often combine contempt with good will, the anti-Semites frequently display a mixture of respect, or even awe, with their malevolence.

An important element in the development of racial anti-Semitism was the growing number of Jewish converts to Christianity. The opening of the ghettos had created new ambitions among the Jews which the slow pace of emancipation could not satisfy. Some found a shortcut through the baptismal font. Benjamin Disraeli would never have become prime minister of England had his father not baptized him in childhood; Heinrich Heine would no doubt have written great poetry, but would hardly have attained his fame and influence without what he called "the entry certificate" of baptism. Once again, as in late medieval Spain, there was some suspicion about the genuineness of these conversions, which might be ascribed, not as in the past to constraint, but to ambition. In an era of religious persecution, the Jew had the option of changing sides. By the substitution of the immutable quality of race, the Jew would be deprived of this option, and even his descendants would be included in the curse.

In general, race was a major, often a dominant, theme in nineteenth-century European writing on national, social, cultural, and often even political questions. Most of these writings were not racist, in the sense that other races were regarded as inferior and to be treated accordingly, and much of it was concerned with identities and loyalties which would nowadays be termed ethnic rather than racial. But in the nineteenth century, and for many well into the twentieth, the two were not differentiated, and perceptions and discussions of these matters often reflect an unholy mixture of different things—the physical classification of the anthropologists, the linguistic classification of the philologists, the aesthetic preferences of romantics, and the realities of historical, cultural, and political identity, which might be tenuously if at all related.

Nineteenth-century Europe attached great importance to problems of nationality, which it often interpreted, especially in Central and Eastern Europe, in racial terms. The Italians, who had few Jews in their midst and no colonies abroad, developed no racist ideologies similar to those appearing further north, and were little affected by anti-Semitism until it was imposed on them in 1938 by the senior partner in the Axis. The fascist regime in Italy, the Italian Empire in

Africa, and the Italo-German Axis all helped to foster its growth, and even after the Empire had crumbled, the Axis was broken, and fascism was overthrown, some of this new anti-Semitism remained, as was clear from certain Italian responses to events in the Middle East. In pre-fascist Italy, when Jews encountered anti-Jewish hostility, it was of the old-fashioned religious, not the modern racial kind.

They were the exception. In Eastern Europe, the Jews with their own separate language, culture, and way of life were self-evidently a race as the term was then used. In Central Europe, where problems of race and nationality were in the forefront of both philosophical and political concern, the Jews were still seen as a distinct race, to be either assimilated or excluded, according to the two prevailing views on how to cope with the Jewish question. Only in England, France, and Holland, where Jewish communities were relatively small, and where political and national identity were equated, in contrast to the confusion of petty states and polyglot empires further east, Jews might hope for acceptance as citizens, as members of the nation. In France, this was taken to imply a renunciation of Jewishness in any but a narrowly defined religious sense. In Britain, where particularism rather than centralism was favored, and where a British nation of four races, English, Scottish, Welsh, and Irish, provided a pattern of pluralism, that sacrifice was not required. In the variegated immigrant societies of the Americas, the Jews could reasonably figure as one group among many, all contributing to the pattern of national life.

Despite the volume and vehemence of anti-Semitic literature in nineteenth- and early-twentieth-century Europe, with one exception, it did no more than delay the advance of Jewish emancipation, and left nothing worse than some remaining educational, professional and social barriers. The one exception was the empire of the czars, where the ideas of the theoreticians of anti-Semitism were given both wider circulation and more practical effect. In Germany, Austria, and France, despite their occasional intellectual and academic successes, the anti-Semites rarely achieved any significant political results—and this despite the support of such prominent figures as the musician Richard Wagner and the historian Heinrich Treitschke, who was responsible for the phrase, much used in Nazi times, "The Jews are our misfortune." The first politician to win an election on an anti-Semitic platform was the Austrian Catholic popu-

list Karl Lueger, leader of the "Austrian Christian Social Party."
Opposed by the grande bourgeoisie, the Austrian upper clergy and
bureaucracy, and the Court, but with the strong support of the Pope
and the Papal Envoy, he was able to win election as mayor of Vienna
with an overwhelming majority. But once installed as mayor, he did
little to harm Jews, but on the contrary even dined in the homes of
Jewish bankers and attended a synagogue service in his mayoral
robes. When reproached by some of his more consistent followers, he
answered with a phrase which later became famous, "Wer ein Jud ist,
das bestimme ich"—I decide who is a Jew.[23]

In France, the Dreyfus Affair seemed for a while to threaten the
civic rights and even personal security of the Jews in France. That
danger passed, however, and despite recurring anti-Semitic agitation, the threat of anti-Semitic action remained remote, until suddenly and devastatingly it was realized by the collaborationist government of Nazi-dominated France.

In the English-speaking countries, anti-Semitism never achieved
the level of intellectual respectability which it at times enjoyed in
France, Germany, Austria, and Russia. The attempts by such figures
as Goldwin Smith and E. A. Freeman to launch German-style racial
anti-Semitism in the nineteenth century, like the later attempts by
Hilaire Belloc and G. K. Chesterton to import the French clerical
variety, had little or no success. This is the more remarkable in that
English literature offers as rich a gallery of Jewish villains as any
literature in Europe—a gallery that begins with the supposed murderers of Hugh of Lincoln in medieval legends and chronicles, and
includes such varied figures as Barabas the Jew of Malta, Fagin,
Svengali, the sophisticated stereotypes of Graham Greene and T. S.
Eliot and the penny plain stereotypes of John Buchan and Agatha
Christie.[24]

Prejudice against Jews has of course always existed in these countries, and on occasion amounted to a factor of some, though never
major political importance. Racist ideas in general, and anti-Semitism in particular, are clearly discernible in the American immigration law of 1924 and the manner of its administration. Significantly,
the Jews figure as "the Hebrew race." Restrictive quotas and exclu-
sions of various kinds continued to operate against Jews in America,
not only at the point of entry into the country but at various subsequent stages. This was particularly noticeable in the 1920s and 1930s,

when racist ideas were prevalent. As late as the 1950s there were still numbers of colleges, clubs, hotels, and board rooms in which Hitler or Stalin would have been eligible and Einstein or Freud would not. I vividly remember a conversation, some thirty years ago, with a student, when as a newcomer to this country I was seeking information about the (to me) mysterious phenomenon of the student fraternity. This student, who incidentally, was the son of the dean of the college, explained how the fraternities were organized and functioned, and remarked that they did not normally admit Jews or blacks because "we feel they would be happier among their own kind." Since the end of World War II, virtually all these barriers have disappeared in the English-speaking countries.

Despite the former prevalence of such attitudes, in modern times the growth of anti-Semitism in the English-speaking world never reached a point when it could be publicly avowed in intellectual or political circles. Anglo-Saxon anti-Semitism, where it exists, is on the whole furtive, disguised, and hypocritical. Both in Britain and the United States, as well as in the other English-speaking countries, the political rights that Jews won in the nineteenth century have never since been seriously challenged, and the Jews of these countries never had to face anything like the barrage of hostile propaganda and political campaigns, the legal restrictions and physical violence encountered by Jews in most countries of the Continent. As a contemporary German Jewish observer noted in 1890: "The Englishman is economically too advanced for anyone to dare to try delude him that he might be dominated by a handful of Jews. He would also be too proud to believe anything of the sort."[25] The Yankee, as Mark Twain has attested, would be even less subject to these Middle and East European nightmares of domination by cleverer businessmen and more astute financiers.[26] It was this same English self-confidence which made it possible for Benjamin Disraeli, a Jewish convert to Christianity, to tell the British Parliament that the Jews were a superior race and aristocrats by nature. This was received with nothing worse than "cries of Oh! Oh! at intervals, and many other signs of general impatience." Disraeli's speech also brought some comments outside Parliament, but the most important—among them a parody published by Thackeray in *Punch*—expressed amusement rather than anger.[27]

Disraeli's own writings are an interesting example of how the assimilated Jew or the ex-Jew could be affected by the notions of the time. Traditional Jews, nourished on traditional literature, might still see themselves as custodians of the Jewish faith and as members of a Jewish community defined by rabbinic law. Jews who stepped outside and became part of Europe were inevitably affected by current European ideas, even those specifically hostile to themselves. While English liberals like William Hazlitt and Lord Macaulay defended Jewish emancipation by arguing that Jewishness was nothing but an accident of birth, no more significant than red hair or blue eyes, Disraeli took the opposite position, proclaiming that "all is race: there is no other truth." Disraeli's obsession with race, and his dithyrambs on Jewish power and greatness, have no basis in Jewish religious or historical tradition. His view of the role of the Jews does not differ greatly from that of the anti-Semites, but is simply reversed —presented in positive instead of negative terms, with pride instead of hate. One characteristic which Disraeli, curiously, shared with the anti-Semites is the attribution of Jewish origins to many people who in fact had no Jewish connections whatever. The difference of course was that whereas the anti-Semites turn those whom they hate into Jews, Disraeli annexed those whom he most admired. Disraeli's fantasies were eagerly picked up and used by anti-Semites, who have always shown an inclination to cite Jewish sources when they can find them, and invent them when they cannot.

The same kind of awestruck belief in Jewish power can be found in some gentile sympathizers with Zionism—even, for example, among some of the promoters of the Balfour Declaration, who saw in it a device to win "international Jewry" to the Allied cause. This belief still appears occasionally even at the present day, though it has lost most of its cogency in view of the manifest inability of "international Jewry" to do anything against either Hitler or his successors in enmity to Judaism. Awe for the mysterious power of Jewry has given place to respect for the political and military power of Israel—but this is not a racial consideration.

Disraeli was probably alone among Jews and ex-Jews in his enthusiastic acceptance and transformation of anti-Semitic fantasies about Jewish power. But other baptized Jews were convinced by what they read of Jewish inferiority and Jewish iniquity, and drew the appropriate conclusions. The prototype, perhaps the archetype, of the phenomenon of Jewish self-hate was a young Viennese Jew called Otto

Weininger, who wrote a long and rambling book about the moral and intellectual inferiority of women and of Jews, the latter being far more serious, and who then, logically, committed suicide at the age of twenty-four. Another baptized Jew, Karl Marx, did not commit suicide, but in his anti-Jewish tirade "On the Jewish Question" seems to recommend this as a collective solution.

The basic themes of anti-Judaism were established at the very beginning of the Christian Era. The first, and by far the gravest, charge in the indictment was deicide. Jews had rejected Christ. They had not only rejected him, but they had killed him, and since Christ was God, they had killed God. Modern scholarship and modern morality have both shed some doubt on the ancient and cherished theory of Jewish guilt for the death of Christ. The Romans were after all the unchallenged rulers of Judaea, and crucifixion was a Roman, never a Jewish, form of capital punishment. True, the Gospel according to St. Matthew is unequivocal in placing the blood of Christ on the head of the Jews, but some modern historical critics have pointed out that the author of this Gospel might have been influenced by a desire to placate and exonerate the Romans, who were and for long remained the rulers of the world they knew. Recently, some Christian moralists have questioned the morality of extending the guilt from those Jews who were present to other Jews living at the time, all the more so to their remote descendants.

But such considerations and such questioning were far from the minds of the early Christians and most of their successors. For almost two thousand years the story of the betrayal, trial, and death of Christ has been imprinted on Christian minds from childhood, through prayer and preaching, through pictures and statuary, through literature and music, through all the rich complexities of Christian civilization. It was not until 1962, after almost two millennia, that the Second Vatican Council, convened and deeply influenced by Pope John XXIII, considered a resolution exonerating the Jews from the charge of deicide. The resolution was strongly resisted, especially by the Near Eastern bishops, and was adopted in a modified form.[28] It may yet be some time before the sermon and the Sunday School syllabus all over the Christian world are appropriately amended and the habits of mind which they inculcate are transformed.

Though the crucifixion was seen as necessary for the fulfillment of God's plan for human redemption, those who were held responsible for it had nevertheless, in Christian perspective, committed a monstrous crime, and they, their compatriots, their coreligionists, and all their descendants in perpetuity were sometimes perceived as subject to a divine curse from which only baptism could save them. No less a person than St. John Chrysostom, in the fourth century, spoke of the synagogue as "the temple of demons . . . the cavern of devils . . . a gulf and abyss of perdition," while St. Augustine explained how those who had once been God's chosen people had now become the sons of Satan.[29]

This curse was interpreted in many forms, the most important being the dispersion and oppression to which the Jews were subject. Those who distrusted and oppressed them were therefore doing God's work. The legend of the wandering Jew, who must wander the earth, knowing neither death nor rest, until the time comes for him to witness the Second Coming, symbolizes this belief. Popular superstition added other details to the curse of the Jews, notably the evil smell—*foetor judaicus*—with which God is said to have afflicted them. This is perhaps an example of ordinary rather than extraordinary prejudice, since similar beliefs occur elsewhere, as for example among whites about blacks, and among yellow men about whites.

During the so-called Dark Ages, Jews in Europe enjoyed a relative tranquility. But the Crusades brought a new Christian militancy, and while this was directed primarily against the Muslims, the Crusaders found their first victims in their Jewish neighbors. This new hostility was aggravated by the relentless attack mounted by the Franciscan and Dominican orders against both Judaism and the Jews. From crusading times onward the Satanic element begins to dominate anti-Jewish polemic. Jews are now seen as children of the devil, whose assigned task was to combat Christianity and injure Christians. By the twelfth century they are accused of poisoning wells, ill-treating the consecrated Host (a somewhat pointless procedure for those who do not believe in it), and of murdering Christian children to use their blood for ritual purposes. The blood libel, as it is known, had originally been used by pagans against the early Christians. It was now used by Christians against Jews, with equal lack of justification, and with far more deadly effect. From time to time, these fantasies were denounced by popes and bishops, but they seem to have been widely accepted and disseminated by the lower clergy, who sometimes managed to convince their superiors. The notion of the Jews as possessing unlimited diabolic powers gained force with every private and public misfortune of Christendom. Before long, we find for the first time the story of a secret Jewish government, a sort of council of rabbis, which the Christians of course located in Muslim Spain, and which was directing a cosmic war against Christendom.

Against such dreadful enemies, only the most drastic measures could suffice. They had to be isolated, segregated, and if possible eliminated. Excluded from agriculture, commerce, and handicrafts, the Jews were driven to the practice of usury, and a new stereotype was formed, of the Jew as the greedy, bloodsucking moneylender. Money was now added to sorcery as an instrument of the Jewish plot to rule the world.

With the growing intellectual sophistication of Christian Europe, such fantasies began to lose their hold, though they—and still more the attitudes resulting from them—have shown extraordinary persistence in some areas, and from time to time make a disconcerting reappearance. The myth of a Jewish conspiracy to dominate the world, directed by a secret Jewish government of which all Jews are agents, reappeared toward the end of the eighteenth century, and has survived. This new accusation was first formulated by French émigré opponents of the Revolution and of the Napoleonic regime that followed it. A French Jesuit called Barruel published a lengthy book proving that the Revolution was the work of a secret conspiracy of Freemasons. Subsequently—no doubt anticipating the later prominence of Jews in continental European Masonic lodges—he made the further discovery that the Freemasons were themselves mere instruments of a deeper and more dangerous conspiracy—the invisible government of the Jews. It was the Jews, according to Father Barruel, who had founded the Freemasons, the Illuminati, and all the other anti-Christian groups. Some Jews tried to pass as Christians in order the better to achieve their deceitful purposes. They had even penetrated the Catholic Church, so that in Italy alone more than 800 priests, including some bishops and cardinals, were really secret Jewish agents. Their real purpose was "to be masters of the world, to abolish all other sects in order to make their own prevail, to turn the Christian churches into synagogues, and to reduce the remaining Christians to true slavery."[30]

Father Barruel, apparently recovering from his nightmares,

made his peace with the new regime to which he had ascribed such evil origins, and accepted an appointment as canon of the Cathedral of Notre Dame. But others emerged to carry on his campaign. Such cataclysmic events as the French Revolution, the rise of Napoleon, the overthrow of most of the old regimes in Europe, and the installation of a new and radically different order in their place, could only be due, in the eyes of some of their less sophisticated opponents, to the working of evil and occult forces. The Freemasons, the Illuminati, the liberal philosophers, and the rest were all outward manifestations of the same underlying cause. The Jews, who had wrought so much evil at the time of the Crusades, had broken their bonds and were at work again. For some, Napoleon himself was a Jew. More commonly, he was an instrument in the hands of Jewish conspirators. Such arguments followed him even after his defeat and exile: according to one German pamphleteer, "although Napoleon is isolated on his rock in the ocean, his Jewish confidants hold the threads of a conspiracy which stretches not only to France but also to Germany, Italy, Spain and the Netherlands, and with objectives consisting of nothing less than world revolution."[31] Another German writer, in a utopian tract published in Nuremberg in 1811, warns his readers against the "philanthropic madness" of emancipation, which could lead to the advent of "circumcised kings on the thrones of Europe."[32]

The enemies of Jewish emancipation could point to some telling evidence. Until the eighteenth century—later in the more backward parts of Europe—Jews had almost everywhere been despised outcasts, living on the fringes of European society, without rights or friends, without claims or hopes outside the limited circle of their own ghetto existence. With very few exceptions, they were excluded from all forms of participation, at the lowest as at the highest level, in the political life of the country where they lived; they made no contribution to its culture, and were excluded from all but specific and in the main, degraded occupations.

When, finally, in Western countries, they were permitted to emerge from the ghetto and enter into the life of European society, they displayed that additional energy and determination often found in penalized minorities that have to struggle to survive. In consequence, they did rather well. Jewish students thronged to the universities from which—with very few exceptions—they had been barred since the Middle Ages, and, not surprisingly, strove to excell. They tried harder, and often they did better than those other students for whom entry to the university required no special effort and was seen as no special privilege. Success breeds envy in any social situation, and it is the more resented when it is won by those previously re- garded as inferiors and outcasts. The idea that Jews wielded some secret and diabolic power, which enabled them to triumph over good, honest Christians, now found new audiences even in the more advanced countries of northern and Western Europe. Only in this way could a few thousand inferior Jews impose themselves on many millions of superior Christians or gentiles.

In the Middle Ages, Jews had sometimes been accused of achiev- ing their evil purposes by means of spells and incantations. The economic developments of the nineteenth century gave new scope to the idea of the other kind of sorcery, the power of money, which they used to conjure up immense forces to obey their commands and fulfill their Jewish purposes, and by which the Jews were able to possess and dominate the Christian world.

For a small but by no means insignificant number of European writers, the successes of the Jews could never have been won in fair competition, and could only be explained by the medieval stories of a dark and devious plot of the children of Satan, able to call on the powers of Hell at will, and seeking, as the French Catholic writer Bonald put it in 1806, "to reduce all Christians until they are nothing more than their slaves." A French sous-préfet in 1808 saw the prob- lem as acute: "It would be better to drive the Jews out of Europe rather than by driven out by them."[33] Such a conspiracy, and such a purpose, obviously required central direction, and in the course of the nineteenth and twentieth centuries a number of different ideas were advanced on the nature of "the secret Jewish government."

To support these and other charges against the Jews, or at least to make them acceptable to those who did not share the presump- tions of the anti-Semites, some sort of evidence was needed. The Jews were known to be a highly literary people, who practiced a very bookish religion. In their religious books, written in strange lan- guages and locked in the secrecy of an unknown script, the evil truth might be found. For Christians, it was difficult to attack the Old Testament, since the Church had made it part of the canon. Hostile attention was therefore focused on those religious books which were distinctively Jewish, namely the rabbinic collections, and especially the most famous and important of them, the Talmud. This is the name given to two great collections of rabbinic law, exegesis, and debate, both compiled during the early centuries of the Christian era, one in Babylonia, the other in the Roman province of Palestine. They are regarded by Orthodox Jews as containing an authoritative formulation of *Halakha,* that is, the rabbinic law that regulates Jewish life and worship. Already in the Middle Ages, Dominican inquisitors staged public burnings of rabbinic writings, and notably of the great codices of the Talmud. The most famous was the burning in Paris in June 1242. Despite the efforts of some Christian scholars, including churchmen, to defend the Talmud, the practice was continued in other Catholic countries, and as late as September 1553 the Talmud and other books were burned by official order, in Rome, Venice, Cremona, and elsewhere in Italy.[34]

A new phase began with Eisenmenger's famous *Entdecktes Judentum,* published in 1711. Johann Andreas Eisenmenger was a professor of Oriental languages, and appears to have devoted some study to the Talmud. The result of his efforts was a massive two-volume work, in which by careful selection, occasional invention, and sweeping misinterpretation, due sometimes to ignorance and sometimes to malice, he presents the Talmud as a corpus of anti-Christian and indeed antihuman doctrines. The title of the book means Judaism (or Jewry) revealed (or unmasked), and indicates its author's purpose. In the course of his book he resumes and attempts to confirm all the lies which had already by his time become standard in the anti-Semitic armory—the poisoning of wells, the Black Death, the ritual murder of children, and the rest. Eisenmenger's book, though disproved again and again by both Christian and Jewish scholars, became a classic of anti-Semitic literature, and has remained a source book for anti-Semitic accusations until the present day. The use of the adjective talmudical, in a variety of negative senses, became one of the characteristics of anti-Semitic writing, and to the present time, its use to denounce the actions or utterances of Israeli leaders is a generally reliable indication that the user is inspired by anti-Semitic prejudice and not merely by concern about the Middle East.

From the mid-nineteenth century some Christian theologians began to launch an attack against the Old Testament itself, despite

its position as part of the Christian canon. A favorite approach was
to contrast the harsh, vindictive, ruthless Jewish God of the Old
Testament with the kind, gentle, forgiving Christian spirit of the
New Testament. It is not difficult to refute this line of argument, by
quoting injunctions to gentleness from the Old, and to severity from
the New, but such refutations had little effect in halting this new line
of attack. It was strengthened by the progress of archaeology and the
decipherment of the ancient Middle Eastern languages, which enabled scholars, particularly in Germany, to find more ancient antecedents for some of the teachings of the Old Testament. The denigra-
tion of postbiblical, i.e., rabbinic, Judaism, already an established
tradition in some Christian scholarship, continued; it was now but-
tressed by what was known as the Higher Criticism, which at once
questioned the theology, the morality, and even the originality of the
Hebrew Bible. The Greek New Testament, for the time being, remained immune to such criticism, and it was not surprising that some
rabbis spoke of the Higher Criticism as a higher anti-Semitism. This
accusation was no doubt unjust concerning many of the distinguished
scholars of the time, some of whom indeed made great efforts to
understand and interpret rabbinic literature, but it received some
color from the practice of putting a distinguishing sign—a kind of
bibliographical yellow star—against the names of Jewish authors
whom they cited.[35]

Eisenmenger's book served as the basis of one of the major classics
of nineteenth-century anti-Semitic literature, *Der Talmudjude* (The
Talmud Jew), by the Canon August Rohling, professor at the Imperial
University of Prague. The numerous misrepresentations and falsifica-
tions in this book were at once challenged and disproved, not only
by Jewish but also by Christian scholars, and in 1885 Canon Rohling,
denounced in print as a liar, a faker, and an ignoramus, was forced
to bring a libel action from which he withdrew in circumstances so
scandalous that he was obliged to resign from his university chair.
This in no way impeded, and perhaps encouraged, the enormous
success of the book. Three French translations, by three different
translators, were published in 1889. Many other editions and translations followed, especially during the Hitler years. The most recent
editions have been in Arabic.

Canon Rohling's book, which was at first endorsed in Rome by the
semi-official Vatican journal *Civiltà Cattolica*, devotes great atten-

tion to the theme of ritual murder, and makes it one of his main charges against the Jews. The wide circulation and academic endorsement of the blood libel in this period had practical effects. Between 1867 and 1914, twelve charges of alleged ritual murder against Jews were tried by jury in German and Austro-Hungarian courts. It says much for the judicial systems of the two Germanic empires at the time that eleven of the twelve trials ended in acquittals; in the twelfth, in Austria, the accused was found guilty of murder, but without ritual implications. This verdict gave rise to many appeals, including one from Thomas Masaryk, and the accused was later pardoned by the emperor. The most famous of these cases occurred at a place called Tisza-Eszlar in Hungary, where in 1882 fifteen Jews were charged with the ritual murder of a Christian girl. The case became an international sensation before the final verdict of not guilty.

Another case, which lasted far longer and attracted far greater attention, was the arrest in 1911 of a Jewish brickmaker called Mendel Beilis, in Kiev in the Ukraine, for the ritual murder of a Christian boy. This followed after the temporary halting of the pogroms in Russia under both international and domestic liberal pressures, and represented a new effort and a new direction on the part of the anti-Semites, by now entrenched at the highest reaches of the imperial Russian government. Two years were spent in preparing the case, which was concocted by an anti-Semitic organization, in cooperation with the minister of justice and the police. It was opposed by an impressive array of Russian liberals and socialists, including such figures as the writer Maxim Gorki and the psychologist Ivan Petrovich Pavlov. The trial opened at the end of 1913, and, like the Dreyfus trial in France, became the focus for a conflict between opposing political forces in Russia, and the cause of widespread protests in the democratic countries of the West. It was no doubt partly because of the latter that the trial ended in an acquittal of the accused, "for lack of evidence," and with no decision on the question of ritual murder.[36]

But if the charge of ritual murder was impeded and in some measure defeated by the courts and the law, the charge of secret conspiracy for world domination, less subject to judicial review, was making greater headway. As Jewish emancipation progressed in the late nineteenth and early twentieth centuries, and Jews became more prominent in business and banking, literature and the arts, journalism and politics, the doctrine that "the Jew is underneath the lot" began to seem, to many who were frustrated and angry, to provide the answer to their questions and to indicate the solution to their problems.

For this doctrine, too, a proof text was needed, and since none existed, not even with the kind of distortions used by the anti-Semitic Talmudists, it had to be invented. It was for this purpose that the famous *Protocols of the Elders of Zion* were devised. Any rational modern reader of the *Protocols* cannot but wonder at the crudity of the inventors of this text, and the credulity of those who believed it. Among the many strange "secrets" revealed in the book is that the Jews make the sons of the nobility study Latin and Greek as the best way of undermining their morals, and that the Jews ordered the building of underground railways in the major cities of Europe so that when the time comes they can blow up any capital which resists their rule. Nor do those who believe in the *Protocols* find it odd that the Jews, in their own secret writings, should cast themselves in the role of agents of evil, and should moreover do so in the specific terminology of Christian anti-Semitism. Yet despite these and many other similar absurdities, the book has gone through countless editions, been distributed in millions of copies, and must rank very near to the Bible in the number of languages into which it has been translated.[37]

The text has a curious history. In its earliest extant form, it has nothing whatever to do with either Jews or anti-Semites, but consisted of a pamphlet written in the 1860s against Napoleon III. The forgers took this pamphlet, substituted world Jewry for the French emperor, and added a number of picturesque details borrowed from an obscure German novel. The *Protocols* first appeared in about 1895, and were almost certainly the work of a group of members of the czarist Russian secret police stationed in Paris. For some time, the book was used only in Russia. It had little influence even there and none at all outside. Its worldwide fame began with the Russian Revolution of 1917. In the course of the bitter civil wars that raged across Russia in the years 1918–1921, the leaders of the White Russians used the *Protocols* extensively to persuade the Russian people that the so-called revolution was no more than a Jewish plot to impose a Jewish government on Russia, as a step toward the ultimate aim of Jewish world domination.

The *Protocols* and the doctrines which it was used to propagate had their effect in the brutal massacres of Jews during the Russian Civil War. At the same time, White Russian agents carried the *Protocols* to all the countries of Europe and the Americas, as evidence of their interpretation of the significance of the Revolution and the nature of the new government in Moscow. In this they achieved quite extraordinary success. In Britain, both the *Times* and the *Morning Post* gave the *Protocols* extensive treatment, and the *Spectator* even demanded a royal commission to decide whether British Jews were in fact "subjects of a secret government." In America, the *Protocols* were widely circulated under the title *The Jewish Peril* and were in particular publicized and distributed by the automobile magnate Henry Ford, an obsessive anti-Semite who wrote a series of articles on "The International Jew," which he later reprinted as a separate booklet.

In 1921, the *Times* newspaper of London published some articles by its Istanbul correspondent, who had discovered a copy of the original French pamphlet and thus exposed the *Protocols* as a forgery;[38] in 1927 even Henry Ford admitted that his accusations were unfounded. From this time onward, in the English-speaking world, the *Protocols* were confined to the lunatic fringe. But in Hitler's Germany, they provided a major theme in Nazi anti-Semitic propaganda, and like the White Russian agents before them, Nazi peddlers of anti-Semitism were instrumental in distributing the *Protocols* all over the world.

The *Protocols*, though by far the most successful, were not the only anti-Semitic fabrication. Another, specially designed for an American audience, is a speech by Benjamin Franklin urging the Founding Fathers not to admit Jews to the new republic, and warning them of the dire consequences if they disregarded his words. The speech is a total fabrication, but was not without its effect. A less troublesome and widely used method was simply to assign a Jewish origin to anyone whom it was desired to discredit, and then to use that person to discredit the Jews.

The advent of capitalism found the Jews well placed to take advantage of the new opportunities which it offered them, and in consequence exposed them to both revised and new accusations. As a community that possessed neither state nor church, neither government nor army, the whole existence of Jews, their very identity, was determined by a book; even the poorest and most backward Jewish communities had a level of literacy higher than that of most of their neighbors. This skill, at the disposal of minds sharpened by centuries of Talmudic study, stood them in good stead in the new era. As outcasts on the fringes of society, struggling precariously for survival, they were better prepared for the rough-and-tumble of early capitalism than were the pampered upper class and cowed lower class of the old social hierarchy. As the moneylenders of the old order, some of them had a skill in the handling of money which enabled them to compete with their less experienced Christian competitors. Finally, possessing neither princes nor prelates in their own ranks, they were unhampered, as were many Christians, by powerful vested interests in the old order.

Significant numbers of Jews began to make money, sometimes very much money, by trade and finance. With that money, they were able to buy a better education for their sons and also—to a greater extent than among the Christians—for their daughters, and to enter the learned professions as far as these were open to them. The political process, at virtually all levels, was still closed to Jews in most countries. But a rising bourgeoisie will seek political expression. Though the Jews could not hold power, their money could sometimes bring them near enough to those who held it to exercise influence. For some Christians, any improvement in the previously humble and despised position of the Jews was an outrage against their Savior. For others, the increasing role of Jewish capitalists was at least a force for corruption, at worst an attempt to take over and dominate the world.

The age of capitalism brought two major accusations against the Jews—one, that they had created and were maintaining it, and two, that they were trying to undermine and destroy it. The first of these accusations came in two variants, from those whose domination was threatened and ultimately ended by capitalism, and from those who themselves hoped to overthrow and replace the capitalist order. The church and the nobility were well aware of the declining power of their orders. Rightly, they ascribed this unwanted change to capitalism; mistaking symptom for cause, they attributed the rise of capitalism to the Jews. A whole literature, much of it written by churchmen and noblemen, developed this theme.

At the same time, another brand of anticapitalist anti-Semitism was beginning among the socialist movements that first rose to prominence in the early nineteenth century. While anti-Semitism was in general a minority view among articulate socialists, it was by no means unimportant. August Bebel, who founded the German Social Democratic Party in 1869, is quoted as saying that "Anti-Semitism is the socialism of fools." If so, there were many such fools, including famous pioneers like Charles Fourier (1772–1837), Alphonse Toussenel (1803–1885), Pierre LeRoux (1797–1871), Pierre-Joseph Proudhon (1809–1865) and, in some of their writings, both Karl Marx and Friedrich Engels. For Fourier, the Jews were "parasites, merchants, and usurers," who devote themselves entirely to "mercantile depravities." Fourier was strongly opposed to Jewish emancipation. "To grant the Jews citizenship was the most shameful . . . of all the recent vices" of contemporary society. Lepers should be segregated and kept away, and "are not the Jews the leprosy and the ruin of the body politic?" Toussenel, a pioneer of both socialism and anti-Semitism in France, gave his retrospective blessing to all the anti-Semites of the past: "I understand the persecutions to which the Romans, the Christians, and the Mohammadans subjected the Jews. The universal repulsion inspired by the Jew for so long was nothing but just punishment for his implacable pride, and our contempt the legitimate reprisal for the hate which he seems to bear for the rest of mankind." Proudhon, in a book published in 1883, gives a classical formulation of the anti-Semitism of left-wing economists:

The Jew is by temperament an anti-producer, neither a farmer nor an industrialist nor even a true merchant. He is an intermediary, always fraudulent and parasitic, who operates, in trade as in philosophy, by means of falsification, counterfeiting, and horse-trading. He knows but the rise and fall of prices, the risks of transportation, the incertitude of crops, the hazards of demand and supply. His policy in economics has always been entirely negative, entirely usurious; it is the evil principle, Satan, Ahriman, incarnated in the race of Shem.[39]

Proudhon, it will be noted, in his modern socialist exposition, has adopted the medieval charge of satanism, and has indeed developed it, by adding the evil spirit of the old Indo-Aryan pantheon, Ahriman.

One of the pioneers of Utopian socialism, the philosopher Johann Gottlieb Fichte (1762–1814), was also alarmed at what he saw as the Jewish danger to the West. In his book on the French Revolution, published in 1793, he sees the Jews as a major cause of the troubles of Europe and offers what may well be the first suggestion of a possible solution: "I see no other means of protecting ourselves against them than by conquering their Promised Land and sending them all there."[40]

Even Jews, or to be more precise, ex-Jews, in the socialist ranks, were influenced by the anti-Jewish ideas current in these circles, and developed their own brand of left-wing Jewish self-hate. The outstanding example of this is of course Karl Marx, the baptized grandson of a rabbi, whose famous essay "On the Jewish Question," published in 1844, has become one of the classics of anti-Semitic propaganda. In this, Marx identified the Jew and even Judaism with all the most disagreeable characteristics of the greedy and predatory capitalist order which he was seeking to overthrow. He also provides a solution: "An organization of society which would abolish the basis of huckstering, and therefore the possibility of huckstering, would render the Jew impossible." Even when not discussing specifically Jewish questions, the remarks of Marx and Engels, especially in their journalistic writings, contained many anti-Semitic allusions and expressions. One article speaks of the Polish Jews as "that dirtiest of all races." When a German historian remarked that in modern Poland as in ancient Egypt, Jews were increasing rapidly, Marx paraphrased this to say that "they multiplied like lice." In Marx's view, Jews were not only responsible for capitalism but even for sometimes strongly anti-Semitic capitalistic governments: "We find every tyrant backed by a Jew, as is every Pope by a Jesuit. In truth, the craving of oppressors would be hopeless, and the practicability of war out of the question if there were not an army of Jesuits to smother thought, and a handful of Jews to ransack pockets."[41] Engels even uses the language of streetcorner anti-Semitism, mocking at Jewish names and using Jewish origins to attack political opponents like Lasalle, while Marx himself, in a letter to Engels, dated July 30, 1862, combined two different kinds of racism in a sneer at Lassalle's alleged negroid features: "Now this union of Jewishness with Germanity on a negro basis was bound to produce an extraordinary hybrid. The importunity of the fellow is also nigger-like."[42] Later, however, Engels, though not Marx, seems to have changed, and in 1890 he published a denunciation of anti-Semitism.

In Britain and North America there was far less anti-Semitism in the socialist movement than in France and Germany, though it is not

entirely absent. It was, however, powerful elsewhere on the Continent, even in Russia, where from the start there was a strong anti-
Jewish strain in the revolutionary opposition to the czars. The anar-
chist Mikhail Aleksandrovich Bakunin (1814–1876) was a bitter
anti-Semite, seeing the whole of world Jewry as constituting "one
exploiting sect, one people of leeches, one single devouring parasite
closely and intimately bound together not only across national
boundaries, but also across all divergences of political opinion."[43] In
Bakunin's view, the Jew is not fit for socialism, certainly not for
socialist leadership, for which he is disqualified by "that mercantile
passion which constitutes one of the principle traits of their national
character." For Bakunin, there was no difference between Marx and
Rothschild; both were from the same stock of speculators and parasites.

Bakunin's disciples in Russia were consistent. When the pogroms
broke out against the Jews, far from condemning or trying to prevent
them, they actively encouraged them. The attacks on the Jews, in
their view, marked the beginning of the social revolution, and were
therefore a positive step forward. The Jews, in the opinion of the
Bakuninists, represented, in magnified form, all the "vices and ul-
cers" of society, so that "when anti-Jewish movements begin, one
may be convinced that in them is hidden a protest against the whole
[social] order, and that a much more profound movement is beginning."[44] No doubt in this spirit, the executive committee of the
Bakuninist organization issued a proclamation on September 1, 1881,
calling on the masses to rise against the "Jewish czar," the Jews, and
the nobles: "Only blood will wash away the people's afflictions. You
have already begun to rebel against the Jews. You are doing well. For
soon over the whole Russian land there will arise a revolt against the
Czar, the lords, and the Jews. It is good that you, too, will be with us."

Such views were by no means universal in the socialist movements, neither in Russia nor elsewhere, and the majority of socialist
leaders were strongly opposed to this kind of argument, whether
deriving from bigotry, as with Proudhon, self-hate, as with Marx, or
cold calculation, as with the Russian Bakuninist organization. But the
extent to which even the socialist leadership had to take account of
the strength of anti-Semitic feelings among their followers was revealed in an incident at the Congress of the Socialist International,
held in Brussels in 1891. Abraham Cahan (1860–1951), a Jewish trade

union leader from New York, asked the Congress to issue a statement of sympathy for Jewish workers under threat of anti-Semitism: "All Russian newspapers," he said, "attack the Jews and say that socialist working men hate the Jews. You are asked to state that this is not true, that you are enemies of all exploiters, be they Jews or Christians, and that you have as much sympathy for Jewish workers as for Christian workers." Some of the delegates were unwilling either to express special sympathy for Jews or unreservedly to condemn anti-Semitism, and eventually a compromise resolution was adopted by which the Congress condemned "both anti-Semitic and philo-Semitic incitements." Edmund Silberner, the historian of left-wing anti-Semitism, has remarked that "the Brussels resolution is a unique document in the annals of international socialism. To the best of our knowledge, it is the only instance in which friendliness towards any oppressed nationality was ever condemned by an international socialist body."[45]

Some Jews, wounded by the continuing anti-Semitism that they encountered in the socialist rank and file and even sometimes in the socialist leadership, lost hope of a solution to Jewish problems through socialist internationalism, and instead began to think in Jewish national terms. Socialist ideologies are an important strain in the development of Zionism in the late nineteenth and twentieth centuries. A number of different forms of socialist Zionism evolved, all of which laid the main stress not so much on the creation of a sovereign Jewish state, as on the social regeneration of the Jewish people by a return to productive labor.

Many Jews, however, remained in the socialist movements which, despite the presence of some anti-Semitic elements, still offered them a warmer welcome than any other political party in Europe at the time, and virtually their only road to political power. This in turn gave rise to the second anti-Semitic interpretation of the Jewish role in capitalism—that of a radical subversive seeking to destroy it. This perception was strongly reinforced in the aftermath of World War I, when the Bolshevik regime in Russia and abortive communist revolutions in Hungary, Bavaria, and elsewhere brought significant numbers of Jewish leaders into international prominence. White Russian anti-Soviet propaganda made the fullest use of this, both at home and in the West. Their arguments seemed to be confirmed by the prominence of such figures as Trotsky, Zinoviev, and Kamenev in the Soviet leadership.

For a while, certain Jews were indeed prominent in the Soviet leadership and exercised great power. But after the rise of Stalin, all this came to an end. In due course, Trotsky was driven into exile and later murdered, Zinoviev and Kamenev and many other Jews were executed for crimes against the state. While these prosecutions and executions were in the first instance ideological rather than anti-Semitic, they hit a disproportionate number of Jews, and prepared the way for the total exclusion of Jews from the higher Soviet leadership and the initiation of a campaign against "world Jewry" which in its language as well as its content is remarkably reminiscent of the older anti-Semitism, both of the left and of the right.

The long record of anti-Jewish action and utterance in Europe should not lead us to overlook the other side—that of the Christians and gentiles who were able to recognize and willing to combat this evil in their midst. During the Middle Ages in Western Europe, much longer in Eastern Europe, hostility to Jews was an accepted norm, but even then there were prelates and magnates who were willing to defend the Jews against their attackers and Judaism against its detractors. In the years of humanism and enlightenment, of liberalism and constitutionalism, there were many, including some churchmen, who were willing to fight for Jewish rights.

All in all, the record is one of steady improvement. After the expulsions from Spain and Portugal at the end of the fifteenth century, no such action was taken against Jews in Western Europe, and on the contrary, Jews were gradually admitted to places from which they were previously barred. Even in Eastern Europe, despite such fearsome events as the pogroms in Russian cities and the great massacres in the Ukraine, the overall picture was one of an increasing desire for tolerance, at least among politically articulate and active elites, and a gradual retreat by the exponents of bigotry and persecution.

That retreat ended in 1933, with the accession to power of a declared anti-Semite in Germany, and the inauguration of a new and terrible campaign against the Jews.

There had been avowedly anti-Semitic movements in Western Europe before Hitler's National Socialists. But they were mostly of minor significance, and although they occasionally won some electoral successes, they were not usually able to put their ideas into effect. There were governments that pursued sometimes anti-Jewish policies, and statesmen who made anti-Jewish remarks, but it was not until 1933 that an avowedly anti-Semitic government, with anti-Semitism as a major plank in its ideology, came to power. Until then, accusations against the Jews had fallen mainly into two familiar categories. On the one side there was the complaint that the Jews stayed in their ghettos, kept their own peculiar ways and shunned Christian society; on the other, that they emerged from the ghetto, adopted European dress and manners, and thus infiltrated Christian society. In Hitler's *Mein Kampf,* the two are combined.[46] He became an anti-Semite, he tells us, when he first saw Hassidic Jews from Eastern Europe in Vienna, and, observing their black hats, sidecurls, beards, and long black coats, he realized that they were an alien race who deliberately kept themselves apart from Aryan Europe. At the same time, he felt an even more passionate hatred against those Jews who cast off their strange garb, unlearned their grotesque accents, and passed themselves off as part of Aryan society.

Once in power, he had personally to confront this dilemma, and others arising from it. The Jews must not remain in their ghettos, because they are an alien presence that cannot be tolerated in an Aryan land. They must not enter Aryan society, because they are a deadly germ that would destroy it. They must not stay in Germany, because their presence pollutes the pure German soil. But it is dangerous to let them go elsewhere, because wherever they go, they will form centers of anti-Nazi agitation. To this multiple dilemma, there could be only one solution. It was Hitler's historic achievement to have devised and applied it.

CHAPTER FIVE

The Muslims and the Jews

THE ARGUMENT is sometimes put forward that the Arabs cannot be anti-Semitic because they themselves are Semites. Such a statement is self-evidently absurd, and the argument that supports it is doubly flawed. First, the term "Semite" has no meaning as applied to groups as heterogeneous as the Arabs or the Jews, and indeed it could be argued that the use of such terms is in itself a sign of racism and certainly of either ignorance or bad faith. Second, anti-Semitism has never anywhere been concerned with anyone but Jews, and is therefore available to Arabs as to other people as an option should they choose it.

A great deal of modern writing about Jews, in the Arab lands as in other parts of the Islamic world, might suggest that many have indeed chosen this option.

For most of the fourteen hundred years or so of the Arab Jewish encounter, the Arabs have not in fact been anti-Semitic as that word is used in the West—not because they themselves are Semites, a meaningless statement, but because for the most part they are not Christians. In Islam, the Gospels have no place in education, and Muslim children are not brought up on stories of Jewish deicide. Indeed, the very notion of deicide is rejected by the Qur'ān as a blasphemous absurdity. Like the Founder of Christianity, the Founder of Islam had his encounter with the Jews, but both the circumstances and the outcome were very different. Muḥammad and his companions were not Jews, and did not live and preach their message in a Jewish society. The Jews whom they knew were the three Jewish tribes of Medina, a religious minority in the predominantly pagan Arabian community. The Muslims did not conceive or present themselves as the new and true Israel; they did not therefore feel threatened or impugned by the obstinate survival of the old Israel. The Qur'ān was not offered as a fulfillment of Judaism, but as a new revelation, superseding both the Jewish and Christian scriptures, which had been neglected and distorted by their unworthy custodians. Islam, unlike Christianity, did not retain the Old Testament, and no clash of interpretations could therefore arise.[1]

The founders of both religions, in different ways, came into conflict with Jewish leaders. But there the resemblance ends. Jesus was crucified; Muḥammad triumphed in his own lifetime and became the head of a state as well as of a community. His fight with the Jewish tribes of Medina resulted in their defeat and destruction, not his, and the clash of Judaism and Islam was resolved and ended with his victory. There is thus no Muslim equivalent to the long and in the theological sense still unresolved dispute between the Church and Israel. There was also a profoundly significant difference between the Jewish denials of the Christian and Muslim messages. Muḥammad never claimed to be Messiah or Son of God; only God's apostle. The Jewish opposition to his apostolate failed while he was still alive. It was in any case less significant, less wounding, less of a reproach than the Jewish rejection of Christian claims. While Christ's dealings with the Jewish priestly establishment in Jerusalem form a central part of the sacred history, Muḥammad's conflict with the Jewish tribes of Medina is—or rather was—of minor importance. Of late, there has been a change in this respect.

In the Western world, it has become the common practice to speak of the "Judeo-Christian tradition." This term, which is much used nowadays, is obviously fairly recent, and would probably have shocked some of the forebears of both the Jewish and Christian exponents of that tradition at the present day. It has, however, been generally accepted, and rightly so since it designates a historical and cultural reality. The term "Judeo-Islamic," in contrast, exists as a term of scholarship, used only in a historical context, and to designate an increasingly remote past. It was never used by either Jews or Muslims in the Muslim lands, and would have been accepted by neither of them as denoting their own beliefs, aspirations, and way of life. It certainly has no bearing on the Islamic lands at the present time.

Yet, in the past, when a large part of the Jewish people lived, and sometimes prospered, under the rule of Islam, the term "Judeo-Islamic tradition" would not have been inappropriate to denote the symbiotic relationship of the two religions and cultures, and the civilization which they created. In Islam as in Christendom, that civilization was dominated, shaped, and directed by adherents of the majority religion, but the Jews who lived among them came to share many of their values and to play a role, not indeed as contributors but rather as participants in a common endeavor. Though the term was never used in the past and is hardly appropriate in the present, it nevertheless designates a historical reality in the Islamic Middle Ages, similar in some respects, dissimilar in others, to the share of the Jews in modern Christendom.

The position of Judaism, which is the predecessor—some indeed would say the parent religion—of both Christianity and Islam, is in many ways intermediate between the two. In some matters, Judaism, even in Christian lands, is closer to Islam; in others, even in Muslim lands, it is closer to Christianity. A glance at the similarities and differences may help to clarify the contrasting relationships between Judaism and the successor religions, between the followers of those religions and the Jews.

The first, most obvious, and probably the most important meeting point between Jews and Christians is in the sacred Scriptures which they share. Jews do not accept the New Testament, but Christians accept the Jewish Old Testament. True, they have done so with uneven enthusiasm, but at least the formal position of all forms of Christianity is that the Old Testament is part of God's Book, and indeed, the Old Testament has played an important part in the formation and development of Christian civilization; its art, its literature, even its languages are profoundly impregnated by the stories, ideas, spirit, and the idiom of the Old Testament. This is a very important component of the Judeo-Christian heritage. It has no parallel in Islam, where both Testaments are considered to be replaced by the Qur'ān.

Concerning the mission and crucifixion of Christ, Islam occupies an intermediate position between the other two religions. Both Judaism and Islam reject the notion that Jesus was the Son of God; neither accepts that he brought redemption and salvation to mankind. But while orthodox Judaism assigns him no place at all, the Qur'ān recognizes Jesus as a messenger of God—not as Redeemer, but as a prophet and one of the series of prophets which culminated in the mission of Muhammad and the final and perfect revelation which he brought. Many of the features of the Gospel version are mentioned, or at least alluded to in the Qur'ān. But in addition to the denial of divine fatherhood, there is a second significant departure from the Christian version in the Muslim account of the Crucifixion. In the Qur'ān, as in the Gospels, the Jews reject Christ and seek to crucify him. But while in the Gospels they succeed, in the Qur'ān they fail. In answer to the Jews, who claimed that they killed "Jesus, son of Mary, the Messenger of God," it is written: "But they did not kill him, nor crucify him, but only a likeness that was made to appear to them ... certainly, they did not kill him, but God raised him up to Himself" (Qur'ān, 4:156–157). Muslim commentators explain that God rescued Jesus and raised him up to Heaven, while on the cross he was re- placed by a double or a phantasm. Thus, while Islam accepts the Christian account of Jewish evil intentions toward Christ, it sees their efforts as ending in unequivocal failure. "They [the Jews] schemed [against Jesus], but God also schemed, and God is the best of schem- ers" (Qur'ān 3:54). The Crucifixion, in the Muslim view, was a delu- sion, and the whole theology and imagery arising from it have no place in Muslim thought or belief.

In general, Jewish and Muslim theology are far closer to each other than is either to Christianity. Both Jews and Muslims profess the strictest monotheism; both of them—no doubt because of an imperfect understanding of the Christian doctrine of the Trinity— have sometimes suspected the Christians of leanings towards polytheism. The first major attempts to formulate a Jewish theology —that is, a systematic statement of religious principles and beliefs in philosophical terms—were made in the Muslim lands in the Middle Ages, and are profoundly influenced by Muslim patterns of thought. These formulations have remained a powerful factor in Jewish reli- gious life everywhere to the present day.

Perhaps the most important area of Muslim–Jewish convergence is in the Holy Law, and the men who are its accredited upholders. Both Judaism and Islam are legal religions, and the Jewish Halakha and the Muslim Shari^ca have much in common. Obviously there are many differences in matters of detail. But these are transcended by the shared idea that there is a Divine Law, coming from God and promulgated by revelation, which regulates every aspect of both public and private, both communal and personal life. This idea, common to Judaism and Islam, is alien to Christianity. Jews and Muslims did not observe the same dietary laws, but they agreed that there are dietary laws, and both looked with disapproval at Christians and others who knew no such restraint. Exceptionally, this affinity is even recognized on the Muslim side. Jewish dietary laws, though different, were stricter, and Muslim jurists therefore ruled that meat killed and prepared by Jews was lawful for Muslims. This rule was confined to Sunni Islam, since for the Shi^{c}a, anything touched by non-Muslims, Jews or others, was unclean, and if taken by Muslims brought pollution. But the Shi^{c}a were always a minority, and the Sunni ruling could have considerable social effects. Similarly, both Jews and Muslims practiced circumcision, and although their rules and procedures were different, they shared a common distaste for the uncircumcised.

The convergence of religion and law in Judaism and Islam gave rise to another point of resemblance—the emergence of a quasi-clerical class of men who are both theologians and jurists, but who are not priests. Since the destruction of the Temple, there has been no sacerdotal priesthood in Judaism. There has never been any in Islam. In contrast to Christianity, there is no ordination, no sacraments, no priestly office of any kind, no functions which cannot be performed by any adult male believer who possesses the necessary knowledge. The ulama in Islam, like the rabbis in Judaism, are primarily men of learning, the doctors of the holy law. At some time, both religions evolved a system of certification, which is, however, in no sense an ordination as that word is used in the Christian churches. The rabbis and the ulama became a clergy in the sociological sense; they never became a priesthood in the theological sense.

In the light of these resemblances and these differences, how did Muslims perceive Jews, and how did they treat them? Jews have lived under Islamic rule for fourteen centuries, and in many lands, and it is therefore difficult to generalize about their experience. This much, however, may be said with reasonable certainty—that they were never free from discrimination, but only rarely subject to persecution; that their situation was never as bad as in Christendom at its worst, nor ever as good as in Christendom at its best. There is nothing in Islamic history to parallel the Spanish expulsion and Inquisition, the Russian pogroms, or the Nazi Holocaust; there is also nothing to compare with the progressive emancipation and acceptance accorded to Jews in the democratic West during the last three centuries.

In considering these questions, a clear distinction must be made between different periods of Islamic history. The first, which we may call classical Islam, begins with the advent of Islam in the seventh century and continues until the great retreat before the advance of Europe. In the far west of Islam, this came with the reconquest of Spain and Portugal, and the Christian threat to North Africa. In the heartlands of the Middle East, it was delayed by the Ottoman Empire, still, even in its decline, a redoubtable military power, and was not felt until the late eighteenth and nineteenth centuries.

This first period was one of strength and confidence, when the Islamic world, apart from some regional setbacks, was advancing in power and expanding in territory. It was a period also when external influences, though present and sometimes important, did not dominate or direct the course of events, and when Islamic civilization was still developing along the lines of its own inner logic.

There are many passages in the Qur'ān, and in the biography and traditions of the Prophet, in which hard words are used about the Jews. These passages are concerned, for the most part, with the Prophet's own conflict with the Jews, in which he was completely victorious. They are to some extent balanced by other passages speaking more respectfully of the Jews as the possessors of an earlier revelation, and prescribing a degree of tolerance to be accorded to them. Most important of all, there is no tradition of guilt and betrayal, such as has colored popular and sometimes ecclesiastical Christian attitudes to the Jewish religion and those who profess it.

The position of the Jews, as of other minorities under Muslim rule, varied enormously, and was of course greatly affected by both internal and external events. Sometimes they prospered greatly; at other times they had to endure bitter persecution. But even at their worst, these persecutions were of the kind that I earlier described as normal, that is to say, arising out of genuine differences and specific circumstances. Most of the characteristic and distinctive features of Christian anti-Semitism were absent. There were no fears of Jewish conspiracy and domination, no charges of diabolic evil. Jews were not accused of poisoning wells or spreading the plague, and even the blood libel did not appear among Muslims until it was introduced to the conquering Ottomans by their newly acquired Greek subjects in the fifteenth century.

In the Islamic lands the Jewish communities enjoyed toleration, in the form and manner prescribed by the laws and customs of Islam. Jews like other non-Muslims enjoyed limited rights, with a formalized acceptance of inferiority—but these limited rights were legally established and enforced. In these countries, before the penetration and adoption of such Western notions as nationalism and patriotism, basic loyalty belonged to one's religious community, and political allegiance to the state, which in practice usually meant to the dynastic rulers of the country. In the Ottoman Empire, for example, the Jews owed and gave their allegiance to the Sultan, and some of them were even able to perform secondary but not unimportant tasks in his service. Like the Christians, they were not required, nor indeed —with some exceptions—permitted to bear arms. To fight for the defense or advancement of Islam was the privilege and duty of the Muslims; unbelievers, even those subject to the Muslim state, were not called upon to share it. It was not until comparatively late times that the acceptance of Western notions of national identity and patriotic loyalty on the one hand, and the introduction of the European practice of the draft on the other, brought a change. Even so, it was slow and reluctant. For a long time Jews and Christians were exempted from military service and required instead to pay a commutation tax. And when finally they were drafted, it was usually in noncombatant and—apart from doctors and engineers—in noncommissioned duties. The full integration of religious minorities into the armed forces did not come until comparatively modern times, and by then it was too late for the Jews in all Muslim countries but Turkey.

All this does not of course mean that Jews under traditional Muslim rule lived in the interfaith utopia invented by modern mythmakers. Jews, like Christians, were both in theory and in practice second-class citizens. But this situation was by no means as bad as the modern connotations of this term might imply. As members of a recognized and protected community, they enjoyed limited but substantial rights, which were at most times effectively maintained. They were expected to keep their place, and the rare outbreaks of violence against Jews or Christians almost always resulted from a feeling that they had failed to do so. They have conspicuously failed to do so in recent years.

Unlike some of their Christian colleagues, most Muslim theologians and polemicists devoted very little attention to Judaism, which they saw as of minor importance and offering no serious challenge. Instead, they directed their main polemics against Christianity, in which they correctly saw their main rival as a world religion and civilization. Anti-Jewish polemics in Muslim controversial literature are for the most part due either to Jewish converts trying to justify their change of religion, or to Christian converts transferring some of their concerns from their old religion to their new one. What the Jew under Muslim rule had to suffer was not hate, fear, or envy, but contempt; what he received was a kind of condescension which could swiftly change to repression if he seemed to be overstepping the limits.

Violent persecution, forced conversion, and banishment were rare, though not unknown. They usually occurred at times of stress and danger, when the Islamic world was threatened from within or without, by pestilence or famine, religious division or foreign invasion. The war against the Crusaders led to a harsher and more repressive attitude to the non-Muslims, who were now, for the first time since the rise of Islam, subjected to a kind of social segregation. The great troubles of the thirteenth and fourteenth centuries, arising from the Mongol invasions and their aftermath, led to a wave of mistrust, expressed in polemics against the non-Muslims and attempts to reduce their economic role. In all this, the Christians were the main target, but the Jews were also affected, especially in North Africa, where after the extinction of the indigenous Christian communities the Jews became, as in Christian Europe, the only religious minority. It was an exposed and vulnerable position, which was not to their advantage. In the East, under Ottoman rule, the change was slower, but by the late eighteenth or early nineteenth century the Jews of the Ottoman lands and still more of Iran had declined into the degradation so vividly depicted by the European travelers. Held back by ignorance and poverty, spurned by Muslims and Christians alike, they were unable to maintain even the positions they had previously held, and were outmatched and replaced by Greeks, Armenians, and Arab Christians. They did not begin to recover until the late nineteenth century, when Western protection and patronage (including that of Jewish organizations) on the one hand, and the new Muslim liberal patriotism on the other, favored their emergence. But it was too late, and the collapse of Western power, followed by the retreat of Westernizing rulers, brought doom to all who were associated in Muslim minds with the external enemy.

Of the three external enemies that successively invaded Islam, the Crusaders, the Mongols, and the modern European empires, the third proved to be the most deadly and the most enduring. In the age of European ascendancy, Muslim society underwent profound changes. The succession of Muslim defeats at the hands of their European enemies, a growing sense of weakness, the increasing domination of Muslim lands and populations by the European empires, the traumatic economic, political, and finally even cultural and social changes resulting from Western paramountcy in the Muslim world, all combined to weaken Muslim self-confidence, and with it, Muslim willingness to tolerate others. The non-Muslim subject populations were now seen in a different light, as disaffected and disloyal subjects whose sympathies lay with the European enemy and who thus constituted a serious danger to Islam. Such suspicions were reinforced by the wealth and prominence which Christians and to a much lesser extent Jews were able to acquire in times of European domination or even of European influence. This gave them a degree of influence, sometimes even of power, which they had never been able to attain in traditional Muslim states.

The change, which began in the late eighteenth century, gathered force in the nineteenth, when the Islamic world found itself threatened by the Christian empires expanding from both Eastern and Western Europe, and ultimately bringing almost the whole of the Islamic world under their rule or at least influence. It was an age when confidence gave way to anxiety, when new notions and institutions were adopted in imitation of the previously despised infidel, and when the trickle of foreign influences became a flood.

In the course of the nineteenth and twentieth centuries an important change took place in the very nature of Muslim hostility to Jews. The old hostility was traditional, one might even say normal. There was of course considerable variation in different times and places, and Muslim treatment of non-Muslim minorities ranged from almost complete tolerance to severe repression. In general, their attitude was that of a master people to a subject people whom they were prepared to treat with a certain lordly condescension as long as they behaved themselves. With the changed circumstances of the era of European domination, the non-Muslim ceased to be contemptible in Muslim eyes and became dangerous. In the case of the Jews, this new attitude was further encouraged by the importation of certain ideas characteristic of European anti-Semitism, but previously unknown even to the most prejudiced Islamic opponents of Jews and other non-Muslims.

Between the Christian and Muslim attitudes to Judaism and the Jews, there was one difference of fundamental importance. Christianity recognized only one predecessor, Judaism; Christendom only one religious minority, the Jews. Islam had two predecessors, of which Christianity was the more recent and more important; at least two minorities, of whom the Christians were far more numerous and far more influential. Christianity was also the religion of the major external enemies of Islam, first the Byzantine Empire, then the Crusaders, finally the states of the modern world; Christianity was a rival missionary religion, competing with Islam for the conversion of the rest of the world. Judaism, in contrast, was professed only by small minorities, who had long since given up any hope of adding to their numbers by conversion. Its adherents disposed of neither political nor military power, and offered no threat to Islam or to the Islamic state. On the contrary, Jews could sometimes be useful to Muslim rulers, because unlike Christians, they were not suspected of sympathies with the external enemy.

The outstanding characteristic, therefore, of the Jews as seen and as treated in the classical Islamic world is their unimportance. In classical Islamic writings, whether religious, philosophical, or literary, there is nothing resembling the concern with Jews that characterizes certain Christian writings from the earliest times to the present day. Muslim religious polemicists devote their main efforts to refuting the main enemy—Christianity. Few of them waste time and effort in refuting Judaism; and the few, as noted, are mainly Muslims of recent Christian or Jewish origin. With one exception, the Spaniard Ibn Ḥazm (994–1064), there is nothing in Muslim religious literature, whether theology or homilectics, that can be compared with refutations of Judaism of Peter the Venerable and Raymond Lull, the ferocious anti-Jewish diatribes of Martin Luther, or the activities of the Franciscan saints John of Capistrano and Bernardino of Siena, as well as a host of lesser figures.

The same may be said of the philosophers. In Europe, even in the enlightened eighteenth and nineteenth centuries, most of the great French and German philosophers gave vent at one time or another to anti-Semitic utterances. Nothing comparable can be found in the writings of the great philosophers in classical Islam. Similarly, classical Islamic literature, though it does occasionally portray a Jewish figure, usually a minor one, offers no such demonic monsters as Fagin or those other Jewish villains that haunted the literary imagination of France, Germany, and Russia, and have begun to invade contemporary Arabic fiction and drama.

The philosophical and literary anti-Semitism of Christendom is an expression of certain deep-rooted and persistent fears and accusations. These too are for the most part unknown to the classical Islamic world. The Jews under the Muslim rule received little praise or even respect, and were sometimes blamed for various misdeeds. They were not, however, accused of being inherently evil or conspiring to take over the world. It was not until many centuries later that this kind of paranoia began to infect the Muslim world. When it did, the sources and stages of the infection are clearly discernible.

If the anti-Semitism of Christian literature is absent in Islam, so too is the philo-Semitic response which it provoked. Muslim literature does not devote much time and effort to speaking evil of the Jews; it has even less to say in their favor. From the Qur'ān, the Tradition, and the Commentaries, and from later literature, historiography, and folklore, it is, however, possible to reconstruct the stereotype of the Jew as he appeared to Muslim eyes.

The earliest Arab recollections of Jews date from the century immediately preceding the rise of Islam, and are on the whole favorable. Three Jewish tribes lived in Medina, and other small groups of Jews were scattered through the oases of Northern Arabia. Nothing very definite is known about their origins, and they have variously been described as Arabized Jews and Judaized Arabs. It was not a problem for their contemporaries. By the sixth century, they were Arab in speech, culture, and way of life, and thoroughly integrated into Northern Arabian tribal society, of which they formed an accepted, indeed a respected part. One of them, the poet, Samaw'al

(Samuel) ibn ᶜAdiya, who flourished in the mid-sixth century A.D., is remembered not only for his poems but also, more especially, for his faithfulness and loyalty, which became proverbial.

The conflict began with the migration of the prophet Muḥammad from Mecca to Medina, where there were three Jewish tribes. The Jews for the most part rejected his apostolate, and resisted his political and military leadership. The resulting struggles, and the hostility which they engendered, are reflected in the Qur'ān, in the Tradition, and in the Commentaries, where the Jew is depicted as stubborn and perverse, rebelling against the commands of God and rejecting and killing, or trying to kill, His prophets. In modern times, under external influences which are easily recognizable, Muḥammad's conflict with the Jews has been portrayed as a central theme in his career, and their enmity to him given a cosmic significance. This is new, and related directly to new situations and influences. The classical Islamic literature takes a more relaxed view, and treats the struggle with the Jews as a relatively minor episode in the career of the Prophet, and one which in any case ended with their utter defeat. Though the Qur'ān, reflecting the Prophet's own dealings with Jews and Christians, states quite clearly that of the unbelievers, the Jews are the most hostile, the Christians the most friendly to the Muslims, later Muslim law made no distinction between the two, and treated both equally. This was also the normal practice of Muslim governments until relatively modern times.

In the Qur'ān and the sacred biography, the important thing about the Jews of Medina is not so much that they opposed the Prophet, as that they were defeated and humbled. The standard Qur'ānic text is in Chapter 2, verse 61, which says of the children of Israel: "They were afflicted with humiliation and poverty, and they felt the wrath of God. This was because they used to disbelieve the signs of God and kill his messengers unjustly. This was because they disobeyed and transgressed." The terms "humility" and "humiliation" occur frequently in the Qur'ān and later writings in relation to Jews. This, in the Islamic view, is their just punishment for their past rebelliousness, and is manifested in their present impotence between the mighty empires of Christendom and Islam. In Arabic poetry and folklore, the humility of the Jew becomes a prototype, and figures commonly in metaphors and stories. Some see this abasement of the Jews as a punishment from God for their rebelliousness and therefore as a condition to which they are perpetually condemned. Sometimes this enduring punishment is linked to the enmity which they displayed towards the Prophet, and which is presumed to continue in the feelings of later Jews towards later Muslims. This perception appears occasionally in the traditions, but is not a major theme in Muslim writing. The theme of humiliation becomes particularly important when, from time to time in Islamic history, individual Jews became prominent, and were seen in the too visible enjoyment of wealth and power, bringing a sharp, sometimes a violent reaction. But this happened more frequently with Christians than with Jews.

In the Islamic as in the Christian foundation narratives, the Jew is hostile, even malevolent. The great difference is that in the Islamic texts his hostility is ineffectual, his malevolence ends in defeat. In the Qur'ān, the Jews disobey Moses, and are quelled; they try to crucify Jesus, and fail—they are deluded into thinking they have done so. In the biography of the Prophet, the Jews oppose him, but they are overcome and are condignly punished, some by expulsion, others by enslavement or death. The same picture appears in the Tradition, the Commentaries, and other later religious writings, of the Jew as hostile, but without the strength or power to make his hostility effective.

This basic difference between the Jew's success against Christ and his failure against Muhammad had a decisive influence on the attitudes of the Jew-haters of the two religions. For the Christian, he represented a dark and deadly power, capable of deeds of cosmic evil. For the Muslim, he might be hostile, cunning and vindictive, but he was weak and ineffectual—an object of ridicule, not fear. This image of weakness and insignificance could only be confirmed by the subsequent history of Jewish life in Muslim lands.

Like the Christian under Muslim rule, the Jew was not allowed to bear arms, or even to ride a horse. Unlike the Christian, this was his fate everywhere. The stereotype of humility is therefore accompanied by a stereotype of cowardice, exposing the Jew to a special derision among the martial peoples of Islam. In popular humorous anecdotes, poking fun at the peculiarities of the various ethnic and religious groups in the Islamic world, the quality most commonly attributed to the Jew is cowardice. One example may suffice, from Turkey in the last years of the Ottoman Empire. Under the influence of both liberal ideology and practical necessity, non-Muslims were at last being admitted into Ottoman military service. For obvious reasons, the Jews were better trusted than their Christian compatriots, but they were less respected. A story current at the time was that some Turkish Jews, fired with patriotic ardor during the Balkan wars, formed a volunteer battalion to defend the fatherland. When they were trained and equipped and ready to set off for the battlefront, they asked the government to give them a gendarme as escort, as there were bandits on the way.

Against this background of humility and powerlessness, the emergence of a Jewish military power and the smashing victories which it was able to win came as a fearful shock. A partial answer to the agonizing questions posed by this change was found in another early stereotype, commonly associated with weakness and humility, that of deceit. Ibn Khaldūn (1332–1406), the greatest of medieval Arab historians, offered a sociological explanation: "[Injury has been done] to every nation that has been dominated by others and treated harshly. The same thing can be seen clearly in all those persons who are subject to the will of others, and who do not enjoy full control of their lives. Consider, for instance, the Jews, whose characters owing to such treatment had degenerated so that they are renowned, in every age and climate, for their wickedness and their slyness. The reason for this is to be found in the causes mentioned above."[2] Others, lacking Ibn Khaldūn's sociohistorical insights, perceived this quality of trickery and deceit as inherently Jewish. In earlier times, it was a minor theme in discussion of Jews and Jewish matters. In modern times, it has provided a useful explanation of military defeat.

In their treatment of the non-Muslim subject peoples, Muslim rulers and populations generally made no distinction between Christians and Jews, according both the same measure of tolerance. From time to time, there were outbreaks of persecution, usually linked to specific events—such as a threat from an external enemy, or, most commonly, the feeling that the non-Muslims were doing too well for themselves and should be cut down to size. Such events, however, were the exception rather than the rule, and the position of the non-Muslims was on the whole tolerable though never totally secure.

In general Jews and Christians were not subject to expulsion. The one major exception appears to have been in Arabia. The common version is that, citing the tradition that "two religions shall not re-

main in the land of the Arabs," the Caliph ᶜUmar expelled all Jews
and Christians from Arabia, which was to be an exclusively Islamic
land. In fact, Jews and Christians seem to have remained in Southern
Arabia, and the expulsion was limited to the Hijaz. Both had remained there in the lifetime of the Prophet, but the exclusion rule
was applied with increasing strictness under his successors.[3] To the
present day, non-Muslims are in principle barred from all the Hijaz
with the exception of Jedda and Taif and Jews are barred from the
whole of Saudi Arabia.

Unlike the Jews and heretics of Christendom, non-Muslims under
Muslim rule were rarely called upon to face martyrdom or exile, or
compulsorily to change their religion. Unlike the Jews of Europe,
they were—with certain exceptions, for example in Iran and Morocco—confined in neither territorial or occupational ghettos, but
were fairly free in their choice of residence and profession. They
enjoyed freedom of worship, and some autonomy in their own communal affairs. They were subject to a whole series of social, political,
and fiscal disabilities, the actual enforcement of which, however,
varied considerably from time to time and from place to place. The
most burdensome, which was never relaxed until the impact of the
westernizing reforms in modern times, was the payment of higher
taxes. The most degrading—though in this the enforcement was
highly erratic—was the wearing of special clothes and signs and
badges, to mark them off from the true believers. The yellow badge,
which was to have so long a history in the Christian West, had its
origins in early medieval Baghdad. This was one instance where the
West learned intolerance from the East.

One characteristic feature of later European anti-Semitism was
entirely lacking in the Islamic world, even in the pattern of discrimination which it imposed, and that was racism. There were Christians
as well as Jews in ancient Arabia, and both were seen as part of the
Arab family. Judaism, like Christianity, was seen as a religion, which
one might join or leave, and not as an inherent and unchangeable
racial identity. A sense of racial identity was by no means lacking
among the Arabs, and it expressed itself in early times in the doctrine
of the superiority of Arabs over non-Arabs, and in later times in the
relationships between whites and blacks. There may perhaps be racial overtones in some references to the Jews, as for example when
the ninth-century Arab writer al-Jāḥiẓ speaks of the deterioration of

the Jewish stock because of excessive inbreeding, or when a controversialist like Ibn Ḥazm of Cordova, in his attacks on Jews, implies rather than asserts racial qualities. But Ibn Ḥazm was writing in Spain, where different conditions prevailed, and he had neither predecessors nor successors in the Arab East. It was not until comparatively modern times that the idea was imported from Europe that the Jews are a separate race, with evil and enduring racial characteristics.

The situation of the non-Muslim minorities in classical Islamic states falls a long way short of the standard set and usually observed in the present-day democracies. It compares, however, favorably with conditions prevailing in Western Europe in the Middle Ages, and in Eastern Europe for very much longer.

It did not, however, last. As the Muslims felt themselves to be weak, threatened, and surrounded, they became increasingly suspicious of their own non-Muslim subjects, most of whom were Christians and therefore suspected of at least sympathizing with the enemy. And from that same enemy the Muslims were soon to learn new ideologies of hatred and new techniques of repression.

The percolation of the distinctively Christian kind of hostility to Jews into the Islamic world can be traced through several stages. In a sense, it began in the high Middle Ages, with Christian converts to Islam. The second stage came with the Ottoman expansion into Europe and the conquest of Constantinople, all of which brought great numbers of Greek Orthodox Christians under Muslim rule. The blood libel was endemic in these parts, and was brought to the notice of the Ottoman authorities through the usual disturbances which it caused at Eastertime. This was the first time that this particular story had become known in Muslim lands.

The real penetration of modern-style anti-Semitism, however, dates from the nineteenth century.[4] It began with the Christian Arab minorities, which of all the communities in the Middle East had the closest contacts with the West. It was actively encouraged by Western emissaries of various kinds, including consular and commercial representatives on the one hand, and priests and missionaries on the other. The Christian minorities had good practical reasons to oppose the Jews, who were their main commercial competitors, and it is significant that outbreaks of anti-Jewish agitation were invariably accompanied by calls for boycotts. In the course of the nineteenth century, accusations of ritual murder became almost commonplace, cropping up all over the empire, in the Arab as well as the Greek and Turkish provinces.

During the second half of the nineteenth century, the first Arabic versions of European anti-Semitic writings were published. The earliest anti-Semitic tracts in Arabic were all translations, mostly if not entirely from French originals and by Christian Arab translators. The very first appears to be a tract published in Beirut in 1869, a translation of a forgery, popular in anti-Semitic circles at that time, purporting to be the confessions of a Moldavian rabbi converted to Christianity, and revealing the horrors of the Jewish religion.[5] The second anti-Semitic tract in Arabic was a free translation of a lengthy French book by one Georges Corneilhan, published in Paris in 1889, and purporting to deal with the Jews in Egypt and Syria. An Arabic version appeared in Cairo in 1893.[6] The translator was the local correspondent of the English-language newspaper *The Levant Herald*. This book is a good sample of the French anti-Semitic literature of the time, denouncing the Jews as the source of all the corruption that was destroying France and indeed the rest of the world, and proposing their total expulsion.

The immediate cause of this sudden outburst of anti-Semitic literature was the trial and condemnation of Captain Dreyfus and the ensuing controversy. The passionate outbursts of anti-Semitism in metropolitan France had repercussions all over the area of French influence. The relationship between France and the Uniate Maronite Christians of Lebanon was a particularly close one, and the Maronites, increasingly influenced by French education and culture, were immediately affected by these as by other events. Some of the Muslim press, in both Turkish and Arabic, was sympathetic to the falsely accused captain, and took the opportunity to score some points against the vaunted liberal civilization of Europe.[7] No less a figure than Rashīd Riḍā, one of the outstanding religious and intellectual leaders of the Muslim world at the time, commented caustically on the humiliation and persecution of the Jews in France. This was not due, he observed, to religious fanaticism, since the French were very far from religious beliefs. He ascribed it rather to racial prejudice and envy of Jewish success. Rashīd Riḍā remarks with some justification that had these events occurred in the East, the same journalists who were harrying Dreyfus and the Jews would have denounced the

people of the East in venomous terms, and "screamed for unconditional freedom and universal justice." Significantly, he condemns
some Egyptian journalists for following the French line and attacking
the Jews.[8] Support for the anti-Dreyfusards was in the main confined
to the Christian minority, and even there was limited in impact and
visibly foreign inspired. It did however provide the occasion for the
first batch of translations of European anti-Semitic literature into
Arabic.

The introduction of the Talmudical theme in Muslim anti-Jewish
polemics dates from this period and was at first exclusively Christian
both in origin and in its diffusion in Arabic. As early as 1890, a
Christian author called Ḥabîb Fāris published a book in Cairo called
Surākh al-Barî' fi Būq al-Ḥurriyya (The Call of the Innocent with the
Trumpet of Freedom), later reprinted as *al-Dhabā'iḥ al-Bashariyya
al-Talmūdiyya,* (The Talmudic Human Sacrifices). This is a compila-
tion of anti-Semitic myths, largely but not entirely culled from European sources, accusing the Jews of ritual sacrifice and ascribing this
to talmudic teachings. In addition to the standard European material, the author added a number of examples from the Middle East,
and examined in some detail the various ritual murder accusations
in nineteenth-century Syria, in Damascus, Antioch, and elsewhere.
The book was reprinted in a new edition, with an introduction and
notes, in Cairo in 1962. Another early work of the same vintage was
al-Kanz al-Marṣūd fi qawāᶜid al-Talmūd. This is a translation of
Canon Rohling's well known anti-Semitic text, originally published
in German. The Arabic version is made from a French translation
and was translated by one Yūsuf Naṣrallāh. The first edition was
published in Cairo in 1899, the second in Beirut in 1968. In both
cases the first edition was almost unnoticed, even among the Christian minorities; the second received considerable attention. The
same is true of some other similar writings produced in the same
period.

These early attempts to spread anti-Semitic literature in Arabic
were by no means unresisted. In the Ottoman lands, the authorities
stopped the circulation of the tract published in 1869, and from time
to time closed down newspapers which published anti-Jewish incitements, seen as a threat to public order. Eminent Christian Arabic
writers and journalists of the day wrote condemning such attacks on

Jews and pleading for a better understanding between the three religions.[9]

It was not forthcoming, and in the years that followed the situation became steadily worse. The rising tide of hostility to Jews, and the sweeping away of the ancient Arab-Jewish communities, must be seen against the background of the larger events of the time. Of these, the most far-reaching and ultimately devastating in its effects was the change in the balance of power between Islam and Europe. For some centuries, Islam was growing weaker, Europe stronger. For a while, Muslims in the heartlands of the Middle East could still close their eyes to the realities of change. By the late nineteenth century, and still more the twentieth, few illusions remained. Much of the Islamic world had been conquered and incorporated in the four great European empires of Britain, France, Holland, and Russia, and even the two remaining independent states, the Ottoman Empire and Iran, were increasingly subject to the political and economic influence of Europe.

Political force and economic pressures opened the way to intellectual influences too. For the first time, Muslim Arabs, Persians, and Turks began to learn European languages, read European books, and even go to European schools. The overwhelming danger threatening the whole Islamic world was domination by Europe. To confront that danger, it was necessary to understand the enemy; many also felt that it was necessary to imitate him.

Europe at the time, from east to west, offered a wide range of institutional models and ideologies of action. They found followers both among the servants and the critics of Middle Eastern governments. On the one hand, the forms and procedures of administration were reshaped along European lines; on the other, the small westernized elites who ruled Middle Eastern states began to think of themselves, their nations, and their countries in the new and hitherto unfamiliar language of patriotism and nationalism.

All this brought important changes in the status of the non-Muslim minorities and in the way they were seen by their Muslim compatriots. The old relationship prescribed by Muslim law and usage, which combined tolerance with inequality, had worked well enough for a millennium. But it was no longer acceptable to the enlightened nineteenth century—neither to the powers of Europe, nor to the

Christian subjects of the Ottoman Empire, who, increasingly, were becoming their protegés.

With the gradual abandonment of the old order, what replaced it was not always an improvement. On paper, the religious minorities were far better off than before. Instead of subject communities in a state defined by Islam, they were now members of a nation and citizens of a country. In the old order, nations were subdivisions of a religion; in the new order, religions were subdivisions of the nation, in which followers of all religions could in principle at least claim an equal share. Among Christians and Jews, these changes aroused great hopes, and even among Muslims, especially in the Arab provinces which had been less directly associated with the exercise of Ottoman supremacy, there were many who shared in the aspirations of the liberal patriots, and their belief in a common national identity transcending religious differences.

But there were enormous difficulties, not least of which was the favor shown by the European empires to the Christians, and, to a much lesser extent, the Jewish minorities, and the rapid advance of these communities in education, wealth, and ultimately even power. Such changes inevitably aroused resentment among the Muslims, who saw no good reason to accept as equals those whom they had long been accustomed to regard as inferiors, and who were the more resentful when these erstwhile inferiors seemed to be acquiring, with foreign encouragement and protection, a kind of superiority. Even the Christians were not always entirely happy with this new equalization, which meant leveling downward as well as upward. A contemporary memorandum, by a high Ottoman official, on the great reform decree of 1856 proclaiming the equality of Muslims and non-Muslims, notes some of the reactions of both communities.

. . . In accordance with this ferman, Muslim and non-Muslim subjects were to be made equal in all rights. This had a very adverse effect on the Muslims. . . . Many Muslims began to grumble: "Today we have lost our sacred national rights, won by the blood of our fathers and forefathers. At a time when the Islamic community is the ruling community, it has been deprived of the sacred right. This is a day of weeping and mourning for the people of Islam."

As for the non-Muslims, this day, when . . . they gained equality with the ruling community, was a day of rejoicing. But the patriarchs and other spiritual chiefs were displeased. . . . Whereas in former times, in the Ottoman state, the communities were ranked, with the Muslims first, then the Greeks,

then the Armenians, then the Jews, now all of them were put on the same
level. Certain Greeks objected to this, saying: "The government has put us
together with the Jews. We were content with the supremacy of Islam."[10]

While these new Muslim resentments were directed primarily
against Christians, the major beneficiaries of the change, Jews were
also affected. And since they enjoyed few of the advantages possessed
by the Christians in numbers, wealth, weapons, and foreign protection, they were on occasion the immediate scapegoats. The local
Christians themselves sometimes contributed to this by stirring up
anti-Jewish feeling, partly through commercial rivalry, partly to deflect Muslim anger away from themselves. In this, they often had the
support of their European friends and patrons.

There was more than one European model for aspiring Middle
Easterners to follow. For a long time, the most admired of these
European models was that of Western Europe—the model of liberal
democracy, limited constitutional government, and equal rights
without discrimination by race or creed. But there were other European models—of religious bigotry, of ethnic nationalism merging
into racism, which also had powerful exponents in Europe and ready
followers in the Middle East. The beginnings of new-style anti-Semitism in the Middle East may be ascribed largely to such foreign mentors and their local disciples. The channels through which they came
were normally of two kinds—religious and official. The clergy of both
the Greek and Catholic churches made great efforts to mobilize their
followers among the subjects of the Ottoman Empire, the one in the
interests of Russia, the other of the Catholic powers and especially
of France. Accusations against Jews of ritual murder in Middle Eastern cities for a long time continued to derive exclusively from Christian sources. The most famous, the Damascus Affair of 1840, began
with some Capuchin monks and was energetically fostered by the
French consul. Consular and clerical intervention can be seen in a
number of other similar cases. By the end of the nineteenth century,
such accusations are already coming from Muslim sources; in the
course of the twentieth century this became commonplace. A new
theme was a call for a Christian–Muslim alliance to confront the
common Jewish enemy. This line of argument still recurs from time
to time, though it has won only limited support.

Another important step in the dissemination of European-style

anti-Semitism in the Middle East came in the aftermath of the Young
Turk Revolution of 1908, which ended the despotism of Sultan Abdul
Hamid II, and installed a constitutional regime. At the time, the
revolution was welcomed by many Muslims as well as most Christians
and Jews, and was seen as portending the dawn of a new age of
liberty and cooperation. There were however many conservative
Muslims who were deeply offended by it, and who saw in the deposi-
tion of the Sultan and the limiting of the powers of his successor a
blow against Islam. They were particularly outraged by the equalization of religions which the Young Turks promised, and although this
promise was never completely fulfilled, the changes went far enough
to arouse serious opposition in the capital and especially in the Arab
provinces.

At a fairly early stage, opponents of the Young Turks alleged that
their revolution was due to Jewish machinations. This was no new
departure in the Islamic lands, where for centuries, to ascribe a
Jewish origin to a movement was a recognized way of trying to
discredit it.[11] In the past, such accusations were rarely pursued, and
formed little more than part of the generalized vocabulary of abuse.
This time it was different. The accusation was given a new sophistication and consistency, and based on the anti-Semitic doctrines and
beliefs which had in the meantime been imported from Europe.
Some European journalists and diplomats took up the theme, notably
the British ambassador, Sir Gerard Lowther, and his chief dragoman,
Gerald H. Fitzmaurice, both of them addicts of conspiracy theories
about Jews. Stories of this kind began to circulate among the foreign
community. They appeared in the local Christian newspapers—
Greek, Armenian, and Christian Arab—and by 1911 even penetrated into the Turkish press. They received a new lease of life during
World War I, when the imperial powers, finding themselves at war
with Turkey and fearing the disaffection of their Muslim subjects,
tried in every way to discredit the Ottoman Empire and in particular
the Young Turk regime that was ruling it. The argument that the
Young Turk regime was not truly Islamic but was dominated by Jews
and Freemasons was of some value in Allied propaganda directed to
the Arabs and, more generally, to the Islamic world.

Contemporary evidence indicates that the reactions against the
Young Turk revolution in the Arab provinces and elsewhere were
concerned with the equalization of non-Muslims in general and not

directed specifically against the Jews. But the dissemination of anti-Semitic notions and writings in the Middle East had begun. For the time being, it was confined to small, insignificant fringe groups, with little or no impact on either the political or the intellectual mainstream of the time. But some of the basic texts of anti-Semitic literature, and the ideas which they contained, were now available in Arabic, ready for use and for wider dissemination when the time came.

The subsequent growth of Arab anti-Semitism to its present tidal proportions is due to many causes—to the imperialist challenge and the nationalist response, to the mingling of imported chauvinism and home-grown fanaticism, to the rise, in a time of violent and painful change, of a new intolerance that exacerbated all hatreds and endangered all minorities. For the Jews, two developments were of crucial importance. One of them was the accession to power of Adolf Hitler and the Nazi Party in Germany, and the tremendous propaganda effort made by them. The other was the beginning of Zionist settlement in Palestine leading to the emergence of the state of Israel and the succession of Arab–Israeli wars.

CHAPTER SIX

The Nazis and the Palestine Question

THE CLOSE and at times active relationship that developed between Nazi Germany and sections of the Arab leadership, in the years from 1933 to 1945, was due not to a German attempt to win over the Arabs, but rather to a series of Arab approaches to the Germans.

For a long time, the Nazi government showed a surprising lack of interest in the Arab world and its affairs. There were several reasons for this. One, the importance of which should not, however, be overrated, was ideological. The Arabs were, in the German classification, Semites, and as such shared the inferiority ascribed by Nazi ideology to the Jews. Such views are indeed expressed from time to time in Nazi writings, and were given dramatic expression by Adolf Hitler himself, when, in a speech to military commanders delivered in August 1939, shortly before the outbreak of war, he is reported as referring to the peoples of the Middle East, among other non-Europeans, as "painted half-apes, who want to feel the whip."[1]

More important than the ideological consideration was the generally low assessment, by German experts, of the Arab potential. The surprisingly negative German policy toward the Arabs was basically determined, however, not so much by ideological or practical judgments, as by their system of priorities. No doubt, the ultimate Nazi aim was world domination. Their immediate objective, however, was Europe, and all other considerations were subordinated, for the time being, to the need to establish their paramountcy on the European continent. The Middle East was seen as relatively unimportant—certainly not worth the sacrifice of other interests, nor the risking of other possible alliances. As long as they retained any hope of remaining on good terms with Britain, the Germans were careful to refrain from any overtly anti-British act. The Nazis did not, at first, depart greatly from the traditional view formulated by Bismarck in a famous phrase, that "the whole Eastern Question is not worth the bones of a single Pomeranian grenadier."

With the international crises of 1938–1939, an accomodation with Britain was no longer seen to be possible, but there was no lack of others to whom Germany was prepared to relinquish parts at least of the Middle East. After the French surrender in June 1940, the Nazis were willing to recognize the continuing rule of the Vichy French government in both Syria and North Africa. At the meeting between Hitler and Molotov in November 1940, they accepted the Soviet demand for German recognition of "the area south of Batum and Baku in the general direction of the Persian Gulf . . . as the center of the aspirations of the Soviet Union."[2] More important than either of these were the claims of Germany's Axis partner, Fascist Italy. German foreign policy consistently recognized the priority of Italian interests and claims in the Middle East, and carefully refrained from any action or undertaking likely to bring Germany into collision with her Italian ally. German Middle East experts were no doubt keenly aware of the troubles which the British had confronted in the inter-war period, as the result of some rather rash political promises to the Arabs, and of insufficient attention to the interests and sensitivities of their French allies. The Germans were determined not to repeat this particular mistake.

Several different factors were involved in the formation of the Nazi attitude to the Middle East, and these were represented by different groups or factions in the Nazi establishment. In this as in other matters, disagreements and even arguments between different interests and opinions within the Nazi state were possible, but only until Hitler made up his mind, after which his will was law and could not be questioned.

In the early years of the Nazi government, the paramount interest of the leadership, therefore of the government, was to get rid of the Jews. The notion of accomplishing this by physical extermination had already been suggested by some Nazi leaders, but was not yet seen as a feasible official policy. Instead, the choice was emigration, and anything which might speed this process and bring Germany nearer to the desired objective of being completely *Judenrein,* Jew-free, was seen as desirable. But in the depression-ridden world of the 1930s, few countries were willing to admit destitute immigrants, and the options for German Jews were severely limited. The Germans therefore saw in Mandatory Palestine a useful dumping ground for their unwanted Jews, and were even willing to take some practical steps to this end. If this served the additional purpose of making trouble for the British and stirring up anti-Jewish feeling, so much the better from the Nazi point of view.

Nazi attitudes toward Zionism and towards the idea of a Jewish state were at first contemptuous, later hostile. According to Nazi racial theories, only Aryans were entitled to political sovereignty; only they were capable of exercising it. The Jews lacked both the creativity and the idealism necessary to establish and maintain a state. For Alfred Rosenberg, Zionism was "a step taken by specula-tors to insure for themselves a new field of activities in order to exploit the world."[3] According to Hitler, if the Jews were left among themselves, they would be like a pack of rats fighting one another to death: "If the Jews were alone in the world, they would choke in filth." A characteristic Nazi view was expressed by the editor of the party newspaper *Angriff,* who toured Palestine in 1937. In a letter to the head of the Near Eastern division of the German Foreign Ministry, he observed: "it is good that the Jews from Germany came to Palestine and spent their fortune here. . . . Palestine is a suitable place for German Jewish immigration. They will not take root there, their fortunes will be spent and the Arabs will liquidate them. . . . The Jews in Palestine are doomed, their end will be to leap from the frying pan into the fire."[4]

Clearly, to those holding such opinions, the idea of a Jewish state was incapable of realization, and therefore posed no problem to Germany. But in the meantime another school of thought had begun to develop, particularly in the German Foreign Office, and found expression in two important memoranda issued in June 1937. One, written by von Neurath, the German minister of foreign affairs, was sent on June 1 to the German Embassy in London, the Consulate General in Jerusalem, and the legation in Baghdad. The other, dated June 22, was prepared in the *Referat Deutschland,* the Nazi depart-ment in the Foreign Ministry, and was circulated to all German diplomatic and consulate posts abroad. In no small measure because of Nazi persecution, the Jewish settlement in Palestine had risen considerably in numbers and resources during the mid-thirties. More important, the British Royal Commission, headed by Lord Peel, was completing its report after a lengthy investigation of the Palestine problem. Although the Peel commission report was not published until July, its general purport was already known. The report was remarkable for the sympathetic understanding which it showed both of Zionism and of Arab nationalism. Its most important recommendation was to give partial satisfaction to both by a partition of Mandatory Palestine and the creation of two separate states, one Jewish, the other Arab. The notion of partition, which long dominated all consideration of the Palestine problem, was here given official expression for the first time. With these recommendations, the idea of a Jewish state was no longer a figment of Zionist imagination. It had become a practical proposal, contained in the recommendation of a British, i.e., Aryan, government report.

German policymakers were quick to take account of this change. In the words of von Neurath's instructions: "Heretofore it was the primary goal of Germany's Jewish policy to promote the emigration of Jews from Germany as much as possible. In order to achieve this goal, sacrifices are even being made in foreign exchange policy [a reference to the currency transfers allowed to Jews leaving Germany for Palestine]."[5] In this new situation, the document explains, the German attitude to Palestinian affairs can no longer be determined by internal political considerations: "The formation of a Jewish state or a Jewish-led political structure under British mandate is not in Germany's interest, since a Palestinian state would not absorb world Jewry, but would create an additional position of power under international law for international Jewry, somewhat like the Vatican state for political Catholicism or Moscow for the Comintern." Opposition to a Jewish state obviously implies support for its Arab opponents: "Germany therefore has an interest in strengthening the Arab world as a counterweight against such a possible increase in power for world Jewry." German opposition to the Jewish state is also expressed in similar terms in the circular of June 22, with an added ideological argument: "In reality, there is a greater German interest in maintaining the dispersion of Jewry. Even when no member of the Jewish race is settled on German soil, the Jewish problem will still not be solved for Germany. Rather, the developments of recent years have shown that international Jewry will necessarily always be an ideological and therefore also a political enemy of National Socialist Germany. The Jewish question is thus also one of the most important problems of German foreign policy."[6]

Instructions were therefore sent to German missions in the Middle East to adopt a more sympathetic but still rather cautious attitude towards the Arabs. Fritz Grobba, the German minister in Baghdad, was told that "the German understanding of Arab national aspirations should be expressed more clearly than before, but without making any definite promises."

The reason for this continuing caution was still the hope to avoid a final breach with England. Even the financial help to Arab rebels, which had been provided from German Secret Service sources, was still small and irregular. Germany was willing to give general encouragement and some secret help to Arab opponents of British power, but, until Munich, stopped well short of the point where this might endanger German–British relations. In the aftermath of the Munich Pact of 1938, and especially after the invasion of Czechoslovakia in March 1939, it was clear, in Berlin if not in London, that Germany and Britain would be on opposite sides in the approaching war. German propaganda to the Arab world became correspondingly more active and more assertive. Radio broadcasts in Arabic were begun in the summer of 1938 and proved immensely effective at a time when radio audiences had not yet developed the jaded palate of our own time. Supplemented by many other forms of propaganda —including broadcast and print—they evoked a powerful response. Even so, however, the Arabs were still not getting the specific promises and tangible help that they desired and expected from Germany. Though British feelings might no longer be a consideration with German policymakers, there were still other powers with interests in the Middle East, whose goodwill was more important than that of the Arabs.

German policymakers and officials dealing with Arab affairs were thus subject to a number of constraints. Those Arab spokesmen who favored a German alliance suffered from no such restrictions. As they repeatedly explained to high German personalities, including the Führer himself, the Arabs supported and trusted Germany because they were fighting against the same enemies. At first this meant the British, the French, and the Jews. Later, with the realignment of forces in the war, the French disappeared from the list and their place was taken first by the Soviets and then also by the Americans.

To fight against the same enemies is certainly a powerful inducement to make common cause. But there were other, deeper, factors which favored German propaganda in the Arab lands and helped to earn it a sympathetic reception. Not only were Britain and France the empires which for a while dominated the Middle East. They were old and secure nations, and their nationhood was expressed in nation-states that satisfied their national and territorial aspirations. The low-key patriotism of Western Europe, and its commitment to a rather legal definition of nationality, had little in common with the emergent nationalism of the Arab world. Unlike the English or the French, the Arabs had no one single nation state, but were divided into a large number of political entities, almost all of them under a greater or lesser degree of foreign control. Their sense of nationhood was old and deep-rooted, but in its traditional forms it had found expression in terms of language, culture, and sometimes descent. For many centuries past, the sense of Arab nationhood had neither affected, nor been affected by, political identity or allegiance. Only very recently, under the impact of changing circumstances and new ideas, Arab intellectuals and, to a lesser extent, politicians had begun to think in terms of an Arab nation, possessing political rights and aspirations, and entitled to express its nationhood in statehood. For the Arab nationalists, the experience of the British and French nations was of little relevance, and their conceptions of nationality and of patriotism alien and confusing. In contrast, the recent history of Italy and still more of Germany offered a much closer parallel to their own travails. The German nation too, like the Arabs, had been split up into a great number of separate states and principalities, some of them incorporated in non-German kingdoms. The successful struggle by which Prussia had achieved the unification of most of the Germans provided an example, indeed a model; and in their own day Adolf Hitler seemed to be continuing and completing the work of bringing all the Germans into a single mighty pan-Germanic state.

More than a strategy of political unification was involved. Unlike that of the British and the French, the German sense of nationality was not defined in terms of citizenship and allegiance—of membership in a political community and of loyalty owed to its duly constituted rulers. German identity was defined, not by frontiers and sovereignty, but by language, culture, history, and, for the Nazis, blood. The situation in the German lands, especially in the nine-teenth century, corresponded much more closely to the ethnic con-fusion and political fragmentation of the Middle East; German-style nationalism, for the same reasons, was more intelligible and more appealing than British or French-style patriotism.

Even before the Germans began to direct large-scale propaganda to the Arab world, the impact of their ideology was felt. The anti-Jewish theme, which had been at most a minor element in earlier versions of German nationalism and became a major theme in the Nazi version, gave it an added appeal for a people who felt them-selves threatened by the development of a Jewish National Home in their midst and the prospect of the creation of a Jewish state. Hostil-ity to Jews was stressed both in German propaganda to the Arabs and in Arab appeals to the Germans. German officials reporting on Arab affairs referred repeatedly to the value of anti-Jewish feelings in promoting their cause.

In principle, of course, the Germans were not just anti-Jewish, but anti-Semitic, and the Arabs as well as the Jews were theoretically subject to the hostility and contempt implicit in Nazi racist ideology. Some Germans, including the Führer himself, did indeed view the Arabs in this light, and there is no lack of derogatory references, in the German documents, to Arab racial origins and attributes. But this racist doctrine seems to have had remarkably little effect on Ger-man–Arab relations. Both sides, especially from the summer of 1937, when a new and more active German policy towards the Arabs was initiated, tried to avoid raising this awkward issue. Some of the Ger-man Arabists, like others elsewhere, became deeply committed to Arab causes. Some even attempted to persuade the National Socialist Party to amend the racial clause in its rules and limit it to Jews. There were even suggestions from German ambassadors and consuls in the Arab lands to amend the anti-Semitic passages in *Mein Kampf* so that they would merely be anti-Jewish. These proposals to tamper with the sacred text were naturally rejected, but there were some signs in Nazi circles of a willingness to accord honorary Aryan status to at least some Arabs.

One candidate nominated for this honor was the mufti of Jerusa-lem, the leader of the Palestine Arab Higher Committee, the Ḥājj Amîn al-Ḥusaynî, principal architect of the wartime alliance between German Nazism, Italian fascism, and Arab nationalism. The mufti made his first approach to the German consul in Jerusalem in 1933, soon after Hitler's accession to power. His objectives, as he explained on numerous occasions to German officials, were far-reaching. His immediate aim was to halt and terminate the Jewish settlement in Palestine. Beyond that, however, he aimed at much vaster purposes, conceived not so much in pan-Arab as in pan-Islamic terms, for a Holy War of Islam in alliance with Germany against world Jewry, to accomplish the final solution of the Jewish problem everywhere.[7]

A writer in the Nazi party newspaper *Völkischer Beobachter*, December 4, 1937, rejects the idea that the Arabs are pure Semites, and speaks of partial Aryanization through Armenian and Circassian elements. He cites as example the mufti of Jerusalem, whose red beard and blue eyes reveal the dominant Circassian strain of his mother. Even more convincing than his facial features, in the view of this writer, was his character: "Had the Mufti been pure Arab, he would have lacked the will and the endurance to carry on a sustained struggle against the British, and would certainly have been open to bribery."[8]

Such dubious compliments from Nazi ideologists do not seem to have bothered their Arab clients, who rightly saw in Nazi anti-Semitism a war against the Jews and the Jews alone. They soon realized that references to other Semites were no more than ideological claptrap with no relevance to the political and military realities of their relationship.

A first attempt to found an Arab Nazi movement seems to date from the summer of 1933, when the Jaffa correspondent of the Cairo newspaper *al-Ahrām* applied to the German consul for help. It was not forthcoming. Despite this rebuff, motivated by larger strategic considerations, the influence of Nazi ideology continued to grow. The mood of the 1930s was vividly described by Syrian Sāmī al-Jundī, an early leader of the Ba^{c}th party, in an autobiographical memoir:

We were racists, admiring Nazism, reading its books and the source of its thought, particularly Nietzsche. . . . Fichte, and H. S. Chamberlain's *Foundations of the Nineteenth Century*, which revolves on race. We were the first to think of translating *Mein Kampf*.

Whoever lived during this period in Damascus would appreciate the inclination of the Arab people to Nazism, for Nazism was the power which could serve as its champion, and he who is defeated will by nature love the victor.[9]

Later al-Jundî describes how in 1940 he was looking for a copy of Rosenberg's *Myth of the Twentieth Century* in Damascus, and finally found a French abridgment of it belonging to Michel Aflaq, one of the two founders of the Ba^Cth.

Several of the political parties founded at this time reveal the influence of the Nazi model. In 1934, when the anti-Jewish Nuremberg Laws were promulgated, telegrams of congratulation were sent to the Führer from all over the Arab and Islamic worlds, especially from Morocco and Palestine, where German propaganda had been most active. By September 1937, when a major pan-Arab congress was held at Bludan with the struggle against Zionism as its main theme, the only European present was a German.

Before long, political parties of the Nazi and fascist type began to appear, complete with paramilitary youth organizations, colored shirts, strict discipline, and more or less charismatic leaders. Even some of the older parties were affected by these trends. Notable among these new parties was the Syrian Popular Party, also known as the Syrian National Socialist Party (more recently renamed Social Nationalist Party), founded by Anṭūn Sa^Cada, which exercised a powerful attraction on Arab youth in Syria and Lebanon during the 1930s. The party was in due course suppressed by the French mandatory authorities, and again by the successor states, but its spirit lived on in the Qawmiyyūn al-^CArab, the Arab nationalist party of the postwar years. More obviously Nazi in form was the Young Egypt Society, formally established in October 1933. Popularly known as "the Green Shirts," it consisted of a paramilitary hierarchy of sections, troops, squadrons, and brigades, all under the command of a "general staff." The major Egyptian political party, the Wafd, felt obliged to counter its popularity by organizing its own youth corps of Blue Shirts.

The Nazi inclinations of Aḥmad Ḥusayn, the founder and leader of the Young Egypt Party, were clear from the start. In June 1934 he called on the German ambassador to Egypt "to express his sympathy for the new Germany." In 1936 he sent a delegation to the Nuremberg rally, and in the summer of 1938 he himself went on a visit to Germany, where he was very well received and from which he returned full of enthusiasm. This enthusiasm ended abruptly with the Munich crisis in September 1938, after which the leaders of Young Egypt denounced the Axis powers for their aggression against small nations. Their ideology and form of organization and activity remained, however, thoroughly Nazi, including such devices as fascist salutes, torchlight parades, leader worship [their slogan was "One party, one state, one leadership"] and, most characteristically, their use of gangs of toughs to terrorize and silence their political opponents.

Not least among the borrowings of Young Egypt from Young Germany was its racism and anti-Semitism. This included support for Nazi philosophy, viciously anti-Jewish propaganda in the party press, and the organization of boycotts and harassment directed against the Jewish community in Egypt.

Despite the public breach with the Germans after the invasion of Czechoslovakia, the inner circle of pro-Axis politicians congregated around the king, and led by ᶜAlī Māhir Pasha, who was prime minister in 1939–40, remained in touch with Young Egypt, to which they gave both political and financial support. General ᶜAzīz ᶜAlī al-Maṣrī, a leading pro-German in Egypt and a close associate of the Young Egypt leader, formed and led an espionage ring to work for German intelligence. A number of these officers seem to have had connections with Young Egypt.

The impact of the Young Egypt Party on Egyptian politics before the outbreak of war in 1939 was comparatively slight, and the efforts at espionage of the young officers grouped around General al-Maṣrī were somewhat inefficient and cannot have been of great value to the Germans. The party did, however, exercise a considerable intellectual influence on the group of officers who finally made the military revolution of 1952, and installed the Nasserist regime in power. Both Gamal Abdel Nasser and Anwar Sadat came from this circle, as did a number of the other officers who conspired with them against King Faruq and governed Egypt after their success.

In the summer of 1940, the crushing Allied defeat on the West European mainland, the entry of Italy into the war, and signing of a separate peace by France, made many Arab leaders believe—with some plausibility—that their moment had come at last and that they would be able to throw off the hated British and French yoke. For this, however, they needed German help, since the British, and even the Vichy French, still disposed of sufficient military force in the Middle East to deal with any Arab rising. An inter-Arab mission was organized by the mufti and sent via neutral Turkey to Berlin, to establish direct contact with the German government at the highest level. This committee included government-appointed representatives from those Arab states—such as Iraq and Saudi Arabia—which already possessed the necessary degree of independence to enable them to do so, and from nationalist committees in those countries which were still controlled by the Allied powers.

The mufti had in the meantime transferred himself from British-ruled Palestine to Lebanon and thence, in October 1939, to Iraq, where he continued his activities. He played some role in the establishment and activities of the strongly pro-German regime of Rashîd ^CAlî al-Gaylânî, who became prime minister of Iraq in March 1940. Rashîd ^CAlî and the mufti sought and obtained promises of Axis support, and in April 1941 carried out an anti-British and pro-German coup. From Iraq they tried to extend their influence to other Arab countries, and notably to Syria, then under the control of the Vichy French authorities. In Damascus two schoolteachers, Michel Aflaq and Salâh al-Dîn al-Bîtâr, formed a "Society to help Iraq." This was the nucleus of what later became the Ba^Cth party. German help was too little and too late to save Rashîd ^CAlî from defeat by a small, scratch force of British, Jordanian, and some other troops. The mufti escaped to Iran together with Rashîd ^CAlî and various members of his regime.

Iran was becoming unsafe for friends of the Axis which, however, looked after its own. In August 1941, the mufti was taken first to the Japanese and then to the Italian legation, where he stayed for a while in hiding. On October 8, 1941, when the new masters of Iran, the Russians and the British, compelled the rupture of diplomatic relations with the Axis powers, the mufti—with shaven beard, dyed hair, and an Italian service passport—left for Italy with the staff of the Italian legation. On his arrival in Rome, on October 11, he immediately made contact with Italian military intelligence (Servizio Informazioni Militari) and very soon after with Mussolini himself, who gave him a warm welcome, no doubt hoping to be able to use him for his own Arab policies. The mufti claimed to be head of a secret Arab nationalist organization with branches in all Arab countries, which, he said, would be willing to join the Axis forces in their war against Britain "on the sole condition that they recognize in principle the unity, independence, and sovereignty of an Arab state of a Fascist nature, including Iraq, Syria, Palestine, and Trans-Jordan."[10] In return, the Arabs, according to the mufti, would be ready to discuss political and military issues of concern to the Axis powers in general and to Italy in particular, such as "the Holy Places, Lebanon, the Suez canal, and ᶜAqaba."

The mufti's proposal was approved by the Italian Foreign Ministry, which recommended that he be given an initial grant of one million lire (about $40,000 at that time) and passed the papers to Mussolini. The Duce gave his blessing, and agreed to meet the mufti. The two men met in Rome on October 27, 1941, only two weeks after the mufti's arrival in Italy. In the mufti's account of this meeting, the only one that has so far come to light, Mussolini expressed hostility to the Jews, whom he described as spies, agents and propagandists for the British. "They are our enemies . . . and there will be no place for them in Europe, even in Italy where at most there are 45,000 of them out of a population of 45 million. They are few, but nevertheless only those who are deserving will remain. Not more than 2,500." According to this report, Mussolini, "a veteran anti-Zionist," fully agreed with the mufti's opposition to "a Zionist state in Palestine . . . they have no historical, racial, or other reason to establish a state in Palestine. . . . If the Jews want it they should establish Tel Aviv in America."

From the mufti's point of view, the meeting with Mussolini went well and achieved general agreement between the two parties. But much remained to be done. The declaration to be issued by the Axis in support of the Arabs was not yet drafted, and more important, Germany, very much the senior partner in the Axis, still had to give her consent. On November 3, a few days after his meeting with the Duce, the mufti prepared yet another draft of the declaration. After some minor emendations by the Italian Foreign Office, the draft was presented to Mussolini and then forwarded with his approval, on November 6, to the German Embassy in Rome. On the same day the mufti reached Berlin, where he met with Ernst von Weizsäcker, secretary of state in the German Foreign Office. After discussions of the draft declaration with him and other German officials, the text was approved with minor changes which in turn were accepted by the Italians. The declaration, according to the summary that has been

published,[11] was no more than a bland statement of general principles. It did, however, include a provision by which the Axis powers
declared themselves ready to give their approval for the elimination
(Beseitigung) of the Jewish National Home in Palestine. This declaration of intent was "in the near future to be set forth in a formal
document which would seal the sincere friendship and close cooperation in the future between the Axis powers and the Arabs. Negotiations for the conclusion of such a treaty would be undertaken as soon
as possible."[12]

The situation, therefore, seemed very promising, from the mufti's
point of view, when he had his meeting with Hitler on November 28,
1941. In fact, the mufti was somewhat disappointed with what he
heard. In answer to his opening statement on what the Arabs were
willing and able to bring to the German cause and what they hoped
for in return, the Führer began with the strongest reaffirmation of
his anti-Jewish position:

The foundations of the bitter struggle which he was waging were clear. He
was waging an uncompromising struggle against the Jews. To this belonged
the struggle against the Jewish settlements in Palestine, because by this
means the Jews wanted to create a state base for their destructive activities
in other countries. It was clear that the Jews had carried out no constructive
work in Palestine. This assertion was a swindle. All the work that had been
done in Palestine was done by the Arabs. He was determined to solve the
Jewish problem step by step, and to address a corresponding appeal to other
peoples, also non-European peoples.[13]

But while the Führer was generous with anti-Jewish declarations,
he was much more cautious in making the pro-Arab statements that
the mufti wanted. "Platonic assurances," said the Führer, "would be
completely useless; only assurances supported by a victorious power
would have any real value." The real issue was being determined in
the great battles in Eastern Europe. Meanwhile, assurances to the
Arabs, unsupported by real force, would only strengthen the Gaul-
lists against the Vichy French. A declaration now would do the Arabs
no good, and could do harm to their common cause. In answer to the
mufti's suggestion that the Führer should give him or Rashīd ᶜAlī a
secret written declaration, the Führer replied that a declaration of
which several people had knowledge was not secret but public. He
had given few declarations in his life while the English had given
many. If he gave a declaration he would stand by it. Meanwhile, he

would carry on the struggle until the Jew–Communist empire in Europe was completely destroyed. In the course of this struggle, in the not too distant future, German troops would reach the southern slopes of the Caucasus. "Then he would be willing to issue such a declaration, for the hour of Arab liberation would then have struck. Germany had no other interest there other than the annihilation of the power that was protecting Jewry." With this German penetration, the destruction of the British Empire would begin. And then it would be a matter of indifference to him what Western Europe would say. He reminded his listener that the way from Rostov to Iran or Iraq was shorter than the road from Berlin to Rostov. He ended his statement with friendly remarks to the mufti and his cause and repeated that: "When we come to the South Caucasus then also will come the liberation of the Arabs. The Grand Mufti could rely on this word."[14]

A few days later, the Germans informed their Italian allies of this meeting and of the Führer's decision that the issue of the declaration should be postponed "for military reasons." The Italians disagreed but deferred to German wishes. The mufti, though disappointed, now tried a new diplomatic tack and asked the Axis powers to issue two statements, one to Rashîd ᶜAlî, recognizing Iraq's independence, and the other to both himself and Rashîd ᶜAlî, assuring the independence and unity of the Arab countries of the Fertile Crescent. After much negotiation with both the Axis powers, the mufti received very limited assent to this proposal. Two letters were sent by the foreign ministers of Germany and Italy to the two Arab leaders. One of them, dated March 31, was sent to Rashîd ᶜAlî and promised recognition of Iraqi independence; the other, dated April 28, 1942, was addressed to both Rashîd ᶜAlî and the mufti, and promised Axis support for the sovereign independence of the Arab countries of the Middle East as well as support for their unification if they wished it, and the "elimination" of the Jewish National Home in Palestine.[15] The texts of these letters are full of carefully worded escape clauses, and were moreover to be regarded as secret. As Hirszowicz remarks: "Only the promise to liquidate the Jewish National Home in Palestine was unambiguous."[16]

The Axis powers do not seem to have attached any great importance to these documents, and the mufti and his associates can have had few illusions as to their value. They continued, however, their strong support for the Axis, in the belief, probably well-founded, that an Axis victory would create a world more congenial to their aims and purposes than one dominated by the Western Allies.

In the years that followed, the mufti, with Rashîd ᶜAlî and some others, continued to shuttle between Rome and Berlin in the hope of obtaining the public declaration of support for Arab political aims that they desired. Curiously, he received more sympathetic answers from the Italians than from the Germans. The Italian Fascist government, with its own imperial plans for the Arab world, was more conscious of the mufti's potential value, and more willing to make use of him. Less encumbered than the Nazis with racist ideologies, they may have placed a higher value on the usefulness of the Arabs as allies or agents. In the last analysis, however, both Axis powers were unwilling to commit themselves publicly, or for that matter even privately, to full support for the mufti's pan-Arab and pan-Islamic projects, or even to grant him the full personal recognition which he sought as the Führer of the whole Arab nation.

In addition to his work among the Arabs, mainly channelled through the "Arab Bureau" in Berlin, the mufti made himself useful to his German hosts in other ways, notably in organizing support among Soviet and Balkan Muslims. This had a military as well as a political effect. The German–Arab legion, based in Greece, was never of any great significance. Of far greater importance were the Muslim units in the German army, raised in the main from among Soviet Muslims, prisoners of war and others. The mufti played some part in stimulating and organizing this movement, and in acting as liaison between the Germans and anti-Soviet Muslim groups in the Crimea, the Caucasian lands, and Central Asia. He seems to have been particularly concerned with the formation of a Waffen SS volunteer division of mountain troops, raised among the Muslims of Bosnia and Herzegovina. These troops played some part in the destruction of Yugoslav Jewry.[17]

While the mufti's diplomatic efforts for the Arab cause were a failure even within the context of a Nazi victory, his propaganda efforts for the Axis cause were remarkably effective. The one point on which he and his Nazi hosts were completely and unequivocally in accord was the Jewish question, and it was on this that the mufti laid the main stress in the vast barrage of propaganda which he addressed to the Arab world and more generally to the world of

Islam. The mufti's perception of the war is vividly expressed in a speech which he broadcast on November 11, 1942, in commemoration of the martyrs of the Arab cause:

Before the outbreak of this war and before the Axis took arms to put a stop to Anglo-Saxon Jewish greed, there was one nation which had fought alone against these forces for more than twenty years.

That nation is our own Arab nation, which has fought against the English and the Jews in Egypt, in Palestine, in Iraq, in Syria, and in all parts of the Arabian Peninsula. After the outbreak of the present war our nation continued this struggle, determined to achieve its aims, that is, liberty, independence, unity and sovereignty. . . .

From the outbreak of this war, the Arab nation had neither peace nor neutrality. It was engaged alone in the hardest struggle against the Anglo-Saxon Jewish policies. This war was for the Arab people none other than the continuation of the uninterrupted struggle which it has sustained alone for twenty years. Today the Arab people has at its side the powerful enemies of its own enemy. In this war the Arabs are not neutral. They cannot be neutral for the reasons I have already given and for the interest which they have in the result of this war. If, God forbid, England should be victorious, the Jews would dominate the world. England and her allies would deny the Arabs any freedom and independence, would strike the Arab fatherland to its heart, and would tear away parts of it to form a Jewish country whose ambition would not be limited to Palestine but would extend to other Arab countries. . . .

But if, on the contrary, England loses and its allies are defeated, the Jewish question, which for us constitutes the greatest danger, would be finally resolved; all threats against the Arab countries would disappear, millions of Arabs would be freed, and many millions of Muslims in Asia and Africa would be saved.[18]

The question that inevitably arises from these remarks is how far the mufti was aware of the full implications of his reference to a "final solution" to the Jewish question. In his postwar memoirs, the mufti insists that his aim was not to destroy European Jewry, but merely to prevent their emigration. Unlike so many of his wartime German comrades, he does not claim that he had no knowledge of the death camps.

For the mufti, the struggle against the Jews was the major theme of World War II, a point which he made frequently in broadcast and other statements. He made his own not insignificant contribution to the destruction of European Jewry.

This happened in several ways. One of them was by obstructing

Jewish emigration from Europe. The Jews of Hungary, Rumania, Bulgaria, and Italy were subject to governments allied with Germany. This was bad enough, but not nearly as bad as the position of Jews in those countries which were conquered and ruled directly by the Germans. These Axis allies showed some willingness to get rid of their Jews by emigration rather than by extermination. In May and June 1943, the mufti sent letters to all four governments demanding that they withdraw their authorization for Jewish emigration and urging them instead to send their Jews to Poland "where they are under active control."[19]

How far the mufti understood the real nature of this "active control" is not entirely certain. In the course of the Nuremberg trials of Nazi war criminals, one of the accused, Dieter Wisliceny, made some statements on this point. Wisliceny was an aide of Adolf Eichmann, one of Hitler's chief executives in the extermination of the Jews. According to Wisliceny, the mufti was a friend of Eichmann and had, in his company, gone incognito to visit the gas chamber at Auschwitz. Wisliceny even names the mufti as being an "initiator" of the policy of extermination. This was denied, both by Eichmann at his trial in Jerusalem in 1961, and by the mufti in a press conference at about the same time. There is no independent documentary confirmation of Wisliceny's statements, and it seems unlikely that the Nazis needed any such additional encouragement from outside.

Some points may, however, be noted. The mufti, unlike the German leaders, had a compelling motive to oppose emigration as a way of disposing of the Jews of Europe, and had actively intervened—on this there is ample written evidence—to prevent Jews from leaving. The mufti's own testimony, contained in his published memoirs, is of some interest. The letters he sent to various European governments, he remarks, produced "positive and useful results for the Palestinian cause." They served however as the basis of a Jewish complaint to the UN in 1947, and an unsuccessful attempt by them to have him tried, with the other accused at Nuremberg, as a war criminal. Their case, he observed in his memoirs, rested on the testimony of Krumey, another of Eichmann's aides: "They promised him that they would save him from the death penalty if he would sign their false testimony. But they—who are notorious for perfidy and falsification and distortion and cruelty, of which the noble Qur'ān provides the strongest testimony against them—never fulfill their promises to anyone, and he was condemned to death at Nuremberg." The mufti does not mention Wisliceny, though he praises Eichmann as "gallant and noble" for having denied, while in Israeli custody, that there had been any connection between the two men. Of his own role the mufti has this to say: "The truth is that when I sent these memoranda to the responsible authorities of the German Reich, and of the above-mentioned states, I was not aiming at the extermination of the Jews; I was striving to prevent the flood of aggressive Jewish immigration aimed at drowning Palestine and the expulsion of its people, as happened afterwards with the help of Britain and the USA."[20]

In a broadcast which he made from Berlin on September 21, 1944, he spoke of "the eleven million Jews of the world." The mufti, obsessed with Jewish matters, must have known that in 1939 there were about seventeen million Jews in the world. There is a blood-chilling accuracy in the disparity.

In their discussions with German officials, the mufti and other Arab leaders presented what seems to have been the first of a series of drafts of a declaration in support of Arab aims and purposes which they were asking the German government to publish. With such a declaration, they believed that they would be able to mobilize massive Arab support against Britain and in favor of Germany. One of the clauses in the draft declaration submitted by the Arab committee to the German government for approval and publication is especially significant: "Germany and Italy recognize the right of the Arab countries to solve the question of the Jewish elements which exist in Palestine and in other Arab countries as required by the national and ethnic [völkisch] interests of the Arabs and as the Jewish question was solved in Germany and Italy."[21]

In the summer of 1940, the gas chambers had not yet been built, and the systematic extermination of the Jews was confined to Poland. But the withdrawal from Jews of all civil, political, and human rights was already an accomplished fact in Germany and in the countries under German control or influence, and this was certainly well known to the Arab committee. It is significant that the proposed clause dealt not only with the Zionist settlements in Palestine, but was extended generally to all the Jews in Arab countries, who were to share the same fate—as indeed some of them did. Both the language and the content of the clause reveal clearly the Nazi influence on the formulation of the Arab proposals.

The Germans, for a variety of reasons mostly arising from their dealings with other powers more important in their eyes than the Arabs, gave evasive answers on the subject of the declaration. A revised version was submitted to the Führer's headquarters in February 1941 and again was accorded no definite answer. In the revised version the Jewish clause was amended to read as follows:

Germany and Italy recognize the illegality of the Jewish National Home in Palestine. They recognize the right of Palestine and other Arab countries to solve the question of the Jewish elements in Palestine and in the other Arab countries as required by national Arab interests, and in the same way as the Jewish question in the Axis lands is being solved. From this it follows that no Jewish emigration to the Arab lands is permitted.[22]

This differs in two significant respects from the June 1940 version. One is the change from the past to the present tense in the reference to the solution to the Jewish problem in Europe, now defined as "the Axis lands," and not merely as Germany and Italy. The other, linked with it, is the ban on Jewish emigration to the Arab lands.

The first Axis-style attack on a Jewish community in an Arab land occurred in Baghdad on June 1 and 2, 1941, in the brief interregnum between the collapse of the pro-German Rashīd ᶜAlī regime and the arrival of the British troops. On this occasion it was the mob, not the authorities, that took action. According to official sources, 600 Jews were killed and 240 injured, 586 business premises sacked, and 911 houses destroyed. Unofficial estimates were much higher. The massacre was carried out by troops, police, and other elements incited by the fallen Rashīd ᶜAlī regime, and seeking vengeance for its defeat. For two days the massacre continued unopposed, while the British army, which by this time had the city at its mercy, took no action but waited in the outskirts. Somerset de Chair, who was serving with the British force as an intelligence officer, explains what happened:

Reading came to me. "Why do our troops not go into Baghdad?" he asked. "Already they may be looting. I know there will be many people killed if our troops do not enter."

This was my own view and the ways of the Foreign Office were beyond my comprehension. From the hour of the Cease Fire their word had prevailed. Having fought their way, step by step, to the threshold of the city, we must now cool our heels outside. It would, apparently, be lowering to the dignity of our ally, the Regent, if he were seen to be supported on arrival by British bayonets.[23]

The British Ambassador to Iraq, Sir Kinahan Cornwallis, had already stated his view that British forces should not occupy Baghdad "except temporarily to secure favorable government or at request Iraqi government." The Jews of Baghdad had learned in these two terrible days that they were completely at the mercy of their neighbors and masters. They had also learned that Western governments, solicitous for good relations with these same masters, would do little or nothing to help them. Needless to say, the lesson was not lost on the masters themselves.

While the mufti and his associates were at work in Germany, there were many in the Arab lands of the Middle East and North Africa who were at least in sympathy with the same cause, and sometimes active on its behalf. The mood of the young officers in Egypt at that time is vividly described by one of them, Anwar Sadat:

For England, 1941 was a tragic year. For Egypt, it was a year of hope. The British empire was confronted with the most dangerous situation in its history. In the eastern Mediterranean, the revolt of Rashid Ali convulsed Iraq; in the west, the Axis was on the march; and between the two Egypt was stirring, ready to enter the fight. For Churchill it was really a desperate hour. . . .

The Axis had superior forces. The fascist war machine was now in the experienced hands of the Germans. Defeat stared Britain in the face. Egypt owed it to herself to profit from these very favorable circumstances. The morale of our forces was very high, and they were ready to fight.

We made contact with the German headquarters in Libya and we acted in complete harmony with them. For the intervention of Egypt could not take the form of an unsupported internal rising. We were not ready to act alone, and a regular war with the British was out of the question, for weakened though she was, England had built up her armaments on an impressive scale. But if a junction could be effective [sic] between Egyptian insurgents and Axis troops, our war would become an international affair. We followed events from day to day, pushing ahead with our preparations and making the best use of the modest resources at our disposal.[24]

Anwar Sadat was caught and put away, as were a number of his associates.[25] Others were more fortunate, though not more effective. Many ostensibly neutral or even pro-Allied politicians kept a line open to one or other of the Axis powers, at least as long as these seemed likely to win the war, and sometimes far beyond that. King Faruq and some of his ministers were in regular contact with the Axis, and even such old and respected allies of Britain as Ibn Saᶜūd, the founder of the Saudi Arabian kingdom, and Nūrī al-Sa^cīd, the Prime Minister of Iraq, were at times in touch with Berlin. Nūrī al-Sa^cīd went so far as to offer his services to the Germans, and suffered the humiliation of being spurned by them. They did not trust him, unjustly suspecting a British trick.[26]

So strong was the pro-German sentiment, that even after the final defeat of the Third Reich it did not fade away and—what is perhaps more significant—it was not concealed. On the contrary, a pro-Nazi past was a source of pride, not shame. The mufti, with other members of the Ḥusaynī clan, escaped from Germany before the debacle and traveled via Paris to the Middle East, where he was again able to play a role of some importance in the events of the postwar years. Though not admitted by the British to Mandatory Palestine, he was welcomed by the government of Egypt. In 1951, he presided over a world Muslim conference, and in 1955 attended the first Afro-Asian conference at Bandoeng. At no stage did he in any way recant or modify his views on the Jews, though in 1961, at the time of the Eichmann trial, he denied that he had been personally acquainted with Eichmann and that he had visited the death camps.

In the early years of the Nasser regime, before the entry and consolidation of Soviet influence in Egypt, the Nazi sympathies of the new rulers of Egypt were undisguised. It will be recalled that in these years Egypt vied with Fascist Spain, racist South Africa, and the military dictatorships of Latin America in providing a haven and a new field of activity for Nazi war criminals on the run. They offered varying attractions. In South Africa, Nazi émigrés could resume life as members of a privileged master race; in Spain and South America, they could enjoy the congenial atmosphere of a fascist dictatorship and ideology. In Egypt they could continue the war against the Jews. Those who made this choice were given a warm welcome and a new field of activity.

The use of "Nazi" in the Arab countries as a term of abuse is comparatively recent, and dates back to the period of General Qāsim's rule in Iraq. His use of the adjective "Hitlerite" to insult President Nasser during the quarrel between the two was recognized at the time as a sign of Soviet penetration. Arab liberals and socialists—in the more conventional sense of these words—were as horrified by Nazism as were their Western counterparts. But the militant leaders of Arab nationalism, both right and left, saw in Hit-

ler's Germany the model of successful nationalism or national socialism, and an inspiring guide and helper in the struggle against their
two great enemies, the West and the Jews. As this role was taken over
by Soviet Russia, some adjustment in political terminology became
necessary. But the memory of Hitler remained green, and his works
and those of his disciples and predecessors were still being translated
and read even—or perhaps especially—in the so-called revolutionary
socialist Arab lands.

Some signs of this affinity with the Third Reich remained long
after Soviet influence had made "Nazi" and "Hitlerite" dirty words.
Both Gamal Abdel Nasser and Anwar Sadat are on record as expressing their admiration, the latter also his active support, for Hitler, and
their deep regret at the Nazi defeat. In September 1953, when a
rumor was flashed across the world that Hitler was still alive and
living in Brazil, the Cairo weekly *al-Muṣawwar* asked certain public
figures in Egypt what they would write to the Führer if the news
proved to be true.[27] Most of the answers were unflattering. For
example, the writer and journalist Iḥsān ꜥAbd al-Quddūs told him to
"go back to your hiding place, for there is no room in the free world
for a dictator; do you remember the millions you killed, do you
remember the gas chambers?" But one of them had different recollections:

I congratulate you with all my heart, because, though you appear to have
been defeated, you were the real victor. You were able to sow dissension
between Churchill, the old man, and his allies on the one hand and their ally,
the devil, on the other. Germany is victorious because it became necessary
for the world balance of power that Germany be created anew, whatever
East and West might think. There will be no peace until Germany is restored
to what it was, and this is what West and East will bring about in spite of
themselves. . . . As for the past, I think you made some mistakes, such as
opening too many fronts or Ribbentrop's short-sightedness in the face of
Britain's old man diplomacy. But you are forgiven on account of your faith
in your country and people. That you have become immortal in Germany
is reason enough for pride. And we should not be surprised to see you again
in Germany, or a new Hitler in your place—Anwar Sadat.

Anwar Sadat did not speak of the persecution of the Jews, either
positively or negatively, in this document, and later he made it clear
that he had achieved a better and deeper understanding of what had
happened to Jews in German-occupied Europe in the Hitler years.

Others were more faithful to the Führer's memory and principles. On June 26, 1974, the Beirut newspaper *al-Bayraq* reported a conversation in Damascus between the leader of the Lebanese Progressive Socialist Party, Kamāl Jumblātt, and the Syrian president, Ḥāfiẓ al-Asad, accompanied by his foreign minister and leaders of the Syrian Ba^cth party. At one point, one of the Syrians said: "Today the Arabs remember Hitler favorably." To which Jumblātt replied: "At least he would have saved us from the Zionists. We must not take a strong stand against Nazism, just as we must not agree with everything the leftists say. Nazism should be revived somewhat. . . . Some studies say that the number of Jews killed by the Nazis is greatly exaggerated. There are enormously large groups that managed to escape from Germany."

The denial of the Holocaust is of course a favorite theme of pro-Nazi and neo-Nazi propaganda. It occurs frequently in Arabic writings on the subject, and occasionally figures in official statements. Nasser himself, in his interview with the extreme rightist German weekly *Deutsche Nationalzeitung,* published on May 1, 1964, after remarking that "during the Second World War, our sympathies were with the Germans," observed that "the lie of the six million murdered Jews is not taken seriously by anybody." This may well be true of the circles in which the late president moved. At the time of the seizure and trial of Eichmann in Jerusalem in 1961, Arab media comment was mixed. One fairly typical hostile response was a news story in the Saudi newspaper *al-Bilād* of May 31, 1960, under the headline: "Capture of Eichmann, who had the honor of killing five million Jews."

In the meantime, the steady growth of Soviet influence was changing the content and connotation of the term "Nazi" in the Arab lands. The Soviets, for their own good reasons, had systematically understated or even where possible concealed the anti-Jewish component of Nazism and had, for example, preferred not to mention the specifically Jewish reasons why so many of their own citizens were martyred at Babi Yar and elsewhere. To depict the Nazis too emphatically as anti-Semites might have had undesirable consequences. It might have aroused sympathy among some of their people for the Nazis, among others for the Jews, and either of these responses would have been undesirable from the point of view of Soviet officials. "Nazi" thus became a generalized term of abuse, with little or no specific anti-Jewish significance. And since Nazism was now a bad thing, it followed that the Jews themselves must be portrayed as Nazis. This change was the more necessary to fill an ideological vacuum. From 1917 until 1945, and in some regions for long after that, the Jews in general and the Zionists in particular were portrayed in Arab propaganda as communists and bolsheviks and Soviet agents. The communist was, so to speak, the favorite enemy, not only in Nazi Germany but also in the democratic West, and the charge of communism was the quickest and most effective way to discredit an opponent. Even Nasser himself, before his own turn toward the Soviets, sometimes used this label against his opponents. But with the consolidation of Soviet influence, and the general acceptance of some form of socialism or leftism as the new state orthodoxy, such words as "communist" and "socialist" were no longer insults but compliments, and therefore unsuitable for application to Jews. The now-discredited term "Nazi" provided a useful substitute, and the world was thus treated to the strange spectacle of Hitler's erstwhile allies attacking Hitler's foremost victims by calling them Nazis and racists.

More recently, the communist label has been brought back into use, not only in Saudi Arabia, where it was never entirely abandoned, but also in Egypt, where, with the switch from a pro-Soviet to pro-Western alignment, anticommunism has again become respectable, and "communist" is once more an epithet that can be usefully employed to discredit an adversary.

CHAPTER SEVEN

The War Against Zionism

T HE INFLUENCE of Europe and specifically of European anti-Semitism, both by example and by deliberate propaganda, prepared the ground and planted the seeds of the new Arab anti-Semitism. The changing perceptions of religious, national, ethnic, and even racial identity nurtured their growth and efflorescence. The new definitions of loyalty, developing in an age of foreign domination and nationalist struggle, brought a new intolerance of diversity that weakened and undermined the position of other religious and ethnic minorities besides the Jews. But the most important single factor affecting Jews was undoubtedly the Palestine question, and the transformation of Arab and ultimately Muslim attitudes toward them must be seen against the background of the successive phases of the Arab–Zionist and Arab–Israeli conflict.

The evolution of the conflict falls into four distinct periods, punctuated by four decisive events: the beginning of Zionist settlement in Ottoman Palestine in 1882, the replacement of Ottoman by British rule in 1918, the birth of Israel in 1948, and the Israeli victory of 1967, which extended Israeli rule to the whole of Mandatory Palestine.

There had been a steady movement of Jews to the Holy Land throughout the centuries, sometimes in greater, sometimes in smaller numbers according to changing circumstances. But these migrations had always been inspired by religious and what one might call cultural motives, never by political purposes. Sometimes they reached considerable numbers, as in the sixteenth century, when the inclusion of Palestine in the Ottoman Empire created a new security and opportunity for Jews, and enabled them to establish new centers of Jewish population in Jerusalem, Safed, and elsewhere. During the late eighteenth and early nineteenth centuries Jews from Eastern Europe began to move to Palestine, and by 1851 the British vice-consul in Jerusalem described them as an important element in the population. Though their reasons for settling in the Holy Land were religious, and some of them were indeed professional men of religion of one kind or another living on the contributions of their coreligion-ists abroad, many were engaged in economic occupations. In 1851 the vice-consul in Jerusalem reported that "the Jews are almost the only artisans—for it is remarkable that the glaziers, shoemakers, bookbinders, etc. are almost exclusively Jews."[1] To these, Zionist settlement added a new dimension, agriculture, which came to have a key importance in the subsequent development of the Jewish com-munity and of Jewish–Arab relations in Palestine. In 1882, when Zionist settlement began, the Jews of Palestine had reached an es-timated 24,000, being roughly 10 percent of the total population. Their position was no worse than might be expected for a religious minority in a remote province of a declining empire. Some of them, enjoying the protection of foreign governments as well as the tolerance of the Ottoman authorities, were able to do reason-ably well.

The idea of a Jewish buffer state between Egypt and the Turkish empire, first suggested and then rapidly abandoned by Napoleon, reappeared from time to time during the nineteenth century. But such ideas attracted little or no serious attention, least of all from Jews. The first steps towards the realization of the aim of a Jewish state were taken in 1882, with the arrival in Palestine of some three or four thousand Jews from the Russian Empire. Unlike their pre-decessors, they were not old men who came to study, pray, and die, but young men and women who came to work, build and live. This was the first of a series of waves of immigrants, overwhelmingly from Eastern Europe, which by the outbreak of war in 1914 brought the Jewish population in Palestine to between 85,000 and 90,000, of whom a substantial proportion were settled on the land. While the main inspiration for this new immigration and the majority of the immigrants came from Eastern Europe, they were not alone. During the same period some five thousand Jews came from the Yemen, in the remote southwestern corner of Arabia, as well as others from

North Africa and Central Asia, and from other Ottoman provinces, both from the Balkans and the Arab lands.

This movement was well under way before the publication of Herzl's *Jewish State* and the establishment of the Zionist organization, and much of this new immigration, especially from the Islamic countries, was of the older, religious-inspired type. But the new immigration from Russia, though it came before the emergence of political Zionism, was unmistakably driven by the same needs and inspired by the same hopes as those which led Theodor Herzl to write his book and found his new movement. The new Russian immigration began with the "May Laws," the severe anti-Jewish laws which were promulgated in the wave of reaction following the assassination of the Czar Alexander II in 1881, and each successive wave was preceded and in part at least stimulated by some new measure or action against the Jews, some new disappointment of their hopes for emancipation in the lands of their birth. These new immigrants belonged to a movement whose members called themselves "Lovers of Zion," the immediate predecessors of the Zionists. Born among Jewish students in the Russian Empire, the movement was strongly marked by the romantic, nationalist, populist, and socialist ideologies of the time. Their immediate aim was the redemption of Jewish society through creative labor; their more distant aim, at that stage not clearly formulated, was the creation of a Jewish National Home and ultimately a Jewish state. It was natural that when the Zionist movement was launched, they should have given it their enthusiastic support.

From the first the Ottoman government, then responsible for Palestine which was still part of the Ottoman Empire, was aware of the nature of this movement, and alarmed by its possible effects.[2] From the records it is clear that the Ottomans, through their embassies and consulates abroad and their contacts with Jewish leaders, were well-informed about Zionism and the aims of its political leaders and agricultural pioneers. Ottoman official policy was opposed to Zionist plans, and did what it could to prevent their implementation.

It could not do much. There is no evidence that Ottoman opposition to Zionist settlement was inspired by anti-Semitic or even by anti-Jewish feelings. Their policy was determined by calculation, not prejudice, and there were obvious reasons for the policy they adopted. The two main political problems of the Ottoman Empire in

the late nineteenth century were nationalist and secessionist movements among its subject populations, and interference in its affairs by
the great powers of Europe. Zionist settlement in Palestine threatened to aggravate both of these problems. On the one hand, if successful, it would create in an already troubled border province a new
national minority, with autonomist and perhaps ultimately secessionist ambitions of its own; as some Ottoman officials put it at the time,
another Armenia or another Macedonia. And, since most of the Jewish immigrants were protected subjects of European powers, and
therefore, according to the capitulatory regime in existence at the
time, enjoyed extraterritorial privileges, they would provide further
and endless opportunities for great power interference in a country
which already had more than its fair share of such troubles.

The Ottomans used two principal methods to counter Zionist
settlement; by prohibiting Jewish immigration to Palestine, and by
prohibiting or restricting transfers of land to foreign, i.e., non-Otto-
man Jews. Both methods failed. The ban on immigration was far from
complete. It applied only to Palestine and not to other parts of the
Ottoman Empire, to which Jews, like other people, were still admitted freely, whether as visitors or immigrants; and even for Palestine
it prohibited only permanent settlement, but permitted Jews to
enter on business or for pilgrimage. In the bureaucratic confusion of
late Ottoman times, these loopholes were quite sufficient to allow as
many Jews as wished to come, and to stay as long as they chose. The
Ottomans themselves recognized this, and in 1901 granted a kind of
amnesty, allowing permanent resident's rights to long-established
illegal immigrants, in the hope that this would help them to regulate
further immigration. It did not.

Similar difficulties also impeded the full implementation of the
regulations against the sale of land to foreigners. Here again, bureaucratic confusion, the willing complicity of Arab sellers and intermedi-
aries, and the interference of the foreign consuls protecting the
"rights" of their "citizens," were sufficient to reduce, though not to
nullify, the effectiveness of the Ottoman land regulations. The consuls of the powers were most zealous in safeguarding the right which
they enjoyed, under the Capitulations, to intervene for the protection of their nationals. Even the Russians, who at first made no attempt to resist the Ottoman land transfer regulations, and were
suspected by some of having instigated them, changed their line

after 1890, and instructed their consuls to act on behalf of their Jewish subjects in Palestine, who thus received a degree of protection from the Russian authorities which they did not receive in Russia. While the Ottomans were well aware of Russian official anti-Semitism, they could not but view with alarm the growth, in one of their provinces, of a significant minority of foreigners under the protection of that European empire which for centuries they had come to regard as their deadliest and most dangerous enemy.

The Young Turk revolution of 1908 brought no significant change. The Young Turks were certainly more liberal and more open to Western ideas than the old Turks whom they had overthrown, and some of them even showed a sympathetic interest in Jewish problems and in Zionism. But they were also nationalist and centralist, and, in the circumstances of the time, more keenly aware than the deposed sultan of the dangers of autonomy, secession, and foreign annexation. The Young Turks, who, according to the hostile propaganda put about by their enemies, were influenced or even dominated by Jewish conspirators, took stronger action against Zionist immigration and settlement in Palestine than any of their predecessors, and by 1911 the Zionist question even became an issue in the parliamentary politics of the capital. The few Ottoman Jews who played any role—and that a minor one—in Young Turk politics were either indifferent or hostile to Zionism.

The main reason for this new anti-Zionist Ottoman policy was that under the constitutional regime established by the Young Turks, there was now an elected parliament in Istanbul, with a significant body of Arab deputies, including a number from the areas directly affected by Zionist immigration. There was also a relatively free press in Palestine, in which these problems could be discussed.

Arab opposition to Zionism, in its earliest stages, was generated by local friction rather than considerations of imperial policy. The Ottoman Turks were the rulers of a great empire, of which the region settled by Zionists was a small and in most respects minor fragment. For the Turks, it was important only because it abutted on the British occupied province of Egypt, and because it housed a number of Christian religious sites and institutions which made it an object of active concern to the Christian powers. For the Arabs, it was the place where they lived, their home. In the earlier stages, their opposition to Zionist immigration was not national and only in a limited sense religious. The name Palestine,[3] which the Romans had bestowed on the conquered and subjugated land of Judaea, had been retained for a time by the Arab conquerors to designate an administrative subdivision of their Syrian province. But that name had disappeared in the country even before the arrival of the Crusaders nine centuries ago. It had returned in Europe with the revival of classical learning at the time of the Renaissance, and was commonly applied by European Christians to what they had previously called the Holy Land. By the early twentieth century, with the predominance of European influence and with it of the European language of discourse, the name Palestine came to be used even in the country. This use was, however, in the main confined to Christians and to a very small group of westernized Muslims. The name was not used officially, and had no precise territorial definition until it was adopted by the British to designate the area which they acquired by conquest at the end of World War I and ruled under mandate from the League of Nations.

It was therefore not as a Palestinian nation that the Arabs of Ottoman Palestine objected to what they saw as the encroachments of the Zionist immigrants and settlers, since the very concept of such a nation was unknown at the time and did not come into being until very much later. Even the concept of Arab nationalism, in the modern sense of that term, was still comparatively new, and although it was a growing element in the political awareness and activity of the Arab provinces of the Ottoman empire, it had not reached significant proportions before the outbreak of World War I.

The earliest Arab opposition to Jewish immigration and settlement was local and practical. It began with the establishment of Jewish agricultural settlements in a few places in the country, and arose from disputes over such matters as grazing rights, land titles, and the differences of custom and usage that inevitably developed between neighbors of such vastly different backgrounds. These disputes were not of great significance. Comparatively few areas of the country were in any way in contact with the Zionist settlers, and even these before very long evolved a kind of modus vivendi with their Jewish neighbors.

But in general, and the more so as the political aspirations of these newcomers came to be known, the Arabs saw their activities with misgiving, and sought ways to stop them. The first formal Arab action against Jewish settlement appears to be a telegram dated June 24, 1891, and sent by a group of Arab notables in Jerusalem to the Ottoman Grand Vizier in Istanbul. This was nine years after the arrival of the first wave of secular Russian Jewish immigrants. Word had been received that a fresh and larger wave of Jews was about to come from Russia. The notables, in alarm, asked the Grand Vizier to stop Russian Jews from entering Palestine and from purchasing land there. In the years that followed, Arab opposition became more active and more political, especially after the Young Turk Revolution of 1908 and the freedom of expression and indeed of opposition which it for a while conferred. The remedy proposed by the Arab notables was basically the policy unsuccessfully applied by the Ottoman administration—a ban on Jewish immigration and land purchases. These remained basic Arab demands until the end of Ottoman rule and thereafter through the whole period of the British Mandate, until 1948.

In both of these demands, they achieved some successes, notably in the later years of the British Mandate; but they were not sufficient to prevent the growth of the Jewish community, particularly after the triumph of militant anti-Semitism in Europe, nor the emergence of the state of Israel.

The terms in which Arab protest was expressed show some variation. Some of the earliest protesters, as one might expect, spoke as loyal Ottomans, drawing attention to the threat this intrusion offered to Ottoman interests. This view, as they no doubt knew, was shared by successive Ottoman administrations. Some spoke in religious terms, and of the need to preserve the Islamic character of what was by now an old Islamic land. The Arab nationalist argument, for obvious reasons, was rarely expressed either in Jerusalem or in Istanbul. Arab nationalism was not viewed sympathetically by the Ottoman rulers, who saw in it—rightly, as subsequent events demonstrated— a threat to the unity and integrity of the empire. It appeared occasionally in the writings of Arab émigrés in Europe, and became a major theme in the interwar period.

There was also some variation in the definition of the intrusion against which they were protesting. Arab notables in Jerusalem, unlike Ottoman officials in Istanbul, had little knowledge of this new Jewish movement in Europe, or of its ideas and activities, but were concerned primarily with what was happening on the Arab doorstep.

The Arabic press, even in the comparative freedom of British-occupied Egypt, did not show much interest in the activities of the Zionist organization and its various congresses. It was not until the public debates of the Young Turk period that Arab writers began to pay some attention to Zionism; even then it was limited, and not always hostile.

The first in Palestine to warn the Palestinian Arabs and the Arab people generally of the "Zionist danger" was Najīb Naṣṣār, a Protestant Christian Arab of Greek Orthodox background. In 1909 he began to publish, in Haifa, a weekly paper called *al-Karmal*, in which anti-Zionist polemic formed a major theme. *Al-Karmal* was closed by the Turkish authorities, but Naṣṣār continued his activities and in 1911 published what was probably the first Arabic book on Zionism. Entitled *The History of the Zionist Movement, Its Purposes and Its Development until the Year 1905*, it consisted of an edited and adapted translation of the entry "Zionism" in the American *Jewish Encyclopedia*, with rather pointed additional comments and a concluding essay by the translator.[4] Naṣṣār's essay, in which he drew attention to the Zionist threat to the Ottoman Empire, was in part an intervention in the debate which had been developing among Young Turk politicians and publicists in Istanbul on the question of Zionism, and reaffirmed some of the points made by the anti-Zionist participants in this debate.

One of the most important of these was the influential Turkish journalist Yunus Nadi, who in April 1909 had published an article in an Istanbul newspaper of which he was editor, entitled "Down with Zionism, Always and Forever." In it, he put forward, perhaps for the first time, an argument that was later to form a staple of anti-Zionist propaganda. Zionists, he argued, would not be content with a Jewish state in their ancestral homeland, but were aiming at something much greater—"the dream of an Israelite kingdom comprising the ancient states of Babel and Nineveh with Jerusalem as its center."[5] Unlike most other Turkish writers who discussed the matter, Yunus Nadi did not dismiss this alleged Zionist as an empty dream, but saw it as a serious danger, because "behind them is the strongest power in the world—that of money." For good measure, Nadi, apparently at the instigation of the French consul in Salonica, added that Zionism was promoted principally by German Jews, and served as a vanguard of German influence in the East. The theory that Zionism aimed not at a Jewish National Home but at a Jewish Empire was often repeated by later polemicists; the argument that Zionism and the Jewish National Home were puppets or agents of one or other imperial power also became commonplace, though the identity of the power in this accusation varied according to the purposes of the accuser. At first it was either France or Germany, later Britain or the Soviet Union, and at the present time, the United States.

The theme of money—of the Jew as disposing of vast financial power, through which he seeks to control the destinies of nations—was familiar in European anti-Semitic literature. It was new to the Islamic world, but made rapid progress, and appears in a number of Turkish and Arabic writings of the time. Even in this early period, anti-Semitic themes made an occasional appearance in the discussion of the problem, but at this stage true anti-Semitism was largely European and Christian. Clergymen and missionaries of various kinds were strongly represented among the foreign population in Palestine and the immediately adjoining areas, and exercised a considerable influence, at least on their coreligionists.

The Greek Orthodox Arab Christians seem to have been rather less affected by anti-Semitism than were the Maronite and Uniate Catholics, but this was soon corrected by their Muscovite protectors. The Russian Imperial Orthodox Palestine Society, which began work in 1882, maintained more than a hundred institutions, mostly schools, in Syria and Palestine, and contributed largely to the education of the new generation of Orthodox youth. Its attitude to Jews, naturally enough, was an exact reflection of that of the Imperial Russian government. The clinics and medical centers run by the society, for example, operated on the same principles as the famous invitation to Russia issued by Catherine the Great—they were open to all sections of the population, "except Jews."

Even the American Protestant missionaries at the Syrian Protestant College, which later became the American University of Beirut, made their own genteel and indirect contribution, through an Arabic translation, published in 1897, of the evangelical novel *Ben Hur*. This was one of the first novels published in Arabic, and a contemporary Jewish writer in Jerusalem noted the impact on Arab readers of its vivid description of how the Jews killed Jesus.[6] By the 1960s the crucifixion—which according to the Qur'ān never took place—had become a major theme of anti-Jewish propaganda, even among Mus-

lims, some of whom present the story in the old-style Christian version of collective and hereditary Jewish guilt, in disregard of both
Christian modernism and Muslim tradition.

Of the Arab writers who, in the late Ottoman period, devoted
attention to Zionist affairs only one, Negib Azoury, can fairly be
described as anti-Semitic. His writings indicate a rather mild case of
the infection, which he seems to have caught from his French hosts
and teachers. While some favorite anti-Semitic themes, such as "the
universal Jewish peril" and the Jewish "project of universal domination" appear from time to time in his writings, they do not seem
to have been among his major concerns. Negib Azoury was neither
a Muslim nor a Palestinian, but a Maronite Christian, probably from
the area which is now comprised in the Lebanese republic. A gradu-
ate of the Civil Service College in Istanbul and an occasional student
at the Ecole des sciences politiques in Paris, he joined the Ottoman
civil service, and was sent to Jerusalem. Later, after some commercial and political ventures, neither of which went well, he fled to
Cairo and thence to Paris, where he embarked on a new career as
a militant Arab nationalist. His attacks on the Ottomans earned him
a death sentence in absentia; his ideas brought him sympathetic
support from certain French circles. His thought and even his language are strongly reminiscent of the anti-Dreyfusard circles within
which he appears to have moved.

Azoury was one of the first to see in Zionism a serious threat to
the emergent Arab nation:

Two important phenomena, of the same nature but opposed, which have still
not drawn anyone's attention, are emerging at this moment in Asiatic Turkey. They are the awakening of the Arab nation and the latent effort of the
Jews to reconstitute on a very large scale the ancient kingdom of Israel. Both
these movements are destined to fight each other continually until one of
them wins. The fate of the entire world will depend on the final result
between these two peoples representing two contrary principles.[7]

Despite this remarkable piece of prophecy, Azoury was a minor
figure. He wrote in French, not Arabic, and exercised little influence
at the time. His book, published in Paris in 1905, evoked a curious
rejoinder, also in French, by another Ottoman Christian, a Greek
Orthodox Arab from Beirut who was studying dentistry in France.
His name was Farid Kassab. Kassab responded to Azoury with a

pamphlet in which he attacked the idea of an independent Arab state and—no doubt for good reason—defended the Ottoman way of life against its detractors. He had some words of praise for the Jewish settlers in Palestine, whom he described as peaceful and inoffensive, and as having brought benefit to the country and to the Empire in general through their revival of industry and agriculture. For good measure, Kassab accused Azoury of being "a Catholic bigot and a Jesuit," and as being "not only anti-Jewish from the religious point of view, but also anti-Semitic."[8]

In general, in this early period, there is little sign of anti-Semitism in the presentation of the Arab case against Zionist immigration and settlement, and very little even of anti-Zionism. Some Muslim writers even spoke of Zionism with respect, seeing in it a model of religious faith, national loyalty, and active self-help that Arabs and Muslims would do well to imitate. The distinction between Jews and Zionists, which became so important an issue in later debates, was rarely mentioned and with no great precision. A distinction which Turkish and Arab writers did make, frequently, carefully, and precisely, was between Ottoman and foreign Jews. The former, especially in the atmosphere of the Young Turk Revolution, were their compatriots, and in principle shared the same allegiance and the same rights. The latter were foreigners and intruders—subjects of foreign and mostly hostile powers, and serving as a spearhead of foreign intervention. From the literature of the time, it would seem that it was not as Jews or even as Zionists that the newcomers were feared and then hated, but as foreigners and especially as Europeans. Jews as Jews might be a nuisance, but could hardly be a danger, and their political ambitions were laughable. It was as subjects—even second-class subjects—of the European powers that they were seen by Turks and Arabs alike as representing a threat, by the one to their empire, by the other to their homeland.

Some of the pronouncements of the Central and West European Jews who dominated the Zionist movement in its early days gave further color to this perception of Jewish settlement in Palestine as a spearhead of Western imperialism. Herzl and his immediate colleagues were, in every respect but one, typical Europeans of their generation—sharing the cheerful confidence of the nineteenth century in the superiority of European civilization to all others, and the belief in the European mission to lead, and incidentally to dominate, the rest of the world on the path to higher things. Even those who, like Herzl himself, professed liberal or leftist opinions, shared this perception, as did such earlier figures as Karl Marx and Friedrich Engels. In the view of the early Western Zionists, the Jews of Europe —they were hardly aware of any others—were authentic Europeans, participating in the same noble tasks as their Christian compatriots of bringing progress to the backward and enlightenment to the ignorant. Like most nineteenth-century writers, Europeans and others, who considered this matter, they attached great importance to the notion of race, which of course they understood neither in the Nazi nor in the modern American sense, but in the sense current at that time and in that place—that is to say, as what is nowadays called ethnicity. In the accepted language of discourse of their day, such words as race, empire, and colony had positive connotations, quite different from the negative meanings that they later acquired.

On the more practical level, the early spokesmen for Zionism found this language useful in appealing to the imperial powers, and in particular to Britain, without whose support the whole enterprise could never have succeeded.

According to a famous phrase, nowadays quoted by the opponents, not the defenders of Zionism, the aim of the movement was "to bring a people without land to a land without a people." No doubt, Palestine was sparsely populated at that time, but it was not a land without a people, and its inhabitants were not isolated; they were part of such larger historic entities as the Ottoman Empire, the Arab or Syrian nation, and—above all—the community of Islam.

The phrase is attributed to the Anglo-Jewish novelist Israel Zangwill, who in an article published in 1901 remarked: "Palestine is a country without a people; the Jews are a people without a country. The regeneration of the soil would bring the regeneration of the people."[9] Zangwill later became acutely aware of the problem presented to Zionism by the Arab population. At one time he turned away from Palestine, and headed a movement for a Jewish National Home in some empty territory elsewhere. This movement led nowhere, and in 1923, at the time of the agreement for an exchange of populations between Greece and Turkey, he proposed a similar exchange for Palestine. His proposal was ignored at the time, though the events of 1948–49 came close to fulfilling it.

A few of the early Western Zionists simply failed to see any problem, and looked at the Arab population of Palestine in much the same way as other white settlers and colonists looked at the existing inhabitants of the countries where they settled in Asia, still more in Africa, and most of all in the Americas. But most of them were aware from the start that there was an Arab population in Palestine, and tried in various ways to win their acceptance. Even Vladimir Jabotinsky, the apostle of militant and military Zionism, in a famous poem speaks of a land where "the sons of Arabia, the sons of Nazareth (i.e., the Christians), and my sons" would thrive side by side.[10] Theodor Herzl, the founder of the Zionist movement, shows concern for the Arab inhabitants of Palestine. In his Utopian novel *Old-New-Land (Altneuland)*, published shortly before his death, he depicts his ideal Jewish state of the future or rather, his ideal Jewish national home, since his Zionist Utopia is still under a kind of loose Turkish suzerainty. Leaders are however elected, and a candidate who campaigns on a xenophobic program is denounced by all Herzl's heroes and is ignominiously defeated. Throughout the book great stress is laid on the absence of any discrimination by race, creed, or—a remarkable feature for a book published in 1902—sex. In Herzl's dream of Zion, women have equal rights, Arabs have a secure and honored place, and one of them, asked by a European visitor whether the Arabs did not resent the Jewish immigration, speaks eloquently of the many economic and other advantages which the Jews had brought to his people. In the same novel, a prominent Jewish scientist speaks of the blacks. The passage is worth quoting;

There is still one problem of racial misfortune unsolved. The depths of that problem, in all their horror, only a Jew can fathom. . . . I mean the negro problem. Think of the hair-raising horrors of the slave trade. Human beings, because their skins are black, are stolen, carried off, and sold. . . . Now that I have lived to see the restoration of the Jews, I should like to pave the way for the restoration of the Negroes.[11]

Herzl, clearly, was no racist, and showed a concern for black suffering that is unusual in 1902; but he was obviously affected by the naive paternalism of his time, with its characteristic inability to understand either the anger or the aspirations of the colonized peoples. This is the less surprising, since those aspirations were only just beginning to appear, at that time, among the colonial peoples themselves.

The imperial line of argument, and the paternalism that sometimes accompanied it, had little appeal for the East European Jews, who provided the bulk of the immigrants and who, in the course of World War I, took over the Zionist leadership. For the most part, they saw themselves as victims of Europe, fleeing like the American pioneers to create new homes, not as standard-bearers of the European civilization in which they had suffered so greatly. They too had their own illusions about the Arabs, not paternalistic, but equally naive. Many were inspired by a kind of romantic socialism, and a sadly mistaken belief that a rejuvenated Jewish working class would be joined by the oppressed Arab peasants and workers in throwing off the yoke of their oppressors, the bourgeois and the effendi.

It was some time before the socialist Zionist movements, confronted with the hard facts of an Arab opposition transcending all class barriers, renounced these aspirations, at least temporarily. In the meantime, the establishment of the British Mandate over Palestine had created a new situation, in which Jews and Arabs competed for British favor. Some Zionists tried, not very successfully, to persuade the British that Zionism was creating a "loyal Jewish Ulster" in the Middle East, and a potential new dominion, to rank with Canada, Australia, and New Zealand as pillars of the British Empire. Their Arab opposite numbers responded by denouncing the Zionists as Bolsheviks and as Russian-inspired enemies of Britain, and urging the importance of their own good will in preserving British rule over countless millions of Muslim British subjects in India and elsewhere.

During World War I, there were attempts to achieve some Arab–Jewish unity, on both the Ottoman and British sides. On January 3, 1919, an Arab and a Zionist leader, Prince Faisal (later first king of Iraq) and Chaim Weizmann (later first president of Israel) actually signed an agreement approving the Balfour Declaration and its implementation. Faisal's consent was conditional on Britain fulfilling Arab claims to independence. Britain did not, and the agreement was therefore null and void.

The victory of the Western powers over Germany and her allies brought a total transformation of the situation in the Middle East. The Ottoman Empire was defeated and its capital for a while occupied. Its Arab provinces were detached, taken over by Britain and France, and made to undergo a series of partitions. Iraq was separated from Syria and placed under British Mandate. Syria was divided between Britain and France, with Britain taking the southernmost third and calling it Palestine, and France retaining the name of Syria for the remainder. Both the French and British then further subdivided their mandated territories. The British divided Mandated Palestine into separate states east and west of the Jordan, the latter being called Transjordan, the former, Palestine. The French, after some experimentation, also divided their Mandated territory into two states, of which one was called Lebanon, and the other kept the name of Syria. For the most part, these divisions did not correspond to the provincial boundary lines of the preceding Ottoman administration, nor for that matter to any that had existed for centuries past. Even the names used to designate most of these new entities were, with the exception of Lebanon, exhumed from ancient or medieval history.

The area which was designated as Cisjordanian Palestine, and then simply as Palestine, consisted of the southern districts of the Ottoman provinces of Beirut and Damascus, together with the independent district *(Mutaṣarriflik)* of Jerusalem, called independent in that it depended directly on the capital and not on a provincial governor. Within this area, the British government as mandatory power was bound, by its own promise contained in the Balfour Declaration, and by the terms of the League of Nations Mandate under which it governed Palestine, to pursue the policy of a Jewish National Home. This term was never precisely defined, either by the British or by the Zionists. For some it meant a Jewish state; for others it meant something short of that. In either case, it required the removal or at least the alleviation of the two main restrictions imposed in the past, on Jewish immigration and land purchase. At the same time, the Balfour Declaration, confirmed by the Mandate, laid down that in accomplishing this result "nothing shall be done which may prejudice the civil and religious rights of the existing non-Jewish communities in Palestine."

During the thirty years of British rule, the Arabs of Mandatory Palestine were divided among themselves on many issues and at many levels—about leadership, about their attitude toward Britain, about ideology, about their relations with the Jews already living in their midst. But on one issue they were, politically at least, completely unanimous, and that is in their opposition to the policy of creating a Jewish National Home. The struggle to prevent this, which had already begun in the last years of Ottoman rule, was now resumed and intensified.

But the circumstances had changed greatly, to the Arab disadvantage, and new techniques of struggle were required. Palestine was no longer part of an Islamic realm, in which the Muslim population could identify themselves with and even become part of the governing elite, and in which the government regarded their land as an integral part of its home territories, which it could in no circumstances agree to give away. Instead, Palestine was now part of a European empire, governed by a more or less colonial administration, under a government pledged to favor and facilitate the creation of a Jewish National Home.

These two major disadvantages were not compensated, though they were to some extent alleviated, by certain advantages that accrued from the changes that were taking place. Notable among these was rapid economic development resulting from the inflow of Jewish labor, capital, and technological skills, and the even more rapid development of political activity made possible by the British contribution of a free press, free debate, and the rule of law. In the interwar period the Arabs of Palestine enjoyed an extremely high rate of population growth. The relatively high level of state revenues made it possible for the Mandatory power to give them one of the best and most extensive systems of primary and secondary education in the Arab world. All this helped to produce an active, educated, and aspiring Arab elite, increasingly resentful of the barriers placed before its political self-realization by the growth of the Jewish National Home on the one hand, and the continued presence of the British Mandatory power on the other. Arab fears became more urgent as the Jewish National Home gained in numbers and in sympathy with the spread of Nazi anti-Semitic persecution in Europe. Palestinian Arab frustration was greatly increased as they saw one neighboring Arab country after another achieve first self-government and then independence, while they themselves were still deprived of even the most rudimentary political rights.

As in earlier days, the struggle against the Jewish National Home was waged at two levels, at home in Palestine, and in the imperial capital, now not Istanbul but London. The campaign on the home front was directed to the attainment of two objectives, to mobilize

Arab opinion, and to prevent the sale of Arab land to Jews. The first of these aims was in the main achieved, thought at some cost in internecine conflict. In the second, the Arab leadership was much less successful, and some even among the leaders themselves were tempted to take advantage of the rapid rise in land prices resulting from Jewish immigration and settlement.[12] In dealing with land transfers as with Jewish immigration, the Arabs were obliged to resort to political methods, to induce the Mandatory power, by pressures of various kinds, to ban or at least restrict both.

In this they won some measure of success. Arab opposition to the Mandatory government and its policies had been growing steadily. It became much more active after the accession to power of Adolf Hitler in 1933. The Nazis aggravated the problem in several ways. By persecuting their Jews, they gave the Zionist movement a new urgency and new resources and thus increased the threat to the Arabs. At the same time they provided many Arab leaders with propaganda support and some practical help and, perhaps more important in the long run, gave them a new role in the game of great power politics. The Arabs responded vigorously to both the problem which the Nazis had inflicted on them, and the solution which they were proposing. Between 1936 and 1939, a significant part of Arab Palestine was in a state of armed rebellion, which ended only with the acceptance of many of the Arab demands by the British government in London. The British White Paper of 1939 imposed major restrictions both on land transfers to Jews and on Jewish immigration, and in effect set a terminal limit to the latter, which would have excluded the emergence of an independent Jewish polity in any part of Palestine. From 1939 until the end of the British mandate in 1948, the White Paper policy was strictly enforced. The Arabs had won a considerable political success. It did not suffice to prevent the creation of a Jewish state.

From the Balfour Declaration of November 2, 1917, to the British White Paper of May 17, 1939, and then from the White Paper, issued on the eve of World War II, to Britain's abandonment of the Mandate in May 1948, an increasingly bitter struggle was waged to decide the ultimate fate of Palestine. The antagonists were Jews and Arabs. At first this was in effect limited to the Jews and Arabs of Palestine, with comparatively little support outside. But the course of events in the world, and especially in Europe, brought a rapid widening of the struggle. The builders of the Jewish National Home gained increasing support among the Jewish people in general, and, as the sufferings of the Jews in Hitler's Europe became known, they benefited from a great wave of compassion, mixed with feelings of guilt, throughout Christendom. The Arabs of Palestine too were at first more or less alone, with only limited sympathy even in neighboring Arab countries, where nationalist leaders were preoccupied with their own struggles against imperial rule. But as the struggle grew in scale and intensity, they too were able to mobilize increasing support, first in the Arab world, then among non-Arab Muslims, and finally in what later came to be known as the Third World.

Between 1918 and 1939, the Arab, Islamic, and Afro-Asian Worlds still counted for little in the international balances of power. Palestine was ruled by Britain, at the time still one of the great European imperial powers that between them dominated the world. The final decisions were made in London, and then ratified by the League of Nations, which was technically responsible for supervising the administration of the Mandate. The League of Nations in turn was wholly dominated by the European powers, and even though it was shaken by the bitter conflicts which eventually brought it to destruction, these were still predominantly between rival European empires. It was therefore to a Christian European world that the Palestinian Arabs had to address themselves in order to gain sympathy and support for their cause, and to block the advance of the Jewish National Home. This required substantial changes both in the content of their case, and the manner in which they presented it. In particular, it meant finding and using the arguments most likely to appeal to the Western public opinion whom it was now necessary to address. This was a very different problem from persuading Ottoman officials or the Young Turk Parliament in Istanbul.

At least in the early years of the British Mandate, it seemed to Arabs and Jews alike that the British Empire was permanent and unshakable and that the task before them was not to remove but rather to placate their British rulers and win them over to their side. Jews and Arabs alike were therefore concerned to demonstrate that support for them, rather than for their opponents, was most in accord with British imperial interests. And each of the two opponents had a corresponding need to demonstrate the danger to those same interests offered by the other side. After the defeat of the Kaiser's Germany and before the rise first of Japan and then of the Fascist powers, the enemy most feared in the Western world was Soviet Russia and Soviet-sponsored revolutionary communism. The prominence of Jews among the early Soviet leaders, and the intensive and world-wide anti-Semitic propaganda of the White Russians, led many in the Western world, by no means limited to the lunatic fringes, to see not just Jewish radicals but the Jews in general as a dangerous element spreading left-wing subversion. While comparatively few were will-ing to accept the whole anti-Semitic case and see the Soviet regime as a Jewish domination of Russia, there were many who saw in the Jews an intellectually radical and politically subversive element which if left unchecked would plunge the Western World into revo-lution, socialism, and anarchy.

In this situation, the most immediately effective way of turning British and more generally Western opinion against the Zionists was to portray them as Reds.[13] Such a portrayal was all the more plausible in that most of the immigrants and virtually the whole Zionist leader-ship were East Europeans; that many of the Zionist parties, including the most important ones, professed more or less socialistic ideas; and that they were establishing communal settlements, called *kibbut-zim,* which—for those who knew neither at first hand—could use-fully be equated with the Soviet collective farms called *kolkhozy.*

As the Soviet revolution and regime developed, there was some loss of plausibility. Zionism was outlawed and suppressed in Russia, and Jewish emigration was stopped. Jewish Bolshevik leaders were eliminated one by one, mostly by execution, and the Soviet govern-ment adopted a position of implacable hostility both to Zionism and to the Jewish National Home in which it never wavered, except for a brief interval in 1947 and the immediately following period. These changes did not, however, inhibit the continued use of this argument against Zionism and the National Home. It gained added force after the rise of Fascism and Nazism, which exercised so powerful a fasci-nation over Arab political activists in the 1930s and 1940s. For the Nazis, Bolshevism was—except for the interlude of Nazi–Soviet friendship and cooperation between August 1939 and June 1941— the archenemy, and of course Bolshevism and the Jews were inextri-cably—again, except for the same interval—intertwined. For those Arabs who accepted Nazi guidance and leadership, the real enemy was the Jewish Bolshevik, aided and abetted by the British and later also the Americans.

The notion that Zionism and Bolshevism are two faces of the same Jewish-minted coin showed remarkable persistence, especially but not exclusively in the Arab world. It remained an article of faith with the late King Faisal of Saudi Arabia until his dying day, and was used by President Nasser in the early years of his regime. It remains a common theme in the conservative Arab countries to the present time. Its replacement by other accusations in the Socialist Arab countries came for reasons quite unconnected with the merits of the case.

In the meantime, however, the situation had been totally transformed by the end of the British Mandate, the adoption of the United Nations resolution to partition Palestine, the breakdown of civil government in the mandated territory, and the establishment of the state of Israel. These events were preceded, accompanied, and followed by a series of wars, first between Arabs and Jews within Palestine, then between the newborn state and its Arab neighbors. In the course of the Arab attempt to destroy the Jewish state at birth by force of arms, great numbers of Arabs fled or were driven from their homes in Palestine, and took refuge in the neighboring Arab countries. Both before and after these events, great numbers of Jews fled or were driven from the Arab countries, and most of them found new homes in Israel.

For the second time the Arab perception of Zionism underwent a major transformation. Under the Ottomans the Jewish state had been a remote and rather absurd fantasy. Under the British it grew into a serious threat. With the birth of Israel it became a reality.

As the result of these events, the Arabs suffered two material setbacks; the loss of Arab territory to an non-Arab state, and the departure or removal of many of its Arab inhabitants. Most of these who left went either to neighboring countries, mainly to Lebanon and Syria, or to those parts of Palestine that remained in Arab hands, that is to say, the Jordanian-held West Bank and the Egyptian-held Gaza Strip. In all these places, the overwhelming majority of the Arab refugees were kept in camps. When the Israeli forces conquered both the West Bank and the Gaza Strip in 1967, there was a further movement of refugees, from the camps on the West Bank across the Jordan to the East Bank. This time, however, the local population of the West Bank stayed put, as did also the refugees in the Gaza Strip.

There is total disagreement between the Arab and Israeli accounts of the departure of the Palestinian Arabs in 1948 and after. According to the Arab version, they were simply driven out by the Israelis. According to the Israeli version, they were in some areas instructed to leave by their own leaders, and in others fled in the kind of contagious panic that often affects civil populations in war zones. The Jews stayed, because they had nowhere to go. The Arabs could hope for shelter in Arab states. There is evidence for both versions from both sides,[14] and it seems likely that all these explanations are true in different parts of the country. In Haifa, a mixed city where there had usually been good relations, it is clear that the Israelis tried, without success, to persuade their Arab neighbors to stay. In Lydda and Ramla, on the strategic road from the coast to Jerusalem, it is equally clear that they compelled them to depart. Atrocity reports in the Arab media certainly had their effect; it was greatly increased after the attack on the Arab village of Deir Yāsîn by the Irgun and Stern groups, and the slaughter of some two hundred and fifty civilians. Whatever its circumstances and origins, the movement rapidly grew into a mass exodus and to the physical displacement of a large Arab population. The numbers of refugees are disputed. Israeli estimates put them at a little more than half a million; Arab estimates at more than double that figure. The United Nations Economic Survey for the Middle East, sent out in 1949, put the total number of Arab refugees from Palestine at 726,000, as of September 30, 1949.

There were some at the time, including a few Arab statesman, who argued that these were relatively minor setbacks, and that the Arabs would be well advised to cut their losses and accept the situation. The area assigned to Israel by the United Nations Partition Resolution was very small, and had been only slightly increased by the successes of the Israelis in their war of independence. Even the whole of Mandatory Palestine was an infinitesimally small part of the Arab world as a whole. The fate of the refugees was a human tragedy, but in the course of peace negotiations it might have been possible to arrange a return to their homes for some, resettlement for the rest, as happened to millions of refugees in Eastern Europe and the Indian subcontinent in the same years. But in fact there was no negotiation, and no willingness among either the established Palestinian Arab leadership or the governments of the Arab states to recognize the accomplished fact and enter into such a process.

The dominant note in the Arab response to these events was one of shock and outrage that these defeats should have been inflicted upon them by a group of people whom they had been accustomed to stereotype as weak, cowardly, and in general contemptible—the people whom God himself had punished with abasement and humiliation. But now it was the Arabs themselves—as some saw it, the Muslims—who had suffered humiliation. Within a few years every one of the Arab rulers who had launched their armies into the debacle of 1948 had been removed or overthrown.

But the new regimes, most of them installed and led by army officers, did no better against Israel. Indeed, they did significantly worse. In the first Arab–Israeli war, in 1948–49, in the course of heavy fighting and very severe losses, the Israelis managed to survive and somewhat improve their position. In 1956, in a war against Nasser's Egypt, they were able to conquer the whole of Sinai peninsula in a hundred hours, and inflict a crushing defeat on the Egyptian army—particularly humiliating to a resurgent military regime. In the war of 1956, the Israelis had some logistical and other indirect military support from France and Britain. Even this excuse was lacking in the war of June 1967, when the Israelis, alone this time, successively defeated the armies of Egypt, Syria and Jordan, capturing vast territories, and all in six days. In the course of this war, the Israelis captured the Sinai peninsula and the Gaza Strip from Egypt, the West Bank and East Jerusalem from Jordan, and the Golan Heights from Syria. It has been argued—the evidence is conflicting—that in the early days after their victory the Israelis would have been willing to return almost all but East Jerusalem to the Arab states, in return for recognition and peace. But neither was on offer, and before very long the Israelis became accustomed to the many advantages which their new acquisitions brought them. It took somewhat longer to appreciate the disadvantages.

After some hesitations, the Arab response was formulated in the famous "No's of Khartoum"—the summit conference of Arab leaders, which on September 1, 1967, announced in Khartoum that they had agreed that there was to be "no recognition, no negotiation, no peace." This remained the formal position of all Arab governments until 1978, and of almost all of them to the present day.

The war of 1967 brought a further, highly significant change. In 1948, the Arabs left in Israel were relatively few in number and, since almost all their leaders and intellectuals had left the country, were politically inert. The Israelis in theory and to an increasing extent in practice regarded them as citizens, and while their citizenship was never fully effective, it did not compare badly with the position of other national minorities in the Middle East. The Israeli victory in 1967 created a new situation, by establishing Israeli military rule over a subject Arab population of a million to a million and a half, with an active and vocal political and intellectual leadership.

The Israeli conquests in the Six Day War in 1967 had another important consequence—the emergence of the Palestinian Arabs as a combatant force in the conflict, with a strong and growing sense of a common Palestinian identity and, ultimately, nationhood. The formation of this sense of identity began with the establishment of the British Mandate and the creation of a new and separate political entity called Palestine, with different rulers, different institutions, and above all different problems from those of the neighboring lands with which they had previously been associated. Already in the 1920s, Palestinian Arab journalists and politicians began to speak of "the Palestine National Movement" and sometimes even of the Palestinian nation. But this was exclusively in the context of the struggle against British rule and Jewish immigration. Their basic sense of corporate historic identity was, at different levels, Muslim or Arab or—for some—Syrian; it is significant that even by the end of the Mandate in 1948, after thirty years of separate Palestinian political existence, there were virtually no books in Arabic on the history of Palestine, the few exceptions being textbooks prepared for use in the Mandatory government's schools.

In time perhaps, without Zionism, the Anglo-French division of the Fertile Crescent would have created a Palestinian state, as it created states in Iraq, Jordan, Syria, and Lebanon; the United Nations might even have created an Arab state in part of Palestine had any of the partition proposals won Arab acceptance. They did not, but the establishment of Israel and the Arab exodus accelerated and transformed the development of Palestinian national consciousness.

A new era began with the establishment of Israel and the Arab exodus. From the manner of their departure from Israel, perhaps still more from the manner of their reception in the neighboring Arab countries, where they were for the most part confined in camps and, with the exception of Jordan, refused citizenship, the Palestinian Arabs acquired a much stronger sense of identity, based on common experience, and a sense of common suffering, need, and destiny. It may well prove to be the ironic achievement of Britain and of Zionism to have created not one but two new nations, in the small territory cobbled together in 1918 from three Ottoman provincial districts.

The Six Day War brought other changes, which profoundly transformed the situation. The emergence and sovereignty of the Jewish state had been hard for the Arabs to accept. Its devastating victories, and the resulting establishment of Jewish domination over a significant Arab population, was incomparably harder.

Apart from Transjordan, which had never been subject to the policy of the Jewish National Home, no part of Mandatory Palestine was now under Arab rule, and no Arab government—with the limited exception of Jordan—could enforce a claim to speak on behalf of the Palestinians. This also meant that the whole Cisjordanian area was now subject to a single authority, that of Israel. There was now far more communication between Palestinians than previously, and a correspondingly heightened sense of community. This helped the emergence of a new force in the Arab world that was to play a role of great importance. The Palestine Liberation Organization was founded in 1964, but it did not become a factor until after the war of 1967. The policies of the Arab governments had failed; their armies had been defeated. The PLO offered a new policy and aspiration, and a new method of waging war against the Israeli enemy. Both of these won considerable support among the Palestinians, especially in the camps, which before long came under PLO control.

From 1967 onward the PLO played a prominent, some indeed would say the leading role, in the Arab war against Israel. The Arab states, naturally enough, were now principally concerned with the recovery of their own lost territories, and, increasingly, with the open pursuit of their own national interests. There was a growing tendency to regard the Palestinian cause as secondary to these interests, and the Palestinian organizations as instruments to be used where possible for their own national purposes. But while the Arab governments and armies projected an image of defeat and impotence, even to their own peoples, the PLO in contrast was creating a new image of the Arab as a daring revolutionary freedom fighter. In this image, the Arab was portrayed as fighting alone against vastly superior forces instead of, as previously, fighting unsuccessfully against a smaller and weaker enemy. Correspondingly, the Israeli David fighting boldly against the Arab League Goliath suddenly became a Jewish Goliath trying to kill the PLO David.

This new image had considerable impact in the Western world, where for the first time since the birth of Israel the PLO and its supporters were able to win over a large section of public opinion, especially in the media and in the literary and academic worlds, from a pro-Israel to an anti-Israel and pro-Arab stance. The argument that the Palestinians are a nation without a homeland, and that the PLO is waging a revolutionary struggle for national liberation, had much to do with bringing about this result, though there can be no doubt that some other factors, unconnected with the Arabs and their struggle, were also at work.

At first, the Arab states responded very favorably to the new policies and activities of the PLO, and took pride in the new figure of the Arab guerrilla fighter. But second thoughts followed. Nearer to the scene and more involved in events than were Western media men and women, the Arab leaders were better aware of the limited effectiveness of the PLO fight against Israel. And furthermore, problems were beginning to arise between the PLO and its Arab hosts, who had increasing difficulty in accomodating a well-armed and well-funded radical organization in their midst. The PLO presence in Jordan, their first base after the 1967 war, ended in 1970, in massacre, expulsion, and flight. The PLO presence in Lebanon, where they established themselves, gave rise to a whole series of troubles in that already troubled country. When finally they were attacked and expelled from Lebanon by the Israelis in 1982, there was no great eagerness on the part of the Arab states either to help them in their struggle or to rescue them in their defeat.

By the end of 1982, the bright image of the Arab guerrilla warrior was more than a little tarnished. But the image of the Arab armies was not much improved. True, in the wars of 1973 and 1982 the Israelis did not win the swift and crushing military victories to which they had been previously accustomed. But they did not suffer defeat either, and the results can have brought no great satisfaction to the

Arab states. The war of October 1973 began very well for the Arabs, with the Egyptians crossing the Suez Canal—a considerable feat of arms—and both the Egyptians and the Syrians advancing against the Israelis. But the war ended with the Israelis within striking distance of both Damascus and Cairo, and the great Egyptian political success that followed was due more to skillful political maneuvering and American diplomatic help than to military achievements. Similarly, while the war in 1982 brought neither military glory nor political advantage to Israel, it nevertheless once again exposed Arab weakness and disunity.

The succession of Israeli victories and Arab defeats in the battlefield raised profound sociological, psychological, and historical questions. Of more immediate concern in the present context is the Arab perception of the reasons for these defeats, which were all the more lacerating in that they came from a previously despised and unarmed subject people. Time and time again the state of Israel, tiny in comparison with the Arab world, and inhabited by a Jewish population which rose from about half a million when the state was established to about three and a half million, succeeded in defeating the armies of not one but several Arab states, vastly superior in numbers, resources, and weaponry. That this could happen, again and again, posed an agonizing dilemma to Arabs concerned about the condition and future of their countries.

How and why did it happen? To these questions a number of different answers were given. The simplest and most comforting, still frequently heard, is that the Israelis were not able to do this on their own, but received help from others. This was indeed so in the war of 1956; it was not in any of the other wars. The Israelis did of course benefit from large-scale military supplies first from Czechoslovakia, then France, then the United States, with accelerated delivery in wartime. But the Arabs had the same service from their Soviet suppliers, with the added advantage, never sought or accepted by the Israelis, of foreign military officers attached to their forces as experts and instructors. For some, the myth of American intervention on the Israeli side in these wars provided a necessary salve for wounded pride. I remember asking an Egyptian army officer whether he really believed that the American Air Force had fought on the Israeli side in the Six Day War. His answer was a model of honesty: "I don't believe it, but I can't disbelieve it." After the 1973 war, when President Sadat took his first steps toward peace, he justified them by saying he could fight against Israel but not against the United States. He had not of course fought against the United States, any more than Israel had fought against the Soviet Union.

There were others for whom the easy excuse of great power intervention was not sufficient, and who sought the causes of Arab defeats in the structure of Arab society. This inquiry began after the first defeat in 1948, and received a new impetus after each setback. By now it has produced a literature of considerable range and variety, and offers the best hope that the Arabs may yet, by rigorous self-criticism, recognize and remedy some of the flaws in their social and political order.

An analysis of the reasons for defeat requires not only a study of one's own weaknesses, but also a dispassionate examination of the strength of the adversary. This proved an even more difficult task. There were some, chiefly among the Palestinian exiles, who made the effort. But most were unwilling to forgo the scoring of polemical points, and unable to relinquish the familiar hostile stereotypes. The Israeli is above all else a Jew, and the Jew is greedy and cunning, and at the same time cowardly and lacking in all the martial virtues. This kind of portrayal does not always appear in serious analytical writings, but it became virtually universal in more popular journalistic and literary and even many official presentations of Israelis and of Jews generally.

Thus, for example, an article in the Egyptian armed forces weekly *al-Quwwāt al-Musallaha* of November 16, 1964, remarks:

The Jew is his very soul and character has not the qualities of a man who bears arms. He is not naturally prepared to sacrifice for anything, not even for his son or his wife. If there is today in Israel a man who bears arms he does this because he is sure that there is another man who will precede him, who will stand in front of him not behind him in order to defend him when the time comes. Were it not for that, no Jew in the world would agree to bear arms.

This was published in 1964. With a diet of such information, it is understandable that the Six Day War in 1967 came as a shock. But even the succession of wars did not entirely change this basic perception, and Arab writers—novelists and playwrights as well as political and military commentators—continued to portray the Israelis as abject and unprincipled poltroons. An Egyptian literary critic, commenting on the cliché-ridden portrayal of Israelis in fiction and drama, aptly asked: "Before this kind of presentation, I put the question: If the Israelis were really like that, how could they have inflicted a defeat upon us?"[15]

How indeed? If the Israelis are as corrupt and cowardly as their literary image, then their victories become even more inexplicable, or at least require explanations beyond the normal processes of rational thought. To a rapidly increasing extent, the literature of anti-Semitism, becoming known from Europe, provided such an explanation. The malevolent but timorous Jew of the local tradition plots and schemes, but all his efforts would be unavailing against the might of Islam, "for God is a better schemer." The cowards, braggarts, pimps, and whores of the Israel depicted in modern Arab fiction could hardly be expected to do much better. But the sons of Satan, exercising demonic power, engaged in a conspiracy against mankind extending through the millennia and across the world, are a truly formidable adversary. The struggle against such an adversary gives cosmic stature to those who engage in it, and lends some dignity even to those who suffer a defeat, which, they firmly believe, can only be temporary.

CHAPTER EIGHT

The War Against the Jews

I N 1979 THE CAIRO newspaper *al-Da^cwa* (The Call), the organ of the Muslim Brothers, published a series of articles, both in the main paper and in the children's supplement, designed to warn their adult and child readers against the dangers threatening the Muslim world. Under the heading "Know Your Enemy," articles in the children's section list four main enemies against whom the Muslim must guard himself—the Crusader, the Jew, the Marxist, and the Secularist. Each of these is described, and depicted, in some detail. There is an interesting difference between the Crusader and the Jew as portrayed in these articles. The Crusader is an enemy because he is a crusader, not because he is a Christian. It is possible to be a Christian without being a crusader, that is, a militant and aggressive Christian. The articles point out that not all Christians are crusaders. Some Christians are good, as for example the old-style Copts in Egypt, who are appropriately meek. Unfortunately, the article notes, this situation is changing. The good Christians are being contaminated by the bad Christians, and they are all becoming crusaders nowadays.

The Jew is named as "Jew," and not under any more specific labels such as Zionist or Israeli. Unlike the Christians, the Jews are all bad, and there are no good Jews. The Jews are genetically and ontologically evil, and the writers of these articles are not concerned with the distinctions made by spokesmen writing in Western languages, between Zionists and Israelis on the one hand and those who profess the Jewish religion on the other. The enemy is simply the Jew, in whatever disguise he appears.[1]

The discussion of the two remaining enemies reveals that these too are either Jews themselves or manipulated and directed by Jews. The Marxist or Communist is a major enemy, and the reader is reminded that Karl Marx's grandfather was a rabbi, this obviously being a point of profound significance in determining the role of Marxism in history and the ultimate purposes of Marxist Communism. The fourth enemy, in many ways the most insidious and the most dangerous to true Islam, is the secularist modernizer. This group includes such characters as Ḥāfiẓ al-Asad in Syria, Ṣaddām Ḥusayn in Iraq, the late Gamal Abdel Nasser in Egypt, and other leaders who sought to establish secular regimes in Islamic lands, and to disestablish the Islamic faith and repeal the God-given Holy Law.

They are all evil. The first great secularist revolutionary, the arch malefactor who started this process and of whom all the others are imitators, was Mustafa Kemal Atatürk, who after the Turkish defeat in the First World War created the Turkish Republic out of the ruins of the Ottoman Empire, and established the first polity in Islamic history in which religion was separated from the state and secular modern laws replaced the Holy Law of Islam even in matters of personal status. The articles offer a new and startling explanation of the origins of Atatürk and his role in history. According to them, he was a *dönme,* a secret Jew, who overthrew the Ottoman sultans to punish them for having refused to give Palestine to the Zionists. This last item, for which needless to say there is not a shred of evidence, has been widely accepted in fundamentalist writings.

All this is paranoiac conspiracy theory of a familiar type—familiar, that is to say, in Christendom, though hitherto little known in the world of Islam. Its appearance is the more remarkable in that it occurs in the publications of a militant Islamic fundamentalist organization, calling itself the Muslim Brotherhood, and presenting what purports to be an ultra-Islamic point of view. Nevertheless, it reflects an approach to Jewish matters which is very far from that of traditional Islam, and the alien, European origin of these diatribes can be seen both in the specific accusations and in the cartoons which illustrate them. It is very different from the approach reflected in the writings of such earlier thinkers as Sayyid Qutb and his radical successors, for whom the anti-Jewish theme, though present, is of secondary importance, and is still expressed in Islamic terms.

The Muslim Brothers now represent a rather conservative strain of Islamic fundamentalism, and are believed to enjoy substantial Saudi support. The Saudis themselves have frequently sponsored and disseminated this kind of anti-Semitic propaganda. The late King Faisal went on record in interviews in the Arabic press with a series of pronouncements on the role of the Jews in history, as for example, that in the Middle Ages they "started the Crusades in order to weaken Christendom and Islam"; that they still habitually practice the ritual murder of Christian and Muslim children and "mix their blood into their bread and eat it"; that they are engaged in a secret conspiracy to rule the world. Both directly and through organizations which they sponsor in Pakistan and elsewhere, Saudi agencies have circulated anti-Semitic publications produced by neo-Nazi and neo-Fascist groups in the western world. As recently as December 1984, Dr. Ma^{c}rūf al-Dawālibī, representing Saudi Arabia at a United Nations seminar on religious tolerance and freedom, attributed to the Talmud the dictum that "if a Jew does not drink every year the blood of a non-Jewish man, then he will be damned for eternity." Most of Dr. Dawālibī's contribution to religious tolerance and freedom consisted of a detailed account of the Damascus blood libel case of 1840, assuming the complete guilt of the accused and the accuracy of all the charges brought against them.[2]

A comparison of Arabic writings about Jews and Jewish matters in the last twenty or thirty years with those of the past will reveal that certain very significant changes have taken place. The first and most striking novelty in writing about Jews is its obsessive character. Whereas previously the Jews were seen as a minor problem or no problem at all, they now loom as the major threat overshadowing the whole Islamic world. The old contempt and mistrust remain; they have now been joined by the European qualities of fear and envy, which have pervaded the entire spectrum of discourse. The Jew is no longer the petty and ineffectual schemer of traditional stereotypes; he has become a figure of cosmic evil, engaged in devilish plots against all mankind. Even the linkage, made in most Arabic writing on the subject, between Zionism and imperialism is seen in a new light. Whereas previously the Zionists were described as agents or instruments of the imperial powers, now the empires and superpowers themselves are often depicted as helpless puppets manipulated by hidden Jewish hands, in pursuit of their plan to rule the world.

These attitudes color not only political discussion, but also literature and the arts, religion and scholarship. They are no longer confined to fringe and polemical publications, but appear in major newspapers, government television and radio programs, and in school and university textbooks. The level of hostility, and the ubiquity of its expression, are rarely equalled even in the European literature of anti-Semitism, which only at a few points reached this level of fear, hate, and prejudice. For parallels one has to look to the high Middle Ages, to the literature of the Spanish Inquisition, of the anti-Dreyfusards in France, the Black Hundreds in Russia, or the Nazi era in Germany. Some Arab countries, now joined by Iran, have become the main centers of international anti-Semitism, from which anti-Semitic literature and other propaganda is distributed all over the world. This has reached new and previously unaffected audiences in Africa, South East Asia, and other Third World countries.

Another feature of the new-style anti-Jewish literature in the Arab countries is the virtual disappearance of the distinction between Israelis, Zionists, and Jews. This was never very strictly maintained in literature for home consumption, but is in general to be found in writings in foreign languages, produced for dissemination in the West. The PLO Research Center in Beirut, in its many Arabic publications on Israel, has also tried to observe this distinction. While maintaining its unwavering rejection of Zionism and of Israel in any form, it has usually avoided the use of explicitly anti-Semitic material. There are no such restraints in either official or unofficial publications in Egypt, Saudi Arabia, Kuwait, Jordan, Lebanon, and some other Arab and Muslim countries. Some writers from these countries, in discussing the Palestine problem, still argue that they are opposed to Zionism and the state of Israel, and have nothing against the Jews or their religion, but few respect such distinctions in public and in Arabic nowadays, and some even explicitly deny them. Thus for example, in an article published in the economic supplement of *al-Ahrām* on September 27, 1982, Dr. Lutfi ᶜAbd al-ᶜAẓîm writes:

The first thing that we have to make clear is that no distinction must be made between the Jew and the Israeli, which they themselves deny. The Jew is a Jew, through the millennia . . . in spurning all moral values, devouring the living and drinking his blood for the sake of a few coins. The Jew, the Merchant of Venice, does not differ from the killer of Deir Yasin or the killer of the camps. They are equal examples of human degradation. Let us therefore put aside such distinctions, and talk about Jews.

Most speakers, broadcasters, lecturers and writers in Arab countries do in fact just talk about Jews. The Egyptian orientation pamphlets for their troops in the war of 1973, for example, commonly refer to the adversary as "the Jews"; even discussions of purely military matters speak of "Jewish troops" or "Jewish officers." In general, it is clear that many at least have extended the adversary from Israel to the whole Jewish people, and from the present generation of Jews to their ancestors through the millennia.

Perhaps the most significant change of all is the Islamization of anti-Semitism. At first confined to some elements within the Christian minorities within the Middle East, it was adopted and absorbed by the Muslim majority in two stages. In the first phase, the anti-Semitic themes and charges were simply copied and translated, without change. They were still recognizably alien, and had little popular impact. In the second stage, these alien themes have been, so to speak, internalized, and in the process of their adoption and assimilation by the Muslim world, have been given a distinctively Islamic aspect.

A striking example of this process is the transformation, in literature and education, of the Prophet's Jewish adversaries from a minor nuisance to a major enemy, an embodiment of the eternal principle of evil. In some traditional Muslim accounts the Jews of Medina, even in their defeat and death, are allowed a certain dignity and courage. This presentation of their role, tragic rather than diabolic, survived into modern times, as for example in the dramatized version of the life of the Prophet published in 1936 by the great Egyptian playwright Tawfīq al-Ḥakīm. In the new version, the Jews are the perpetual enemies of Islam and the Muslims and therefore—by an easy transition—the cause of all the troubles that befell the Islamic world in early as in later times. For such an interpretation of the Jewish role in Islamic history, the material supplied by the Qur'ān and the Tradition was insufficient, since, while denouncing the wickedness of the Jew, it denies him the strength or courage to do much harm. Nor was the literature of Christian anti-Semitism, the usual standby of Muslim neophytes in this field, of much help. For Christian bigots, to make war against Islam was a holy, not an unholy task, and therefore no work for Jews.

The gap was, however, easily covered by the use of creative imagination. An example of how this functioned may be found in a paper submitted by an Egyptian sheikh, ^CAbdallāh al-Meshad, to the fourth conference of the Academy of Islamic Research, held at al-Azhar, in Cairo, in 1968. In this paper, entitled "Jews' Attitude toward Islam and Muslims in the First Islamic Era," the writer explains that even after the death of the Prophet

the Jews remained the same people of mean disposition and buried rancour so that they never forgot how the Muslims had treated them. They were in wait for their calamities despite their (Jews) dispersion. They tried to seize the chance to revenge on them. They were usually cowards and could not face openly their enemy especially when he was strong. Therefore their methods in attacking the Faith were conspiracies, plots, intrigues, seditions, separation from the believers, distortion of the Call and trials to drive the Muslims out of their purified Creed, which was the cause of their strength.

He goes on to assign the Jews a major role in all the political, social, religious, and other problems which arose in the early centuries of Islam and even charges them with at least complicity in the murder of the Caliph ^CUmar, an accusation hitherto unknown to historiography:

When we look at the recent pictures of the Jews' conspiracie ￬nd how they design precisely and accurately for the long run or forever in such a subtle technique that we never suspect of its safety, we think it not impossible that the Jews were those who drew the plans and plotted for killing Omar or at least, they had known that conspiracy but they did not ferret it out.[3]

The Azhar Conference devoted a great deal of its time to historical analyses of this type. The proceedings were published in three volumes in Arabic and in one volume in English, from which the above passage is cited, and given wide dissemination in the Muslim world. Such accusations have spread from conferences to schoolbooks, from the Arab lands to the whole Islamic world, as far away as Malaysia and Indonesia and the Muslim peoples of tropical Africa.

The penetration of anti-Semitism in its European Christian form was at first slow and limited, and it did not become a major factor in the Arab world until the late 1950s and 1960s.

This does not of course mean that there was no hostility to Jews. This was still present, in two forms. The old Islamic contempt for the Jews as the less important and less estimable of the two religious minorities was still there, along with the prejudices and the stereotypes that had grown up in the course of the centuries. It was however a relatively minor factor in Muslim Jewish relations. From the time of the Crusades, and especially in the nineteenth century, Muslims in Syria and Egypt were much more suspicious of Christians than of Jews. Ever since Bonaparte's invasion of Egypt in 1798, and with the subsequent growth of the economic, strategic and political influence of the European powers in the Middle East, the local Christians had flourished greatly under the protection of their foreign coreligionists, and were achieving a level of wealth and power which would never have been possible under traditional Muslim regimes. Because of their links with the foreign powers, they themselves were coming to be regarded as foreigners by their Muslim compatriots, or, worse than that, as disloyal subjects and allies of foreign enemies. Except in North Africa, where there were no indigenous Christians, the Jews derived fewer advantages from the foreign presence, and therefore incurred less antagonism.

At first, it was the Christians, more than the Muslims, who were affected by anti-Jewish sentiments, and who on occasion engaged in anti-Jewish activities. As a rival minority, competing for the same positions in a predominantly Muslim society, they were at times moved by commercial rivalry, at times by a natural desire to deflect Muslim resentments elsewhere. More open than the Muslims to Western influences, but still by no means westernized, they were often infected by Western diseases before they had developed Western immunities. An example of this was the anti-Semitism communicated to them by some of their clerical mentors and business associates from Europe.

Anti-Semitism of this kind remained a marginal phenomenon among the eastern Christians, with only minor impact among the Muslims. The most important was the spread of the blood libel in the course of the nineteenth century, and the rare Muslim responses to the propaganda of the anti-Dreyfusards and their like. Among Muslims, when anti-Jewish prejudice appeared, as it occasionally did, it was still of the traditional Islamic, not the Christian anti-Semitic type. This remained true for some time after the development of the Zionist enterprise in Ottoman and Mandatory Palestine, and the conflicts to which it gave rise.

In the early years of the Mandate, some Palestinian Arab writers still tried to maintain certain distinctions, not so much between Jews and Zionists, as rather between foreign and local Jews, the latter now being seen as part of the Middle Eastern family instead of, as previously, Ottoman fellow subjects. A few Jews, in Syria, Iraq, and to a lesser extent in Egypt, even played some part in Arab political life. When Faisal was crowned king in Damascus in 1920, one of the committee of Syrian delegates that received him was Joseph Laniado, later president of the Syrian Jewish community. Another Syrian Jew, Eliyahu Sasson, later an Israeli diplomat, was editor of a nationalist newspaper, al-Ḥayāt, during the years 1919–20. There was even an attempt, with some response, to win Sephardic support for the Arab case against Zionism as a European and either Bolshevist or imperialist intrusion.[4] But this Arab appeal to their Jewish neighbors came to nothing when Arab leaders and spokesmen failed to observe the distinction, which they themselves had made, between Jews and Zionists, between foreigners and compatriots, and launched their attack on Judaism and on all Jews alike.

In these attacks, they relied more and more on anti-Semitic writings imported from Europe. Foremost among these were two old anti-Semitic favorites—Canon Rohling's *Talmud Jew* and the *Protocols of the Elders of Zion*. Both had been repeatedly condemned in the Christian world, the one as a distortion, the other as a fake, by both scholarly analysis and legal judgments, and since the end of the Nazi regime both had been forgotten except among the lunatic fringes. In the Arab lands, both have enjoyed, since the late fifties, a new popularity.

The *Protocols of the Elders of Zion* is occasionally mentioned in Arab polemics linking Zionism and Bolshevism in the early 1920s. The first Arabic translation, made from the French, was printed in *Raqīb Ṣahyūn*, a periodical published in Jerusalem by the Latin Catholic community, on January 15, 1926.[5] Another translation, also made from the French by an Arab Christian, was published in Cairo in book form a year or two later. The first translation by a Muslim, from the English, appeared in Cairo with a lengthy introduction in 1951. Numerous editions and translations followed.

In the years that followed, the trickle grew to a flood, and before very long the Arabic reader had at his disposal a wide range of anti-Semitic literature, all of it of Christian and European or American origin. It included the products of clerical and anti-clerical, right-wing and left-wing, socialist and fascist anti-Semitism. Some of these books were translated several times, and went through many editions. As well as books, there were articles in newspapers and magazines, broadcasts, public lectures, and exhortations, all of which helped to familiarize the Muslim Arab reader with a set of themes and images previously unknown to him—the Jew as ritual murderer, as Freemason, as capitalist, as communist, as reactionary, as subversive, and as the center of an evil conspiracy aiming at the domination of the world. With the new literature came a new iconography, and in time Arab cartoonists learned to use, and Arab newspaper readers to recognize, the grotesque stereotypes of Jewish racial features long familiar to readers of the anti-Semitic press in Eastern Europe and elsewhere in the Christian world.

In previous times, Jews had received little attention in Muslim literature, whether religious, historical, or fictional. Now they begin to cast a longer and darker shadow. Works purporting to be scholarly reveal dreadful secrets about Jewish history and the Jewish religion, while writers of popular fiction and drama create an array of malignant Jews worthy to take their place beside the Jewish rogues' gallery of literary Europe. Even that familiar figure of European anti-Semitic literature, the beautiful Jewess, makes an occasional appearance, at the side of the more explicitly repulsive Jewish male, in Arabic fiction and reportage, while the sexual fantasies, characteristic of such Nazi experts as Julius Streicher find their parallels in the orgies of rape and sadism projected onto Israeli soldiers. Much of this is the conventional depicting of the wartime enemy as a stereotype of evil. But he is usually defined or named as a Jew, and non-Israeli Jews are often included in the condemnation.[6] A point of some significance is that while this literature is by now very extensive, few of the major figures of modern Arabic literature are among its authors.

When the antibiblical line of argument against Judaism was transferred from Christendom to Islam, the task of Arab Muslim polemicists was much easier than that of their European Christian predecessors, since for them the Bible had no canonical status. Already in classical times, the principle was adopted that the Jewish, and for that matter also the Christian scriptures were not only superseded; they had also been corrupted and distorted by the Jews and Christians, and could therefore no longer be regarded as authentic statements of God's word. In classical times there was very little criticism by Muslim scholars of the Old Testament. Such attention as they gave to the Bible was directed rather against the New Testament, the scripture of Islam's only serious rival. In modern times the attack on the Old Testament has become a major theme in anti-Jewish propaganda. Some Arab writers claim to see in the Old Testament the roots of all the evil characteristics and dark plots which they attribute to the Jews. Some have even gone so far as to denounce the Fathers of the Church for granting canonical status to the Old Testament and placing it alongside the New, thus permitting the wicked Jews to infiltrate their poison into the Christian religion by means of their corrupt and evil scriptures.

Indeed, the demonization of the Jew in modern Arabic writings goes further than it had ever done in Western literatures, with the exception of Germany during the period of Nazi rule. In most Western countries, anti-Semitic divagations on Jewish history, religion, and literature are more than offset by a great body of genuine scholarship, the work of Christian scholars, while the fictional Jewish villains, though perhaps not matched, are at least challenged by fictional Jewish heroes. In modern Arabic writings there are few such countervailing elements. Interest in the Jews is either absent or hostile. There is virtually no scholarly literature on Jewish matters, even under the highest academic auspices, which does not seek to make some polemical point against the Jews. At the very least, serious scholarly historians of Muslim Jewish relations are concerned to demonstrate Muslim tolerance and, sometimes by implication, more often explicitly, to expose Jewish ingratitude. Most commonly, writings on Jews, past and present, consist of far-reaching accusations couched in violent language. This is the more remarkable if it is contrasted with the portrayal of Arabs and Muslims in Hebrew scholarship and literature in modern Israel. Israeli literature has some negative stereotypes; it also includes many sympathetic portrayals of the Arab—his displacement by Jewish settlement, his predicament under Israeli rule. Most Israeli research on Arab history and culture conforms to the standards, methods, and language that are normal in international modern scholarship, and has produced work of great value and importance. Some books have indeed been of sufficient interest to the Arabs themselves to be specifically exempted from Arab League boycott regulations, and introduced to Arab countries —a few even translated into Arabic.

With the growing conflict, old hatreds were exacerbated and old

associations disrupted. The great Iraqi poet Ma^crūf al-Ruṣāfī, who
taught at the Teachers's Training College in Jerusalem between 1918
and 1920, composed an ode in praise of Sir Herbert Samuel, the
British High Commissioner for Palestine. In the poem, al-Ruṣāfī denies the charge that the Arabs are anti-Jewish:

> We are not, as our accusers say, enemies of the Children of Israel,
>   in secret or in public.
> How could we be, when they are our uncles, and the Arabs are kin
>   to them of old through Ishmael?
> The two are akin to one another, and in their two languages there is
>   proof of their kinship.
> But we fear exile, and we fear a government that rules people by
>   force.[7]

The poem brought a storm of outrage among Palestinian Arabs,
who were shocked by his action in addressing an ode to the Jewish
Zionist British high commissioner. This became so serious that al-
Ruṣāfī found himself obliged to leave the country.

There were still some who insisted on making such distinctions.
An article in the newspaper *Mir'āt al-Sharq* of May 14, 1924, denounced the popular songs current at the time, cursing the Jewish
religion: "Such songs are meaningless and, moreover, opposed to the
principle of a monotheistic religion be it Islam or Christianity. . . . We
should win the respect for our struggle of both our enemies and
friends."[8]

But the trend was in the opposite direction. Before long the
attack was extended from the present to the past, including the
remote past. Even the famous and highly respected ancient Arabian
Jewish poet Samaw'al, famous for his loyalty, was not spared. Ibrā-
hîm Tūqān (1905–1941), one of the best known Palestinian poets of
his time, dismissed the stories about Samaw'al as mythical. As Tūqān
explained, the poems attributed to Samaw'al were so full of the
authentic noble Arab spirit, that they could not possibly have been
composed by a Jew; the famous story of Samaw'al's fidelity, which
became proverbial, is reinterpreted. In allowing his son to be butchered rather than surrender the coat of mail which had been entrusted to him for safekeeping by a friend, Samaw'al demonstrated
not his fidelity but his Jewish love of money.[9]

There were also new elements, among them the accusation that the Jews were an element of disruption, bringing such dangerous forces as communism and sexual libertinism. The main factor however was the growth of Jewish settlement in Palestine, and the mounting Arab and Muslim fear that Palestine would lose its Arab and Muslim character. As the Jewish community grew by immigration, and newcomers swamped the older established Jewish inhabitants, the distinctions between old and new, between foreign and local, between Jews and Zionists were forgotten by most Arabs, and attacks were generalized against all.

The rise and triumph of Nazism in Europe brought mixed reactions in the Arabic press and literature. There are a few signs of awareness that this change in Europe was aggravating their problem by driving Jews from Europe to Palestine; there were occasional expressions of disapproval for Nazi excesses, notably after the invasion of Czechoslovakia. But much more important was the reaction of sympathy for this new force in the world which was opposed simultaneously to the three major enemies of the Arabs, the British, the French, and the Jews. It was natural to welcome such a force, and to give a hearing to its point of view. Responses to reports of Jewish persecution in Europe were generally unsympathetic, and concentrated on two themes, which eventually became universal in Arab comments on these matters. The first theme was that the Jews had greatly exaggerated their sufferings, and were shamelessly exploiting them for political advantage; the second was that the Jews deserved what they got because of their misdeeds. Sometimes these were defined as trying to bring to Germany the destruction and devastation which the Jews had previously brought to Russia. With the growth of Soviet influence in the Arab world, and the consequent change of attitude towards the Russian revolution and communism, this last detail was dropped and replaced by others. The general attitude towards persecutions of the Jews in Europe could be summed up in the phrase: "This is not our affair, it is not our fault, and it should not be remedied at our expense."

Links with Germany began very early, and by the war years were very strong indeed. These links went beyond political tactics, and included a considerable ideological component. The impact of Nazi political, social, and economic doctrines on Arab nationalist theoreticians of the time is easily detectible. This makes it the more noteworthy that the Nazi mixture of old Christian and new racist anti-Semitism had much less influence. There were some, such as the mufti and a number of his associates, who accepted the entire Nazi line. But most, even among those who embraced the Nazi alliance against British and French imperialism and Zionist settlement, stopped short of Nazi anti-Semitism, and continued to express their hostility to Jews in political or at worst in traditional Islamic terms. While these could sometimes be very violent, they were generically different from the Nazi view of the Jews.

In the course of the struggle for Palestine, old stereotypes and new grievances inevitably influenced one another, and the tone of anti-Zionist and anti-Jewish polemics became increasingly bitter, violent, and general. The Jew—not just the Zionist—was depicted as mean, treacherous, cowardly, vicious, cunning, and of course implacably hostile to Islam. These anti-Jewish stereotypes had been present since early Islamic times, but they had been a secondary theme in Islamic literature; even as late as the 1950s, Sayyid Qutb, the leader of the Muslim Brothers, wrote an essay on "our struggle against the Jews,"[10] but accorded them a minor place among the enemies that menace Islam—capitalism, communism, secularism, and worst of all, the neopaganism of renegade Muslim dictators. What was new was not so much the themes, as the nature and extent of their use. The Jew, his religion, his history were abused and insulted in many ways and with growing violence, but the themes, the imagery, even the language were still drawn from traditional Islamic sources. The only new theme borrowed from Europe is that of money. With few exceptions, Muslim writers did not yet present the Jew as an incarnation of evil, a child and agent of the devil, a poisoner of wells, a perpetrator of ritual murder, a drinker of blood, and a wicked plotter seeking to subjugate all mankind and to rule the world.

Even such momentous events as the alliance with the Nazis, the establishment of Israel, and the plight of the Palestinian refugees brought only a slight increase in the use of anti-Semitic, as distinct from anti-Jewish themes. The real change began after the war of 1956 and reached its peak after the war of 1967. It was these shocking defeats—unendurable, inexplicable—and the consequent establishment of Jewish rule over Arab subjects, that finally led to the

massive adoption of anti-Semitism, henceforth the dominant influence in the discussion of Israel and Zionism, of Judaism and the Jews.

The first substantial indication that the enemy was perceived not
just as Israel and Zionism, but as the Jews, was the adoption by Arab
governments of legal measures against both citizens and aliens of the
Jewish faith. After the events in Baghdad in 1941, and for the remainder of the war years, the presence of large Allied armies kept matters
more or less under control. But hostility to Jews was growing, and
with the relaxation of Allied pressure following the end of the war,
anti-Jewish feelings found open expression. The first postwar wave of
anti-Jewish outbreaks came in November 1945, with riots and attacks
on synagogues and Jewish shops in Egypt and Syria, and a massacre
in Libya, where 130 Jewish dead were officially counted and so many
houses, shops, and workshops were destroyed that much of the community was left homeless and destitute. A third wave followed in
December 1947, with massacres of Jews in Aleppo and Aden. In the
latter, official estimates gave 82 dead, a similar number injured, 106
ships sacked, 220 houses damaged or destroyed.[11]

All this preceded the establishment of the state of Israel, though
it was in part stimulated by the growth of the Jewish National Home
in Palestine. The Jews of the Arab countries, with the exception of
Yemen, had hitherto been little affected by Zionism and on the
contrary some of them regarded this predominantly European
movement with suspicion. No doubt, some of the statements by Jewish leaders in Arab countries attacking Zionism and supporting Arab
nationalism may be ascribed to the very strong pressures to which
they were subject—it is for example improbable that Damascus Jewish leaders were really acting, as they stated, "of their own free will"
when they announced that they intended to hold a banquet in honor
of Fawzî al-Qāūqjî, a former Syrian officer who had served with the
mufti's forces in Palestine, with Rashîd ᶜAlî in Iraq, and thereafter
in the German army. There is, however, no reason to doubt their
sincerity in their expressions of loyalty to the countries of which they
were citizens, and their misgivings concerning the new and Western
society that was emerging in Palestine. These loyalties and these
misgivings were both dispelled by the course of events in the Arab
countries between 1945 and 1950.

To a world grown used to the massive slaughter, in battle and in cold blood, of Hitler's Europe, the loss of life inflicted on the Jews in various Arab cities may seem small. It did not seem so to the immediate victims, the more so since such attacks were a new experience for them. The Jews of the Arab world had known persecution in the past. But that persecution had been comparatively mild, and that past was becoming remote. Their more recent memories were of tranquility and prosperity, of a respected and accepted place in the nation, of shared hopes for the fulfillment of liberal, patriotic ideals. The anti-Jewish outbreaks in one Arab city after another, and the hatred that produced them, came as a rude shock to some hitherto comfortable and complacent Jewish communities. Sporadic violence might perhaps have been contained or even accepted. What ultimately made the position of the Arab Jews untenable was the steadily mounting harassment and discrimination directed against them by the governments of their countries, and accompanied by a furious barrage of vicious anti-Jewish—not merely anti-Zionist—propaganda in the press and the radio, in literature and the arts, in political speeches and pronouncements, and even in the textbooks used in schools.

In the summer of 1948, with the establishment of the state of Israel and the unsuccessful attempt by the Arab armies to destroy the new state at birth, the already bad situation of the Jews in Arab countries deteriorated rapidly. In Egypt, Iraq, and Syria they were subject to arbitrary arrest, to interrogation and beating, to large-scale confiscation of assets and compulsory contributions to Arab causes, to dismissal from employment and limitations on movement, and to a whole series of financial and commercial restrictions. The point was driven home by violent outbreaks in many cities, extending as far away as Morocco.

Like the Germans in the early years of the Nazi regime, some Arab governments seemed to have been principally concerned to get rid of their Jews. Emigration was the most obvious answer, and again like the Nazis, they do not seem to have greatly cared where they went. Many of the wealthier and better equipped elements preferred to go to Western Europe and the Americas. Most of the poor found their new home in Israel. At least two Arab governments, those of Iraq and Yemen, cooperated directly in the transfer of their Jews to Israel. Others were willing to turn a blind eye.

Arab government action against their own Jews was practical rather than theoretical, administrative rather than ideological. Comparatively little explicitly anti-Semitic literature appeared at this time—the flood did not begin until several years later—but as the Arab–Israeli conflict grew in scale, intensity, and bitterness, Jews in most Arab countries were subjected to both official and popular pressures so severe that most of them felt obliged to leave. Today only small remnants remain. These anti-Jewish acts were no doubt encouraged by the arrival in the Middle East of a number of escaping Nazi war criminals, some of whom placed their expertise in "Jewish affairs" at the disposal of their hosts. One of them, Johann von Leers, a specialist in anti-Semitic literature, was publicly welcomed in Cairo by no less a person than the mufti Ḥājj Amîn al-Ḥusaynî, who in a speech remarked: "We thank you for venturing to take up the battle with the powers of darkness that have become incarnate in world Jewry."[12] Under the new name ᶜUmar Amîn, von Leers became a political adviser to the Egyptian information department, and stayed in Cairo until his death in 1965.

Of the once great Jewish communities in the Arab lands, only in Morocco and Tunisia do sizeable remnants remain, their safety dependent on the survival of the present political order in both countries. In Syria a few thousand still live, subject to severe disabilities. In Egypt, Iraq, Yemen, Libya, and Algeria, a history of Jewish communal life dating back to remote antiquity has come to an end, and only a few old people are left.

Those Arab countries with no Jewish citizens took care not to acquire any, or even to admit them as visitors. The Jordanian nationality law of February 4, 1954, grants citizenship to residents of the West Bank areas annexed to Jordan, but explicitly excludes Jews. All the independent Middle Eastern Arab states included a question about religion in their visa application forms, and routinely refused visas to travelers, of whatever nationality, who declared their religion as Jewish. Some of the more strongly Islamic states demanded certificates of baptism from West European and American travelers, as proof that they were not Jews.

After the departure of almost all the Jews from the Middle Eastern Arab states, the struggle took a new form, that of political warfare against their perceived enemies—the state of Israel, and behind it world Jewry. With the failure of both military and economic mea-

sures against Israel, governments devoted increasing attention to
ideological weapons. For this purpose, the weapon of European anti-
Semitism was useful in many ways. On the one hand it provided a
ready-made system of themes, issues and even visual images for a war
against the Jews. On the other it brought useful allies, among them
the survivors of the old anti-Semitism and the harbingers of the new.
The former included neo-Nazis in Germany, neo-fascists in Italy,
their imitators in Britain, France, and the USA, and a wide range of
extreme rightist and racist groups in Latin America. The latter put
them in touch and in accord with the resurgent anti-Semitism of the
left.

An early sign of the adoption and adaptation of anti-Semitism was
the enormous output and distribution of anti-Semitic publications.
There were Arab writers who argued against this trend. This dissemination and acceptance of anti-Semitic propaganda, they said, would
injure the Arabs, by weakening their resolve or discrediting their
cause. In a book published in 1972, a Syrian Marxist philosopher,
Ṣādiq Jalāl al-ᶜAẓm, poured ridicule on naively personal and con-
sipiratorial interpretations of events, and warned his readers that
belief in such fantasies would paralyze their will and prevent them
from understanding and confronting their real problems.[13] In a book
on the Talmud published by the PLO Research Center in 1970,
Asᶜad Razzūq complained of the general reliance by Arab writers on
such tainted sources as Canon Rohling's *Talmud Jew*, which "today
are rejected and despised by civilized people," and asked: "Until
when do we want to be our own worst enemies, as we persist in
prejudicing the justice of our cause, and appear to be determined to
nullify its humanistic character?"[14]

But such appeals found little response. Razzūq listed twenty-six
books based directly or indirectly on Rohling, and since these there
have been more. There are at least nine different Arabic translations
of the *Protocols* and innumerable editions, more than in any other
language including German. One of them, published in 1961, was
introduced by the famous and respected author ᶜAbbās Maḥmūd al-
ᶜAqqād; another, published in about 1968, was translated by Shawqî
ᶜAbd al-Nāṣir, the brother of the Egyptian president. The book has
been publicly recommended by Presidents Nasser and Sadat in
Egypt, President ᶜĀrif of Iraq, King Faisal of Saudi Arabia, Colonel
Qaddāfî of Libya, and various other monarchs, presidents, prime

ministers, and other political and intellectual leaders. The *Protocols* were featured in an article published in the official Egyptian cultural journal in 1960, written by a senior government official.[15] The same official was the author of a booklet demonstrating that the United States is a colonial dependency of Israel, and not, as innocent Arab leftists had supposed, the other way around.[16] The case is demonstrated with a great quantity of fabricated statistics, derived mainly from American Nazi publications.

Until a few years ago, the reader with access only to Arabic would not have known that the authenticity of the *Protocols* had ever been called in question, the sole discordant voice coming from Marxist critics who reject personal explanations of history, such as those relied upon in the *Protocols*, but still without indicating they are a fabrication. More recently, a few Arab writers have shown at least some awareness of this, but they still display a curious reluctance to abandon the *Protocols* entirely. One writer, denying Arab reliance on this book, quoted an Iraqi broadcast on the *Protocols* which describes them "as of questionable authenticity."[17] The same writer in an article in *al-Ahrām* of February 22, 1974, observed judiciously that "the prevailing opinion at the present time is that the *Protocols* are a forged document." This cautious formulation no doubt represents some progress, but leaves a number of questions unanswered, such as who forged them and what they represent. Here the article is remarkably equivocal. There is little to indicate that the forgers were anti-Jewish and that the *Protocols* were used by Nazis and others to justify racist action against the Jews. On the contrary, the unwary reader could be left with the impression that if the *Protocols* were not actually fabricated by Jews, they nevertheless accurately reflect the image which the Zionists hold of themselves and which they desire to project to others. Here the writer makes use of a theory which is much used in Arabic writings of this kind—that Zionism and anti-Semitism are one and the same, that Zionists and anti-Semites are natural allies and collaborators, and thus, whether the one or the other was responsible for the *Protocols* really makes very little difference. Some Arab writers are unhappy with the *Protocols*, not because they are forged, but because they project an image of the Jew as the possessor of immense hidden powers. This represents a danger to Arab morale.

It is however precisely the specter of immense hidden power that makes the *Protocols* so attractive to many Arab writers, and ensures it so wide a distribution. By March 1970, a Lebanese newspaper placed the *Protocols* first on its list of nonfiction best-sellers. Besides the great and growing number of Arabic translations and editions, there is a rapidly developing original literature of anti-Semitism in Arabic, much of it based directly or indirectly on the *Protocols*, which are extensively cited as authoritative. The *Protocols* also figure prominently in propaganda distributed internationally by some Arab states and by Iran.

In President Nasser's day, the main source of such propaganda was Egypt. As far back as January 1965, an English-language pamphlet entitled *Israel, the Enemy of Africa* was released by the government information department in Cairo, and distributed in great numbers in the English-speaking countries of Africa. The authors of the pamphlet cite directly from the *Protocols* and also from Henry Ford's *The International Jew,* and on the basis of these authorities denounce the Jewish faith and describe all the Jews as cheats, thieves, and murderers.

More recently, the task of disseminating the *Protocols* has been taken over by various agencies operating in Saudi Arabia, in Libya, and latterly also in revolutionary Iran. The late King Faisal made a practice of presenting copies of the *Protocols* and other anti-Semitic publications to visiting ministers, diplomats, journalists, and other dignitaries.[18] Copies are also distributed via consular and cultural missions. The message has been carried to such countries as Pakistan, Malaysia, and Indonesia, and from there given even further circulation. On September 20, 1978, *The Canberra Times* reported a lecture in the Australian capital by a Pakistani professor called Qazi, who was quoted as saying that "at present Jews were not just a threat to Arabs, but to the whole world. This was not his opinion but had been written in Jewish secret documents." This report appeared under two oddly matched headlines, the first, in quotes, "Jews Threat to Whole World," the second "Professor Hopes for Better Understanding." In a subsequent issue, the professor confirmed that he had been accurately reported, and that the "secret documents" to which he alluded were the *Protocols of the Elders of Zion.* While some intellectuals in the more open Arab countries are beginning to express doubts about the *Protocols,* there are others willing to carry on the task. A publication called *Imam,* published from the Iranian Embassy in London, quotes extensively from the *Protocols* in its issues of 1984 and 1985, with accompanying cartoons in the standard manner of East and Middle European anti-Semitic iconography. In 1985 a new edition of the *Protocols*, printed in Iran, was widely distributed by "the Islamic Propagation Organization, International Relations Department" of Tehran. Most recently, it has been reported that the *Protocols* are on sale at the bookstall in the great mosque in London. Henry Ford's anti-Semitic tract, later renounced by its own author, has been translated into Arabic, and in May–June 1984 the original text, with an introductory note derived from the writings of the well-known Jew-baiter Gerald L. K. Smith, was serialized in the widely circulated English-language *Saudi Gazette*, published in Jedda.

The involvement of some Arab governments in anti-Semitism was not limited to the use of the *Protocols*, the blood libel, and other standard issue weapons from the anti-Semitic armory. There was also more direct involvement through links with extreme right-wing neo-Nazi and other anti-Semitic organizations, especially in Europe and Latin America. The best-known case occurred in London in 1962, when the Egyptian military attaché, Colonel (later General) Muḥammad al-Shazli made secret contacts with the leaders of the "British National Socialist Movement," an extreme right-wing group devoted to nazism, fascism, and anti-Semitism. These links became known when the British police raided the home of one of the British Nazi leaders and discovered correspondence with the Egyptian military attaché. The correspondence, dealing with proposed cooperation for a joint struggle against "the organized forces of Zionism and world Jewry" discussed the provision of Egyptian funds for anti-Semitic propaganda activities. The colonel denied all knowledge of this correspondence, and was very shortly afterwards recalled to Cairo. The fascist leaders, however, at their trial and in subsequent press interviews, gave somewhat fuller information.[19]

By the late sixties, the atmosphere had changed, and links with fascist organizations were as inappropriate as the charges of Bolshevism that had been so common in the immediately preceding years. For some, such as the Saudis, this approach was still possible, but in the great majority of Arab states which claimed in various degrees to be radical, socialist, and revolutionary, such links and such accusations were no longer acceptable. The attack on Israel was now expressed in left-wing instead of right-wing terms, and addressed to an audience accustomed to a somewhat different frame of allusion. In the event, this presented no great difficulty.

Intellectual fashions and international alignments had changed, and so too had the fashionable enemy. In place of the International Jew Communist who had haunted the White Russians and the Nazis and still haunts the Saudi court, a new figure appeared—the Racist. The attack on Zionism was accordingly redefined, and the charge of racism used with telling effect. It was particularly successful with liberal and leftist circles in Western Europe and North America, which had for long favored the cause of both Israel and Zionism, and were now, to a considerable extent, won over to the Palestinian side. The adoption of this line of attack only slightly reduced the use by writers in Arabic of such racist documents as the *Protocols,* and racist arguments directed against the Jews.

Individual Jews or Zionists may of course be racists, as may individual members of any other group or followers of any other nationalist ideology. It would indeed be difficult if not impossible to point to any religious community or ethnic group exempt from this social and moral disease. But Judaism, like Christianity and Islam, does not countenance racism, while Zionism is no more racist than any other nationalist movement, and has hitherto been less so than many of them. As with the Arabs in an earlier period, such frictions and prejudices as appeared did not go beyond what was normal between different peoples in a state of war. There have, however, been ominous signs of deterioration. Negative stereotype of Arabs have recently been noted in Israeli children's literature. In the early 1980s, the Israeli prime minister and the chief of staff spoke of Arabs in the language of ethnic insult, of a kind that would have been inconceivable a few years earlier, and hostile reflections, not just on Israel's Arab enemies but on Arabs in general, began to appear in extremist religious and nationalist publication, though not in the mainstream press. A hundred years after the beginning of Zionist settlement in Palestine, and almost forty years after the establishment of the state of Israel, an explicitly anti-Arab party was established in Israel, with a policy of ethnic hostility against Arabs. It is still a minor fringe group in the Israeli political spectrum—though, if the present situation continues for any length of time, it may well grow into something more important. Racism is an infectious disease.

The Arab case against the Jews was ostensibly concerned with the ideology of Zionism and the actions of the state of Israel, both against the Palestinian Arabs and against the neighboring Arab states. Such indeed were the origins of the indictment—but before long it assumed much greater dimensions, embracing the entire Jewish people, throughout the world and throughout its history.

A common accusation is that the Jews are and have always been racists. Some of the accusers see no inconsistency in describing this trait as a racial characteristic; others, with better logic but equal lack of evidence, ascribe it to the inherently vicious character of the Jewish religion. This latter charge is documented with suitable quotations from the standard anti-Semitic treatments of the Talmud and the Old Testament, with some new and distinctive twists. The story of the Exodus is retold with Pharaoh as hero and the Israelites as villains—a somewhat difficult feat, since it flatly contradicts the version contained in the Qur'ān. Special attention is given to the role of the Jews in Islamic history, from the tribes who opposed Muhammad to the Jewish capitalists of King Faruq's Egypt, who, according to this perception of history, in Egypt as elsewhere abused the tolerance and hospitality which had been accorded to them in order to seek economic and ultimately political domination. A similarly evil role is assigned to the Jews in Europe and the Americas, where by their activities they are said to have brought on themselves the well-deserved hatred of the peoples they were trying to exploit and dominate.

Many of these writings employ the well-tested anti-Semitic device of ascribing a Jewish origin to whatever idea, movement, organization, or individual they may choose. Thus, for example, after the murder of President Kennedy, the Arab press and other media made much of the fact that Jack Ruby, the murderer of Lee Oswald, was Jewish. Some went further, claiming that the assassination was a Zionist or simply a Jewish plot. The famous Egyptian journalist Anîs Mansūr, in an article in the illustrated weekly *al-Musawwar* of December 6, 1963, discussed the preparations for the second Vatican Council, and admonished the Catholics for being "busy making peace with the Jews, while the Jews are assassinating the foremost lay Catholic personality in the world . . . thus the great deception succeeds, and the Jews are exonerated of blame for the killing of both Christ and Kennedy at one and the same time." Ruby's Jewishness was presented with special emphasis in a letter to the editor by one

Nā'if Shablaq, prominently featured in the Beirut daily *al-Ḥayāt* of November 28, 1963. The writer's purpose was to reveal "an important point, which the international news agencies—mostly under Zionist influence—apparently tried to cover up: namely that the killer of Lee Oswald is a Jew on both his father's and his mother's side, a Jew by belief and a Jew by religion, who was born a Jew and lived as a Jew." From this fact, and some additional "facts," such as that "the name Ruby or Rubinstein means Rabbi" and that Ruby was a nightclub owner and the night life industry of the United States is "almost entirely monopolized by Jews," the writer goes on to infer that the assassination was the work of "world Zionist organizations and world Jewry."

This line of argument was taken up by other writers, some of whom added, for good measure, that the Catholic Leon Czolgosz, the murderer of President McKinley and the Protestant John Wilkes Booth, the murderer of President Lincoln, had both been Jews, and "armed by the Zionist organization." This contribution to historiography was published in April 1964 in *The Scribe*, a monthly magazine published in English, French, German, Italian, and Spanish by the National Publications House in Cairo, an agency of the Egyptian government.[20] The kind of imagination that can turn John Wilkes Booth into a Jew and make him a Zionist agent twenty years before the first beginnings of the Zionist movement obviously has no limits. The second point is the less surprising if we recall that the term "Zionist" or "Zionism" is often used by Arabic writers when discussing medieval or even ancient times, when it is clearly a simple synonym for Jews and Judaism. Another remarkable discovery relayed by the same journal, allegedly on the authority of the Moscow newspaper *Krasnaya zvezda*, organ of the Soviet Ministry of Defense, is that the famous gangster Al Capone was in fact an Israeli, whose true name was Isaac Schacher. It will be recalled that Al Capone died in 1947, one year before the establishment of the state of Israel.

Sometimes the tendency to ascribe all that is disapproved to Zionist or even simply to Jewish origins goes to astonishing lengths. Thus, a book published in Cairo in 1970 claims to discover the Zionist roots of the thinking of Sigmund Freud.[21] A broadcast from Tripoli radio on April 11, 1973, attacking the theory of evolution as unsuited to revolutionary Libya, asks rhetorically: "How long will the revolution wait for the monkey to turn into a man, so that it may become sure of the impossible theory of the Jew Darwin?" Perhaps the prize for this kind of imagination should go to the author of a monograph on anti-Semitism, published by Khartoum University Press, which asserts that anti-Semitism is a Jewish invention, and that the term, which "was in use a long time before Wilhelm Marr used it" in 1879, was coined by "the Zionists."[22] It is not clear what propaganda point is served by such stories, except perhaps the general one, common in anti-Semitic writings; not only are all Jews evil but all evil is Jewish.

Once accepted, this principle is capable of indefinite extension, and can be applied to ancient as well as to contemporary events. In an article published in the Cairo daily newspaper, *al-Ahrār*, on February 14, 1983, Rif^{c}at Sa^{c}īd Ahmad offers a new interpretation of the Elephantine documents, a group of Aramaic papyri and parchment scrolls discovered in Elephantine in upper Egypt, and revealing the existence of a Jewish settlement, apparently consisting of military colonists in the Egyptian service, probably dating back to the sixth century B.C. These documents have long been known to scholarship, but Ahmad discovered a new significance that had eluded the attention of scholars. In his view, the documents prove that the Jews conspired against several Pharaohs and were involved in continuous subversion while exploiting their position as mercenaries. "During the Jewish presence in Egypt, many acts of this nature occurred." This history is of significance today because Israel and Egypt have reached a stage of "struggle in the shadow of understanding"—an interesting characterization of bilateral relations after the peace. The Jewish instruments in this struggle, as listed in the article, are history, economics, and espionage, accompanied by treason.

Similar arguments, racially conceived and historically expressed, are used by other Egyptian critics of the policy of peace with Israel, and appear not only in articles attacking the peace as such, but even in discussing temporary hitches in the process of negotiation. The discussion of specific points of policy, both in the media and by government spokesmen, can be similarly affected. Some Egyptian and other Arab criticisms of the policies and actions of the Begin government might well have received the assent of many Israeli and other Jews. They can not, however, receive that assent when they ascribe the errors or misdeeds of Israeli leaders to inherent and eternal Jewish wickedness, and moreover express this view with the stock epithets of anti-Semitic diatribe. Such publications could not fail to cause both anger and alarm in a generation of Israeli and other Jews who knew from personal experience what lay at the end of the road of which such language was the beginning.

In a society in which religion is the innermost core of identity and the ultimate focus of loyalty, it was natural and indeed inevitable that countries at war with a state defining itself as Jewish should see the adversary as "the Jews"; at a time when extreme violence of language is the norm even in internal disputes, it is hardly surprising that they should have availed themselves of the rich armory of themes and images offered to them, indeed urged upon them, by European and later American anti-Semitism. This became easier with the departure of most of the Jewish inhabitants of the Arab countries, so that the Jew was no longer a familiar neighboring presence and could be the more easily depicted as a satanic embodiment of evil.

Perhaps the outstanding example of this kind of writing is provided by Anîs Mansūr, who in many books and innumerable articles has repeated all the standard accusations of Nazi anti-Semitism, and added a few of his own. According to his book, *The Wailing Wall and the Tears,* which has run through many editions, the Jews are instructed by the Talmud to hate all other religions and are told that they are free to commit any crime or offense against followers of other religions. As quoted by him, the Talmud also teaches Jews how to swindle non-Jews;

swindling a non-Jew is not a swindle but is an obligation since the Jew regards all money in the pocket of any other person as being his of right, and taking possession of this money amounts to recovering it, and such recovery by any means is a lawful act. Therefore stealing from a Muslim is not stealing and the only theft is theft from another Jew. . . . The immorality which the Jews direct in Europe and America and which they were the first to introduce in an organized form when they entered the Land of Canaan coming from Iraq is not considered a moral or social crime, because it is the duty of the Jew to rape women of other religions. Similarly when a Jewish girl gives herself to a Muslim or a Christian, this is not considered a kind of fornication, since fornication can only take place between human and human, and the Jews regard anyone other than themselves as animals. Therefore there is no moral crime between an "animal" man and a "human" woman.

After gathering these gems from Canon Rohling's *Talmud,* Mansūr then goes on to cite from his other main source authority, the *Proto-*

cols of the Elders of Zion, which he describes as "the secret constitu-
tion of the Jews." This he says "advises Jews to become obstetricians
and to specialize in abortion, which in fact they do in all the world
and which they used to do in Egypt . . . and the reason for this is that
abortion is a means to reduce the number of non-Jews—one, a thousand, and a hundred thousand."[23]

Anîs Mansûr is a prolific writer on many subjects, including such
topics as ghosts and other manifestations of the occult, visitors from
outer space, and the like. One may reasonably ask whether his anti-
Semitic ravings do not belong to the same intellectual order of
phenomena and constitute no more than an extreme form of normal
vituperation.

The question may be put in this way. Is the predominantly anti-
Semitic tone of discussions of Jews in Arab countries at the present
time merely part of the normally heightened level of emotion and
hostility in time of war, which will fade away if and when the problem is resolved? Or, alternatively, has it already been internalized,
and become part of at least the present phase of Arab and more
generally, Islamic world views?

In seeking an answer to this question, it may be useful to examine
the treatment, by Arab and other Muslims, both official and unofficial, of matters which have no direct connection with the modern
state of Israel, the Zionist movement and ideology, or the Arab–
Israeli conflict. One possible test might be the treatment of the Nazi
Holocaust, which Arab writers and spokesmen tend on the whole
either to deny, in accord with the neo-Nazi line, or else to minimize
or even justify. Discussions of the antecedents of Jewish migration to
Israel make little of the Holocaust, but explain how the Jews, by their
own behavior, brought the hatred of the Europeans upon themselves, and were thus led to seek a home elsewhere at Arab expense.
An Egyptian textbook of the Nasser period, for example, informs
pupils that "the Jews describe and always have described the immigrants [to Israel] as being persecuted in order to arouse sympathy
and extract money and in order to veil the Zionist expansionist
desires, but the fact is the Jews never are (or have been) persecuted."[24] Another example is the contemporary comment on the
trial of Adolf Eichmann in Jerusalem, some of which found him guilty
only of not having completed his task. In 1978, Iraq protested when
the government of Poland—certainly no sympathizer with Zionism

or with Israel—arranged ceremonies to commemorate "the so-called Jewish ghetto uprising" in Warsaw and the martyrdom of the Polish Jews during the war; in Athens, in April 1979, the ambassadors from the Arab countries except Egypt protested even at the screening of the television series commemorating the Holocaust, and in March 1984 Egypt, despite the existence of a peace treaty and diplomatic relations with Israel, banned a film depicting the Holocaust.[25]

But perhaps the treatment of the Holocaust is not a fair test. While it is true that the Holocaust ended three years before the establishment of the state of Israel, it nevertheless contributed very substantially to that event—on the one hand, by launching the desperate and finally unstoppable Jewish drive to a national home and state, on the other, by mobilizing international sympathy and support for that aim. It has been plausibly argued that without the Holocaust there would have been no Israel; indeed, the late Sheikh Ja'abiri of Hebron once remarked, ironically, that "the Jews ought to erect statues of Adolf Hitler and Amîn al-Husaynî in the center of Tel-Aviv, as the co-founders of the Jewish state of Israel." Though no doubt exaggerated, this observation surely contains a kernel of truth.

There are, however, other events, more remote in time, where no connection could possibly be established with the Arab–Israeli conflict. Two particularly revealing cases are the biography of Muhammad and the crucifixion of Christ—the one central to Islamic belief and history, the other totally alien to Islam, which teaches, on the authority of the Qur'ān itself, that the crucifixion never took place.

In the last few decades there has been a significant change in the teaching of the biography of the Prophet. The traditional stereotypes of the Jew as hostile, even malevolent, have been retained and given a new and central importance. But the insignificance of the Jew, the ineffectualness of his hostility, which are a feature of the traditional accounts, have disappeared. Comparison of the traditional and modern versions of these events shows several changes. The first and most obvious is in the violence of the language used, and the nature of the accusations made. Thus in an Egyptian textbook of "Arab Islamic history" used in teacher training colleges in the sixties, we find:

The Jews are always the same, every time and everywhere. They will not live save in darkness. They contrive their evils clandestinely. They fight only when they are hidden, because they are cowards. . . . The Prophet enlightened us about the right way to treat them, and succeeded finally in crushing the plots that they had planned. We today must follow this way and purify Palestine from their filth.

The contemporary relevance is made clear in another Egyptian textbook, a manual on religious instruction for first-year junior high school: "The Jews of our time are the descendants of the Jews who harmed the prophet Muḥammad. They betrayed him, they broke the treaty with him and joined with his enemies the polytheists and the hypocrites to fight against him. . . . Today they are fighting the Arabs."[26] No less a person than the Ayatollah Khomeini, in the foreword to his book on Islamic government, which contains his political creed, remarks: "The Islamic movement was afflicted by the Jews from its very beginnings, when they began their hostile activity by distorting the reputation of Islam, and by defaming and maligning it. This has continued to the present day."[27] In general, school books in these countries are highly political; even such subjects as spelling, grammar, and elementary arithmetic are given a political content through the examples chosen, and are used to strengthen national feeling and to encourage hatred and contempt for the perceived enemy. Hostility to Israel and to Zionism is of course standard and virtually universal, and is usually expressed in very vigorous language. Often, though not always, this crosses the line to explicit anti-Semitism.

In 1968 and 1969, perhaps for the only time, a detailed content analysis of Arabic textbooks was made under the auspices of an international authority. After the Six Day War, the Israelis conducted their own investigation of the textbooks used in the camps maintained by the United Nations in the territories which they had conquered. On the basis of this inquiry they made a formal complaint to the United Nations Educational, Scientific, and Cultural Organization. What Arab governments did in their own countries and in their own schools was an internal matter, and beyond the competence of any international authority, least of all acting on an Israeli request. But the schools in the refugee camps were under United Nations auspices, with teachers appointed by the UN, and operating under a UN budget, the greater part of which was provided by the United States. The Israeli complaint that these schools were inculcating racist anti-Semitism in their pupils could not therefore be ignored, and a UNESCO commission, consisting of an American, a Frenchman, and a Turk, all three Arabic scholars of eminence, was appointed. The commission, which examined 127 textbooks used in the refugee camps on both banks of the Jordan, in the Gaza Strip and in Lebanon, explained the criteria upon which it based its recommendations: "All terms contemptuous of a community taken as a whole should be prohibited since this, obviously intolerable in itself, can among other consequences lead to the violation of the most sacred rights of the individual. Hence, 'liar,' 'cheat,' 'usurer,' 'idiot'—terms applied to Jews in certain passages, and part of the deplorable language of international anti-Semitism—cannot be tolerated." Among many other problems, the commission noted in particular that in textbooks on religion and history

An excessive importance is given to the problem of relations between the Prophet Muhammad and the Jews of Arabia, in terms tending to convince young people that the Jewish community as a whole has always been and will always be the irreconcilable enemy of the Muslim community. Furthermore, in certain passages, pejorative and harmful terms employed to designate the Jewish community are not admissible. . . . Finally, special mention should be made of students' exercises which are often inspired by a preoccupation with indoctrination against Jews rather than by strictly educational aims. Many of these exercises should be removed or entirely rewritten.

The commission finally recommended that 14 textbooks be withdrawn entirely, 65 be modified before further use, and 48 of the original 127 be retained without change. The report was presented to the 82nd Session of UNESCO held in Paris on April 4, 1969. It was never published. The offending textbooks were withdrawn from the UN camps. Most of them remained in use by the ministries of education of the Arab states which had originally published them, or were replaced by others along similar lines.

The biography of Muhammad, including accounts of his struggle with the Jewish tribes of Medina, is of obvious concern to Muslims. Even the presentation of the struggle with the Jews, though given a new twist in modern times, is based in the last analysis on elements in the Islamic tradition. The same cannot be said of the modern Muslim concern with the crucifixion of Christ—an event entirely outside both the theology and the historiography of Islam.

Accounts telling the story of the crucifixion in Christian rather than Muslim terms appeared in Arab writings more and more frequently. This interest reached its apex during the Second Vatican Council held in Rome between 1962 and 1964, and concentrated on the famous "schema of the Jews"—the draft resolution which was to exonerate the Jews from the crime of deicide. From the first, Arab governments exerted very strong diplomatic and other pressures on the Vatican to prevent the adoption of this resolution. Their justification for this action was explained in an Arab League newsletter of October 28, 1964: "Certainly the Arab Christians have raised their voices against the attempts to alter the Holy Scriptures. As inhabitants of the cradle of Christianity the Arabs are in a better position to be able to judge the history of Christianity. That is why they permitted themselves to oppose the attempts of the Council." The following issue of the same newsletter (November 20, 1964) explained the strategy:

All Arab ambassadors to foreign countries have received instructions to keep constant contact with the bishops and cardinals who participate in the Council in Rome and to enlighten them about the political background behind the Jewish schema debated by the Council. The Arab ambassadors will also explain the Arab point of view concerning this document to the Papal Secretariat and other authorities at the Vatican. This action of the Arab nations is to be interpreted as a good-will action, in order to maintain good relations with the Vatican.[28]

The gentle threat in the last sentence was made clearer in more popular publications.

The spearhead of attack was of course the Arab Christian churches, and the one Arab government, that of Lebanon, which had some standing in the Christian world. But others took up the cause. President Sukarno of Indonesia made a special trip to Rome to warn the Pope of the dangers resulting from such a resolution, while the Jordanian Foreign Minister, Qadrî Tūqān, was reported in the Beirut press as warning that the passage of the proposed declaration would be disastrous, since "history testifies to Jewish intentions of destroying Christ and Christianity." Another writer warned that "the Zionizing cardinals . . . are the dupes of an incessant power struggle which uses the supposed sufferings of the Jews as one of its principle aids." The visit of Pope Paul VI to the Holy Land in 1963 was an occasion for much writing on this subject. Thus Kāmil al-Shinnāwî, in an article in the Cairo Akhbār al-Yawm, of December 14, 1963, observed:

The Jews have already exploited this purely religious pilgrimage to create the impression in world opinion that the new pope has an opinion about the accusation against them of killing Christ, and they are talking again of an historic document which will acquit them of this crime, which they want to make public, imagining that it is hidden in some hiding place . . . in the Vatican.

I as a Muslim do not accuse the Jews of killing Jesus, since the noble Qur'ān lays down that they neither killed nor crucified him but only a likeness shown to them.

But the historic facts confirm that the Jews fought against Christ and pursued him and sought his blood and that they accused him of lying and making false claims and denied that he was the awaited Messiah, and the priests assembled in Solomon's temple and sentenced him to death by crucifixion . . . and they sent their sentence to the Roman authorities to be put into effect.

This was about 1934 years ago, and from that day the Jews went on boasting that they had killed and crucified Christ, and the Qur'ān came and confirmed that they had neither killed nor crucified him, but Christian belief holds the Jews guilty of the crime of killing and crucifying him. . . . The Christian religion holds firm to its belief that the Jews shed the blood of Christ because they admitted their guilt and boasted of it, and because of their treatment of Christians and people in general, like murderers and bloodsuckers. I as a Muslim am not shocked by the Jewish claim that they are innocent of the blood of Christ, since this claim accords with my religious beliefs, but I wonder what induces these vagrants today to try and clear themselves of a crime which they admitted perpetrating nearly two thousand years ago. Why do they insist on clearing their conscience of the blood of Christ, at a time when so many fingers are pointed at them to demand justice for the blood of Kennedy? . . . We are convinced that this visit will not influence the Pope's belief as to the nature of the Jews, since he knows them quite enough. And once he has met them, he will get to know them more than enough.

On his arrival in Jordan on January 4, 1964, the Pope was greeted by a broadcast commentary from Radio Amman, which stated among other things:

The events of history will fortify his lofty spirit more and more; his Holiness will consider how the Jews behaved at that time. . . . Some two thousand years ago the Jews crucified Jesus, after beatings, humiliations, and tortures that heap shame upon mankind everywhere. And fifteen years ago, in the most cruel manner, the Jews overran Palestine. They attacked its innocent, unarmed citizens and subjected many of them to the most villainous atrocities. . . . Thus do the Jews prove their responsibility for the infamies of their forebears, and for the crucifixion and humiliation of Christ nineteen centuries ago.

According to the testimony of some Vatican observers, it was principally the influence of the representatives of the Near Eastern churches which caused some toning down of the draft resolution. What remained, however, was still very displeasing to the World Muslim League. At a meeting of the League in Mecca in November 1964, presided over by the chief mufti of Saudi Arabia, and attended, among others, by the mufti Amîn al-Ḥusaynî, it was stated that:

The newspapers of yesterday have brought to our attention the decree, approved by the overwhelming majority in the ecumenical council, absolving the Jewish people from culpability in the crucifixion of the Prophet of God, the Christ, peace and blessings be upon him. Secret and open maneuvers, undertaken for a long time by Zionist circles and their accomplices, the colonialist forces, have precipitated and provoked such a decree, which therefore lost all religious character, and became a purely political move, which is aimed at securing the support of the Christian world for the Zionist idea.

The document produced by the meeting goes on to point to the difference between the Christian and Muslim views of the crucifixion, as set forth in the Qur'ān, and continues:

On the other hand, the initiative of the Catholics in mutilating their own dogmas and altering their own laws, under the influence of whims and passions, will only reinforce among us our adhesion to that which was revealed in the immutable and unalterable Qur'ān. . . . And it is with some astonishment that we consider how the Christian peoples permitted a circle of prelates, seduced by and in complicity with Zionism, to trifle with dogmas and shatter religious convictions that have survived for two thousand years. . . . It has reinforced doubts concerning the integrity of their Scriptures and the solidity of their dogmas, and furnishes a new weapon to the forces of impiety and materialism.[29]

The arguments put forward by Arab spokesmen notwithstanding, it is strange that Muslim leaders should have concerned themselves so intimately with the council of a church which they do not accept, and the definition of a dogma in which they do not believe. Probably the best explanation was that given by the London *Economist*, which remarked that in the Arab view this was no time to be acquitting the Jews of anything.

Perhaps the clearest indication of the way in which the war against Israel was generalized to become a war against the Jews may be seen in the way in which the boycott of Israel, operated by all member states of the Arab League, was put into effect. Officially, the boycott is directed against the state of Israel, and against all firms, institutions, and individuals in other countries who trade with Israel. It is concerned with cultural as well as commercial activities, and for example requires the banning of performers, or of films made by performers, believed to have given aid and comfort to Israel. In practice, however, this was often given a remarkably wide definition. In at least two cases, both of which became public, ambassadors were refused by Muslim countries for no other reason than their Jewish birth. In 1973, a distinguished British diplomat, who had previously served in Saudi Arabia, had already been given *agrément* as ambassador, when a Jewish newspaper in London referred to his Jewish birth. The *agrément* was promptly withdrawn. More recently, the government of Indonesia refused an American ambassador for the same reason. In neither case was there ever the slightest suggestion of connections with Israel or Zionist activity. In the same spirit, a visit by the New York Philharmonic to Malaysia was cancelled in August 1984 when it became publicly known that the Malaysian authorities had demanded and obtained the removal from the program of Ernest Bloch's *Schelomo,* subtitled "A Hebrew Rhapsody for Cello and Orchestra." This piece of music was composed in Switzerland in 1915, three years before the Balfour Declaration; the composer himself died in 1959. No indication was given of how the Malaysian censors were able to establish the Zionist quality of the music. Presumably the name "Hebrew" in the subtitle was sufficient evidence.[30]

An even more remarkable case occurred in Egypt in June 1979 when the organizers of a theater festival in Cairo were ordered to omit three plays by an Egyptian Jew called Ya^{c}qūb Ṣanūa^c. Two things are noteworthy about this action; first, that it was taken two and a half months after the formal signature, at the White House in Washington, of the peace treaty between Egypt and Israel, second, that Ya^{c}qūb Ṣanūa^c, who died in 1912, was a fervent Egyptian patriot and the editor of a nationalist journal, who never in his life showed the slightest interest in Jewish affairs.[31] Indeed, one modern Egyptian scholar has even claimed that he was a Muslim.[32]

The same spirit was in evidence at the Fourth Cairo International Film Festival, held in September of the same year. At first, there were signs of a change of heart. Elizabeth Taylor, whose films had been banned in Arab countries for twenty years because of her support for Israel and perhaps because of her conversion to Judaism, was a guest of honor at the opening night, and was received by President Sadat. A number of Israeli producers, directors, and actors came to the festival as private guests of some of their Egyptian colleagues. The organizers of the festival took pride in the fact that, for the first time, some films with Jewish stories or Jewish characters were to be shown in Egyptian cinemas. But it did not quite work out that way. The first victims were, oddly enough, Yugoslavs—from a country which had always sided with the Arabs and still has no diplomatic relations with Israel. Fifteen minutes were cut from the Yugoslav entry at the festival, on the grounds that one of the characters was Jewish. The Yugoslav delegation walked out. The Swiss delegation threatened legal action, claiming that the censor had mutilated their film beyond repair. An American film, *The Magician of Lublin*, based on a story by Isaac Bashevis Singer, was held up in airport customs throughout the festival. An Italian film, *The Garden of the Finzi-Contini*, describing the fate of a Jewish family in Italy during World War II, was deprived of its final scene, in which a Hebrew song was sung.[33]

In general, the purpose of such censorship, whether imposed by the government or, as often in Egypt, by the journalists themselves, is to eliminate anything that portrays Jews in a favorable light, or, worse still, shows some understanding for an Israeli point of view. Reference has already been made to the subediting of the Kahan Report on the massacre at Sabra and Shatila. In the same spirit, the schoolbooks examined by the UNESCO commission "usually (but not always) explazize the religious significance of Jerusalem to Christians and Muslims, but make no mention of its symbolic importance to the Jews—a regrettable omission to say the least."

Despite the enormous interest in history in the Arab countries at the present time, and the vast output of literature devoted to the Arab and Islamic past, little attention is given to the history of the Jews, or even to the history of their own Jewish communities. As^{c}ad Razzūq's book on the Talmud, in which he makes use of the standard English translation and a wide range of scholarly literature in order to distinguish between Zionism and Talmudic Judaism, appears to be unique. On local history, one short book, a history of the Jews in Iraq, was published by a Christian Arab author in Baghdad in 1924.[34]

Apart from anti-Semitic polemic, which is plentiful, it remained an isolated effort. The history of the Jews in the Islamic lands in both medieval and modern times is almost completely neglected, and the few scholars who have attempted to look at it have for the most part not troubled to learn Hebrew or even the Hebrew script, which would have enabled them to read Judeo-Arabic, the language principally used by Jews in Arab countries in premodern times. They are thus compelled to rely on Muslim and other external sources, mainly the work of Jewish historians available in English. So far the only Muslim country in which local Jewish history has received any serious attention from Muslim historians is Egypt, where a few books and articles have dealt with the history of the Jews in that country. These, while considerably better than the usual anti-Semitic scurrilities, are still much affected by polemical purposes. It is not always clear to what extent this kind of attitude is due to genuine conviction, or to political, social and academic pressures. It may be noted that where an author is seen as being insufficiently severe in dealing with the Jewish role in Egyptian history, he or she may be subjected to harsh criticism, and even accused of being "pro-Zionist." In contrast, scholars and students in Egyptian universities now show an increasing interest in Hebrew studies, including both classical and modern Hebrew literature. These studies have developed far beyond their original concern with understanding the enemy. This new interest is apparently not shared in the PLO Research Center. Among many monographs on political, social, and economic affairs in Israel, only one, a book by the famous Palestinian author Ghassān Kanafānî, was devoted to literature. It deals, not with Israeli, but with Zionist literature, and is limited to books available in English, most of them—as for example Arthur Koestler's *Thieves in the Night* and Leon Uris's *Exodus*—not Israeli.[35]

In the early seventies, and still more after the war of 1973, there were several indications that some Egyptians were willing to think about coming to terms with Israel, some only for tactical reasons, some with a genuine desire for peace. Sadat's journey to Jerusalem in November 1977, and the peace treaty that eventually followed, seemed at the time to herald a profound change in Arab–Israeli relations, and consequently in Arab attitudes toward Jews. The response of the Egyptian public to these events made it clear there was a deep and genuine desire for peace, and a willingness to live side

by side as neighbors. The first Israeli visitors to Egypt were aston-
ished by the warmth and friendliness with which they were received
by the common people. But the new mood did not last, and before
long, the anti-Semitic themes, which had never entirely disappeared
from the Egyptian media, appeared again, if anything with greater
force.

Several factors contributed to this deterioration. One of them was
the long drawn-out and sometimes bitter negotiations, which extended from Sadat's journey until the final signature of the peace
treaty on March 26, 1979. In the perception of the Egyptians, as of
many other people, the Israeli prime minister Menahem Begin had
failed to respond in kind to the courageous and imaginative gesture
of the Egyptian president and had instead initiated a process of
protracted and legalistic wrangling which caused first disappointment and then embitterment. Naturally and justifiably, the Egyptian
media commented critically, sometimes harshly, on Begin's policies
and conduct. Unjustifiably, but equally naturally, they began more
and more to do so in what had become, in the preceding decades,
the familiar language of anti-Semitic stereotypes. And this was of
course duly reported in Israel, and contributed further to a harden-
ing of attitudes and a worsening of the atmosphere. The Israelis for
their part were already disappointed with what they saw as Egyptian
footdragging in the implementation of the Peace Treaty, and in
particular the Egyptian refusal to proceed with what had been called
"normalization," i.e., the development of normal commercial, social,
cultural, scientific, and tourist relations.

The final signature of the peace treaty was favorably received in
Egypt, but without the raptures and enthusiasm engendered by the
visit to Jerusalem. After the signature, things got worse rather than
better. A major cause of complaint against Israel was the lack of
progress on the Palestine autonomy clauses of the treaty; another the
expansion of Jewish settlements on the West Bank; another a continuing dispute between the two countries about Taba, the few hundred yards which the Israelis claimed and retained after evacuating
the Sinai Peninsula. The Israeli invasion of Lebanon in June 1982,
and the devastation that followed, brought Egyptian–Israeli relations
to their lowest point since the treaty, and to the abandonment of
virtually all restraints in the campaign not only against Israel and
Zionism but against Jews and Judaism in the Egyptian media.

From the signature of the treaty until the present day, the Egyptians have had no lack of specific political grievances against the government of Israel. In seeking to remedy these grievances however, the government of Egypt proceeded in the main within the limits of normal diplomatic and political action. They reduced commercial relations with Israel to a minimum, but did not reimpose the Arab League boycott. They discouraged Egyptians from visiting Israel, but did not bar Israeli visitors to Egypt, who continued to come in great numbers.[36] They withdrew their ambassador from Tel-Aviv, but did not close their embassy, nor expel the Israelis from Cairo. One wonders why the Egyptian government did not use its considerable influence with the media to persuade them to show the same restraint in the discussion of these issues, and limit themselves to political argument and polemic, instead of resorting, as they did, to the themes and language of both racist and religious anti-Semitism.

Part of the answer may be found in habit. Anti-Semitism may have been, in the first place, an alien import from Europe, but it had become so much a part of the accepted language of discourse that many writers seem to find it impossible to formulate their complaints against the Jewish state and its leaders without using this ready-made system of anti-Jewish abuse. This comes easily in a society where the level of violence in polemic is noticeably higher than has of late become usual in the Western world.

One of the most powerful influences in this continuance and recrudescence of anti-Semitic writing is the influence of the Arabian countries, in particular of Saudi Arabia and Kuwait. When Sadat negotiated and made peace with Israel, Egypt was expelled from the Arab League and the community of Arab nations, and was subjected to an isolation and a hostility almost as great as those directed against Israel. Since then there has been a considerable improvement in Egyptian–Arab relations, and successive Egyptian governments have been able to win some measure of acceptance.

For the Egyptian professional and intellectual communities this renewal of contact with Arabia is of particular importance. Egypt has for long been the intellectual powerhouse of the Arab world, exporting books, magazines and newspapers, teachers, writers and journalists, both to Southwest Asia and Northern Africa. But this relationship imposes certain restraints. When the Egyptian writer Najīb Maḥfūz, generally regarded as the greatest living Arabic novelist, spoke out in favor of coexistence with Israel and entered into correspondence with Israeli writers, he was denounced as a traitor, and his books placed on the boycott list by the Arab League. They are still widely distributed and read in the Arab countries, but only in pirated editions. Two other eminent Egyptian writers, the dramatist Tawfīq al-Hakīm and the scholar-humanist Husayn Fawzī, were similarly condemned and proscribed for their welcome to the peace treaty. It is natural that writers and publishers, with an eye to the richest Arabic-reading markets, should avoid anything which might provoke a ban, and perhaps give preference to themes and treatments likely to appeal to Saudi taste. The vehement anti-Semitism of many Saudi publications gives an indication of what this might be.

For these and no doubt other reasons, anti-Semitism remains a powerful influence in the Egyptian media. A few examples may suffice. Dār al-Hilāl is one of the best known Egyptian publishing houses, and the publisher of a widely circulated book of the month club. Its choice for April 1981 was a book entitled *Al-Yahūd, Ta'-rīkhan wa-ᶜaqīdatan* (The Jews, History and Faith), by Dr. Kāmil Saᶜfān. The author, described on the cover of his book as an expert on Hebrew and Judaism who will "reveal the secrets of the Jews," begins in ancient times. Pharoah had turned on the Jews because "they tried to take control of the economy of Egypt," and furthermore had "collaborated with the colonialists—the Hyksos—against the people of the country." Pharoah therefore got rid of them. Dr. Saᶜfān is eclectic in his abuse. Though addressing an overwhelming Muslim readership, he uses Christian as well as Muslim themes, including the crucifixion. He tells the story of the Damascus blood libel of 1840 as an historic fact, and claims that there were other such cases which remained unknown because of "Jewish manipulation." Similarly, in the modern period, though apparently committed to Third World and pro-Soviet positions, he does not disdain such standard Western anti-Semitic forgeries as the warning ascribed to Benjamin Franklin and, on a larger scale, the plot to rule the world. Further books of the same kind have followed, including some by Anīs Mansūr, by now one of the leading journalists in Egypt, and known to have been close to President Sadat.

The freedom of the press in Egypt, though considerable and growing, has not hitherto included the right to attack major government policies. There was therefore little or no explicit opposition to the policy of peace with Israel, and this probably lent additional force to indirect criticisms in the form of attacks on Israel and Jews. If Jews, by their very nature, are evil and treacherous—the theme of treachery is greatly stressed—can it be safe or wise to enter into agreements with them? The argument is rarely explicit, but is clear enough.

Since one of the purposes of anti-Semitic diatribe is to criticize the government, it occurs most frequently and in the most violent form in the opposition press, religious, socialist, and liberal alike. The widely read religious daily paper *al-Jumhūriyya* has been particularly active in anti-Semitic propaganda. Thus on November 20, 1983, a journalist called Muḥammad al-Ḥaywān devoted a long article to Jews, more particularly Egyptian Jews, in New York. This enabled him to combine two favorite themes—anti-Semitism and anti-Americanism. New York, he explains to his readers, is a barbarous city, merciless and heartless. It is a pitiless master which consumes its inhabitants. Among the worst things in New York are the Jews, and among the Jews, the Egyptian Jews. The article begins with a reproach which comes rather oddly from an anti-Zionist: "The Jews of Egypt did not go to Israel . . . even those who went there experimentally were not able to stay there for long . . . all of them came to America . . . and particularly to New York." The writer goes on to warn his readers: "My advice to those who go to New York is beware, beware of those who speak the Arabic language, beware of their noses, because they are Jews. They harbor feelings of hatred against the Arabs, and they want to suck them dry of all they have, both information and money." The Egyptian Jews could not live in Israel, he goes on to explain, because they had been accustomed to live by robbing and cheating the Muslims. In Israel they had to deal with other Jews, and, since thieves can not live by robbing other thieves, they had gone to New York, where they batten on Arab visitors. The article then goes on to explain how the Egyptian Jews in New York operate various illegal rackets, under the protection of the Jewish mayor.

The tone of the Socialist press is hardly better. In an article published in *al-Sha^{c}b,* the organ of the Socialist Labor Party, on June 28, 1983, Sa^{c}d al-Faṭāṭirī, a retired ambassador, lists "twenty-three cultural devices for the destruction of Islamic civilization." The starting point for this argument is a characteristic fictional quotation ascribed to Begin: "There must be no compassion for the Arabs until we destroy the so-called Arab civilization and build our own civilization on its ruins." In addition to obvious political and military methods, the ambassador explains, Israel also seeks to encircle the Arabs by encouraging disunity among them, fomenting rebellions and civil wars between them, and inducing economic and social crises inside or between the Arab states. For these purposes Israel has perfected a series of devices for the cultural infiltration of the Arab world, which Dr. Faṭāṭirī then sets forth in detail. They include such things as penetration through official and unofficial institutions (embassies, scientific centers, history societies, friendship societies, and other devices disguised as scholarly research); technical aid to developing countries; scientific and cultural exchanges; the publication of a Jewish encyclopedia in all languages, presenting Israel to the world as it wishes to be seen; trying to win over the Christians, beginning with the [Vatican] document exculpating the Jews of the blood of Jesus; disinformation and exaggeration in discussing the death and destruction in Germany under the Nazi regime; stressing the democratic order in Israel and "causing it to appear in the world as a democratic citadel in the Middle East and as the only modern state in the region." The final paragraph, though somewhat cryptic, deserves quotation: "This continuing danger, great though it is, is not more deadly than the Tyrant whom the Arabs, by putting their trust in God and seeking His help, were able to crush and destroy."

The most viciously anti-Semitic articles appear, not in the Socialist or fundamentalist press, but in *al-Aḥrār*, the organ of the Liberal Party which emerged in the democratization of recent years. In the issue of July 19, 1982, an article by Dr. Yaḥyā al-Rakhāwī, propounds some new theories on Jewish and Israeli history:

When the State of Israel was established and won the good-will of the world and was recognized by many in both East and West, one of the reasons for this recognition was the desire of the people in the East and West to get rid of as many as possible of the representatives of that human error known as "the Jews." Behind this motive there was an additional, secret purpose; to concentrate them in one place, so that it would be easier to strike them at the right moment. There can be no doubt that such hopes occupy the thoughts of politicians more intelligent than Hitler but at the same time more cowardly than he was.

And for us, we must remember, among both bombardments and negotiations, both speeches and landmines, that we are all—once again—face to face with the Jewish problem, not just the Zionist problem; and we must reassess all those studies which made a distinction between "the Jew" and "the Israeli" . . . and we must redefine the meaning of the word "Jew" so that we do not imagine that we are speaking of a divinely revealed religion, or a minority persecuted by mankind. Every word has an origin, a development and a history, and it seems that the word "Jew" today has changed its content and meaning.

We thus find ourselves face to face with the essence of a problem which has recently donned the gown of religion and concentrated itself on a piece of land. In this confrontation we cannot help but see before us the figure of that great man Hitler, may God have mercy on him, who was the wisest of those who confronted this problem . . . and who, out of compassion for humanity, tried to exterminate every Jew, but despaired of curing this cancerous growth on the body of mankind. And now they virtually confirm the accuracy of his intuition.

In the remainder of the article, the writer depicts the cosmic struggle which must now ensue between the forces of good and the forces of evil, the latter personified in the Jews. He stresses that he is speaking not just of Zionists but of Jews, and sees the enemy both in "the Jews as individuals" and "the Jews as a State." He sees the struggle as taking place on two levels. On one the forces of good, i.e., the Egyptians, Palestinians, and other Muslims, will have to Judaize themselves in order to prevail against the Jews—that is to say, they will have to become cruel, ruthless, deceitful, and unscrupulous and thus to some extent endanger their own moral well-being. On this level, he notes that "our teacher Khomeini, may God prolong his life," is probably the most suitable to play this role in the struggle, with the Pope and Father Capucci in reserve. This gives added importance to the struggle at the second and higher level—between humanity and Judaism. In describing the struggle between humanity and the Jews, the writer urges his side, that of "humanity," not to worry about "stupid accusations of anti-Semitism." Defeat in this battle, failure to "excise the Jewish cancer on the body of humanity," could lead to the destruction of humanity itself.

The progovernment press in Egypt, though by no means free from a kind of endemic, low-key anti-Semitism, does not normally publish material of this level of virulence. Since the signing of the peace treaty, and despite the ups and downs in the Israeli–Egyptian relationship, there has been some overall improvement in the tone of discourse, especially after the accession to power in 1984 of a coalition government in Israel and such events as the visit to Cairo of the Israeli minister Ezer Weizman in the spring of 1985. But the antigovernment press has increased the violence and frequency of its anti-Semitic campaigns since the peace treaty, and the progovernment media, with few exceptions, do remarkably little to counteract it.

The cumulative effect of this steady torrent of anti-Semitic propaganda was dramatically revealed in the Ras Burqa affair. On October 5, 1985, at a place called Ras Burqa, in the district of Nuwaiba in Sinai, a mentally disturbed Egyptian gendarme called Sulaymān Khāṭir machine-gunned a group of Israeli campers, three adults and nine young children who were sliding down a sand dune. Five children managed to escape, though two were wounded. The remaining seven—four children (three girls and a boy), two women, and one man, a retired judge, were killed or disabled. According to Israeli eyewitnesses, Egyptian gendarmes who were nearby gave no help to the wounded, and stopped an Israeli doctor and other holidaymakers, at gunpoint, from going to their aid. Those who were not already dead were left to bleed to death.

Demented gunmen may run amok in any part of the world, and the gendarme later stated in the course of his initial interrogation that he had no knowledge at the time of the identity and nationality of the people he had shot, and that they had offered him no offense or provocation. His only reason was that they had, he said, trespassed on a prohibited area. Even the failure to succor the wounded may perhaps be attributed to uncertainty and disarray. Far more ominous was the response of the Egyptian opposition press, echoed in other Arab countries. In no time at all Sulaymān Khāṭir was being celebrated as a national hero, and mass demonstrations were held in his support. To justify this portrayal of his action, the age and the sex of the dead Israelis were suppressed, and all kinds of mutually contradictory fantasies were developed—that they were spies caught photographing secret installations (in a demilitarized zone), they had spat upon and torn up an Egyptian flag, that half-naked Israeli women had offended Sulaymān Khāṭir's Muslim conscience, and even that they had attacked him, forcing him to fire in self-defense. These stories remained uncontradicted in the progovernment media, which for many weeks withheld the facts from readers and viewers. As the celebration of Sulaymān Khāṭir built up, many leading Egyptian intellectuals, of both the leftist and religious opposi-

tions, joined in acclaiming him and his deed. Eventually, he himself
came to accept the role that had been thrust upon him. According
to the well-known Marxist politician and writer Khālid Muḥyi 'l-Dīn,
the trial of Sulaymān was a trial of Egyptian and Arab opinion. For
Nabīl al-Hilālī, the real charge of the regime against Sulaymān was
that he had fired against the Zionists instead of against the workers
and students. The leader of the Muslim Brethren ᶜUmar al-Tilimsānī
observed that, "if every Muslim would do what Sulaymān did, Israel
would no longer exist"—apparently a call to solve the Middle East
problem by genocide. Most indignantly rejected the official statement
that Sulaymān Khāṭir was mad. Luṭfī al-Khawlī, the Marxist writer
and editor, regarded it as an insult to the Egyptian nation to call him
mad, since he alone had stood firm while others had held back. Far
īd ᶜAbd al-Karīm, one of the leaders of the Nasserist Arab Socialist
Party, acclaimed him as "the conscience of this nation," who with his
bullets had "washed away the shame of silence" of Camp David; he
went on to express the hope that "the whole of this nation would
be struck with this same mighty madness." Muḥammad Ibrāhīm Kāmil, a former minister of foreign affairs, said that his action
expressed the anger of every Egyptian and every Arab after the
Israeli aggression in Tunīs. Ali Hillal Dessouki, a professor at the
University of Cairo, addressing the soldier as "my brother Sulaymān,"
expressed his astonishment at an age when such men as Sulaymān
are accused of madness, and his sadness at the so-called sane of this
time. Nūr al-Sharīf, an actor, told Khāṭir that "you are the sanest
among us, for you did what we all want." Aḥmad Nāṣir, of the Egyptian Bar Council, believed that history would always honor Sulaymān
Khāṭir as "a living model of a noble Egyptian who refused to be lead
astray by the treaties of betrayal and surrender." This extraordinary
cult of Sulaymān Khāṭir reached its peak by the end of the year,
when he was brought for trial before a military court. The resulting
demonstrations were seen by the government, with some reason, as
a threat to itself, and for the first time the progovernment press
published the real story of what had actually happened at Ras Burqa,
and who the victims were. Some writers in the Egyptian press even
went so far as to concede that the progovernment media had been
at fault in not publishing the truth and thus giving free scope to the
purveyors of lies, and expressed their horror at a state of mind which
made a national hero of a killer of women and children and called

on others to follow his example. In a particularly striking article published in *Al-Muṣawwar* on December 28,1985, Makram Muhammad Aḥmad, the editor of that journal, examined the whole story at length. Citing the official transcript of the accused man's interrogation, he castigated the opposition press for their dishonest and irresponsible handling of the story, and expressed his belief that if the boot had been on the other foot and an Israeli soldier had killed Egyptian women and children, no one in Israel, not even the most fanatical extremists, would have attributed his action to a patriotic hatred of Israel's enemies, and commended him for it.

The sentencing of Sulaymān Khāṭir and his subsequent reported suicide in prison, in January 1986, seemed for the moment to end this chapter, and it may be that the dawning awareness of the damage that such episodes inflict on the honor and dignity of Egypt will have some effect.

It is no doubt too early to ask Arab writers to give their readers a dispassionate discussion of Israel or of Zionism. But it is not unreasonable to ask them to provide, for the reading public and above all for impressionable and vulnerable children in schools, some account of the history, religion, and culture of their new neighbors, cooler and more accurate than the absurd and evil fantasies of European anti-Semitism. Unfortunately, there is not likely to be any major change in the media while significant numbers of Egyptian scholars and writers, editors and publishers, feel it necessary to conform to the climate of opinion in Saudi Arabia and its cultural dependencies.

And in these and other Arab countries, the atmosphere will not improve, as long as there are few or no Jewish residents and only rare, mostly disguised, Jewish visitors, and as long as the Arabic reader desirous of learning something about Jews will find only a literature dominated by the ignorant bigotry of Canon Rohling and that masterpiece of anti-Semitic fabrication, the *Protocols of the Elders of Zion.*

CHAPTER NINE

The New Anti-Semitism

WITH A BETTER, or at least a fuller understanding of the meaning and connotations of such terms as Jews and Semites, Judaism and Islam, Zionism and anti-Semitism, it should be possible to make a more reasoned and more informed approach to the question with which we began—what importance must we assign, in the Arab–Israeli struggle, to anti-Semitism—more specifically, to the profound and special hatred of Jews that goes beyond normal political conflict, beyond even the normal hostilities and prejudices that arise between different peoples, and attributes to them a quality of cosmic and diabolic evil?

In approaching this question, it is necessary, first, to define precisely with what aspects of the Arab–Israeli conflict we are concerned; second, to dismiss certain very persistent myths which have for long bedeviled all discussion of these matters.

On the first point: this inquiry is concerned only with the incidence, if any, of this kind of hatred in the participants in this conflict, whether directly or indirectly involved—the Israelis and the Palestinians, the Jews and the Arabs, the superpowers and lesser powers pursuing their own various interests in the region; and in particular, with the influence or effect of anti-Semitism in the formation of policy, in the choice of tactics by the participants, and in the public discussion of these matters by the media. Our inquiry has not been directly concerned with the rights and wrongs of the Arab–Israeli conflict, nor with the merits and demerits of the various cases that are put forward. More generally, it is not concerned with any of those aspects—and they are by far the most important—that have nothing to do with race, hate, or prejudice.

Among Israelis, and much more among other Jews and pro-Jews, there is a tendency to equate enmity to Israel or to Zionism with anti-Semitism and to see Arafat as a new and unsuccessful Hitler and the PLO as the present-day equivalent of the Nazi SS. By now it should be clear that this is a false equation. The Arab–Israeli conflict is in its origins and its essence a political one—a clash between peoples and states over real issues, not a matter of prejudice and persecution.

But while the Arab–Israeli conflict is an example of normal conflict, it has certain abnormalities which make it unique. These arise from the continued refusal of all but one of the Arab states to recognize Israel or to meet face to face in negotiation with its official representatives. This refusal is still maintained after nearly forty years of Israeli existence, and after a succession of Arab political and military defeats. Lebanon, which negotiated and signed a direct agreement with Israel in 1984, was compelled to abandon it, and the Lebanese government was not permitted to enter into political contact with Israel even to arrange the orderly liberation of its own territory. Egypt, which unlike Lebanon possessed sufficient strength to take an independent line and enter into such a relationship with Israel, was execrated by almost all the Arab states; most of them broke off diplomatic relations with Cairo and placed Egypt in almost the same kind of isolation as Israel herself. Perhaps most striking is the symbolic, one might almost say the magical, destruction which is constantly repeated and reenacted at the United Nations and its various agencies—a kind of prefiguration of what the Arab States hope ultimately to inflict on Israel. Even the bitterest of conflicts— between France and Germany over Alsace and Lorraine, between Greece and Turkey over Cyprus and the Aegean, between China and Japan, India and Pakistan, or Iraq and Iran have never involved total nonrecognition of one side by the other, the total refusal of dialogue, the declared intention not merely to defeat but utterly to destroy the adversary state and wipe it off the map. And even though statesmen in some Arab countries now speak in private or abroad of coexistence and peace with Israel, few, outside Egypt, have yet been willing to do so in public and at home, and in terms that go beyond the customary careful ambiguities.

In what then does this uniqueness lie—this special sense of outrage which after almost forty years is still unappeased? Some see its cause in the displacement of the Palestinians from their homes to the neighboring Arab countries, where great numbers of them still live in refugee camps. Whatever the causes—whether they were expelled by the Israelis, urged to go by their own leaders, or simply fled in panic as the war exploded around their homes—there can be no doubt about the immensity of the human tragedy which befell them, and about the suffering which they have endured from then till now.

But the intractability of the Palestinian refugee problem is a consequence, not a cause, of the political problem. That the problem was not solved, like others elsewhere in our brutal century, by a combination of resettlement and some repatriation, was due to an act of will on the part of the Palestinian leadership and of the Arab states. It was indeed a considerable feat to have preserved the refugee camps and their unhappy inhabitants for so long, and prevented their absorption into the expanding economies of the oil-rich Arab states, at a time when these were attracting and employing millions of guest workers from Egypt and Yemen, from Africa, from India and Pakistan and Sri Lanka, and even from as far away as Korea and the Philippines.

Does the special sense of outrage then derive—as many have argued—from the fact that the state of Israel was created by intruders who came from across the sea and imposed themselves on a country where they had not previously lived, displacing many of the inhabitants and reducing the remainder to the status of a conquered people? Certainly such events give rise to deep feelings of anger. This perception of the Israelis as outsiders remains even though by now a majority of Israeli Jews originated in neighboring Arab and other Muslim countries. But even these events are very far from unique, and virtually all the sovereign states in the Western Hemisphere, as well as several elsewhere, were created in this way.

For Muslims, in particular, the loss of old Muslim land to non-Muslim invaders is a heavy blow, causing anguish and outrage. But this too is not unprecedented, and has indeed happened many times before. From the loss of Portugal and Spain, at the end of the Middle Ages, to the abandonment of province after province and Muslim community after Muslim community in southeastern Europe during the long-drawn-out retreat of the Ottoman Empire, Muslims have lost many countries to Christendom. Old Muslim lands on the northern and eastern shores of the Black Sea, around the Caspian, and in Central Asia were added to the Russian Empire. They remain part of the Soviet Union and their fate is decided in Moscow. More recently, the invasion and occupation of the sovereign Muslim state of Afghanistan, and its incorporation in the Soviet imperial system, with the exile of millions of its people, has passed with remarkably little protest or concern by Muslim governments or Muslim peoples.

Why then this special anger in the Muslim response to the end of Palestine and the birth of Israel? Part of this is certainly due to its position, in the very center of the Arab core of the Islamic world, and to its inclusion of the city of Jerusalem which—after long and sometimes bitter disputes—was finally recognized as the third Holy City of Islam after Mecca and Medina. But most of all, the sense of outrage, as is clearly shown in countless speeches and writings, was due to the identity of those who inflicted these dramatic defeats on Muslim Arab armies and imposed their rule on Muslim Arab populations. The victors were not the followers of a world religion nor the armies of a mighty imperial power, by which one could be conquered without undue shame—not the Catholic kings of Spain, not the far-flung British Empire, not the immense and ruthless might of Russia—but the Jews, few, scattered and powerless, whose previous humility made their triumphs especially humiliating.[1]

This perception is still not in itself anti-Semitic. It does not deny that Jews have a place in the scheme of things; it insists rather that their place is a modest one, as a tolerated subject minority, and that by appearing as conquerors and rulers the Jews have subverted God's order for the universe. The same sense kind of outrage colored the contemporary Turkish response to the Greek landings in western Anatolia in 1919. The Turks were able to ease their rage by defeating the Greek invaders and hurling them back to Greece. The Arabs have not been able to defeat the Israelis, of whom, in any case, the vast majority have no other place to which to return.

There were occasional unsuccessful attempts at dialogue after the first Arab–Israeli war, but they ceased after the wars of 1956 and 1967. The Israeli victories in 1948 and 1949 had been comparatively small, and had been won after hard fighting and heavy losses. They had left a relatively small and silent Arab population as citizens of Israel. Even these events had left a sense of shock. The swift, vast and apparently effortless victories of the despised "Zionist gangs" over several Arab armies added an unendurable feeling of humiliation, compounded by the continuing affront of Israeli military rule—now reinforced by settlements—over a sizable and vocal Arab population. It was difficult enough for Arabs to recognize Jewish sovereignty. It was much harder to live under or even at the side of Jewish domination. It was in the wake of these defeats, and because of the need to explain them, that Nazi-type anti-Semitism came to dominate Arab discussions of Zionism and Judaism as well as of the state of Israel. The Egyptian successes in crossing the Suez Canal in 1973 and recovering part of Sinai provided only a partial easing of this anguish, but they were an essential prerequisite of Anwar Sadat's journey to Jerusalem. And in this there may perhaps be some hope for the future.

There is another dimension to the question, little if at all related to the politics of the Middle East. Since Israel happens to be a Jewish state inhabited largely by Jews, and since there are people who hate Jews independently of the Palestine conflict, anti-Semitism may sometimes be a factor in determining attitudes, on occasion even in determining policy and action. How far and in what circumstances is this so? This question may be examined in relation to some of the different groups involved. While anti-Zionism or anti-Israelism is not necessarily inspired by anti-Semitism, the possibility cannot be excluded that in some cases it may indeed be so. To determine whether opponents of Zionism or critics of Israel are inspired by honest or by dishonest (clandestine anti-Semitic) motives, one must examine each case—government, party, group, or individual—separately, and in doing so look for specific ascertainable criteria.

The distinction is often difficult to discern. The sometimes rather savage oratory and journalism of a society accustomed to violent invective and involved in a long and bitter war may easily be taken —not necessarily correctly—as an expression of anti-Semitism. In contrast, the carefully modulated reproof of a more sophisticated culture may also lead those who do not know the coded language to accept it, with an equal possibility of error, as the expression of an honest conviction. In the Arab world, where tempers run high and language is strong, fair comment may sometimes look like bigotry. In the West, where restraint is prized and different social norms prevail, the opposite can happen.

The distinction is easier to recognize in the Arab world than in the West, since the Arabs after all are directly involved, with vital interests at stake. When the Arabs accuse the Israelis, their leaders, and their supporters of all kinds of fiendish misdeeds, they may be doing no more than engaging in normal wartime propaganda against the enemy. The content and language of this propaganda may seem intemperate, especially when contrasted with the tone of the vast majority of Israeli politicians, scholars, and journalists in discussing the Arabs, but ample parallels could be found for it in the conduct of both sides during the two world wars. When Arab spokesmen liken Begin to Adolf Hitler and Jengiz Khan, these accusations may shock the West and infuriate the Jews; but we may better evaluate their impact within the Arab circle if we recall that Adolf Hitler was until not so long ago a much admired hero, and that the secretary general of the Arab League, announcing the Arab invasion of Mandatory Palestine in 1948, stated—mistakenly as it turned out—that the destruction which the Arab armies would bring to Israel would rank with the deeds of the Mongol invaders, i.e., the followers of Jengiz Khan. In this context, we may recall that not so many years ago young Americans with a sufficient level of education to be admitted to major universities were likening the campus police to the Nazi Gestapo and comparing American politicians and academicians to the obscene tyrannies that devastated Europe, inflamed the world, and brought death to countless millions. If American students could not see the difference between the flaws of democracy and the essential evil of fascism, young Arabs, having no direct acquaintance with either form of government, could hardly be expected to do any better.

The use of the term Nazi to describe Israel, in Western and more especially in Eastern Europe, from which the Arabs first learned the practice, is a very different matter. The Europeans, unlike most Arabs or Americans, know at first hand what Nazism was, and what Nazis did to Jews. Knowing this, they must also be aware of the absurdity of such comparisons. In making them, they raise profound and disquieting questions concerning their own attitudes and motives.

Even the frequently reiterated Arab intention of dismantling the state of Israel and "liquidating the Zionist society" is not, in itself, necessarily an expression of anti-Semitism. In the view of most Arabs, the creation of the state of Israel was an act of injustice, and its continued existence a standing aggression. To those who hold this view, the correction of that injustice and the removal of that aggression are legitimate political objectives.

The same cannot be said of the great and increasing body of Arab writing about Israel and the Jews. When Arab spokesmen, not content with denouncing the misdeeds of the Israelis, attribute these misdeeds to innate Jewish racial characteristics discernible throughout history; when furthermore, they accuse the Jewish people as a whole of practicing such monstrous crimes as ritual murder and of seeking through secret conspiracies to attain world domination; when they document these accusations with the standard fabrications of European anti-Semitic literature; when finally they devote great efforts and resources to disseminating these same fabrications all over the world—then no doubt remains that those Arabs who write and distribute these things are engaged in anti-Semitic activities, not different from those which disfigured the history of Christian Europe for many centuries. Given the scale on which all these activities are taking place, the question is no longer whether some Arab governments are pursuing anti-Semitic policies; the question is why were these policies adopted, how far have they gone, and how deep is their impact.

The Arabs are not the only group for whom opposition to Israel arises from a clash of interests. Arab hostility to Israel rests on a genuine grievance, a real conflict over mutually exclusive interests and claims. This conflict may be clouded by prejudice; it may be influenced in its expression by prejudice. It is not caused by prejudice. Much the same may be said—in varying degrees—of some other opponents of Israel. The Soviet Union, for example, has clear political reasons, both domestic and international, for its hostility toward Israel. Obviously, Soviet interests are not served by the presence in the Middle East of a powerful state which is not merely politically aligned with the United States, but is linked to the West by institutions and way of life. The Soviets know very well that strategic alliances are more effective and more secure when they are underpinned by real affinities, and not merely political choices of current leaders. It is for that reason that the Soviets are rarely content with political and strategic alliances, but rather seek to refashion societies and regimes, in the countries where they have sufficient influence, in their own image. Functioning Western-style democracies are more difficult to create, and in this respect America is at a disadvantage. They are also, however, more difficult to destroy, and their presence is a corresponding Soviet disadvantage. While the Soviets have often made some political gains by playing on Arab hostility to Israel, these have usually proved transitory.

But Soviet hostility to Israel and to Zionism may at times have other causes, unrelated to the struggle in the Middle East. Unlike the Nazis, the Russians are not committed, publicly and ideologically, to an anti-Jewish policy, and their official attitude to anti-Semitism is to denounce it. They would be perfectly capable of changing sides if they thought it desirable, and indeed, for a brief period in the late 1940s they did so. Soviet diplomacy supported Israel against Britain, and it was arms from the Eastern Bloc which enabled the infant Jewish state to withstand the onslaught of the Arab armies in 1948. Since then, however, the Soviet Union has turned the other way, and has, with its satellites and followers, pursued a policy of unrelenting hostility to both Israel and Zionism.

While this policy can be explained and, in the Soviet context, justified on political grounds, certain features are noteworthy. One of these is the violence of language used both in addressing Israel and in discussing Israel, in diplomatic and scholarly utterances as well as in overt propaganda. Even by the standards of communist political vituperation, the invective used in condemning Israel and Israeli actions is remarkably strong. It has remained consistently strong over the years—far more so than the language employed against any of the other governments, regimes, movements, peoples or ideologies that have at one time or another incurred Soviet displeasure.

Perhaps even more remarkable is the fact that the Soviet Union has on two different occasions broken off diplomatic relations with Israel. This is a step which the Soviets have never taken since early times, even with their most dangerous and avowed enemies. The Soviets, for good reason, have always attached the greatest importance to the maintenance of their diplomatic and consular missions even in politically hostile territory. They were careful to maintain diplomatic relations for as long as possible with Pilsudski's Poland, even after the murder of a Soviet ambassador in Warsaw; with fascist Italy, and with Nazi Germany, even after the Anschluss with Austria and the German occupation of Czechoslovakia. Nor have they found it necessary in more recent times to break off diplomatic relations with states opposed to them or which they regard as puppets of hostile powers, in Europe, Asia, Africa, or the Americas. They were always careful to maintain relations with regimes which they denounced as imperialist or fascist, and even with fiercely anticommunist regimes, such as that of Indonesia, which suppressed communism and executed communists in great numbers. They did not break off relations with dissident communist regimes, such as those of Yugoslavia and China, despite fierce ideological and political battles. The only rupture of relations with such a regime, with Albania in 1961, came on an Albanian, not a Soviet initiative. Most of the Soviet satellites retained their diplomatic relations with Albania, and the Soviets tried unsuccessfully to restore them.

In contrast, they have twice broken off diplomatic relations with Israel. The first occasion was in 1953, at the time of the so-called Doctors' Plot in Moscow, when a small bomb was exploded in the courtyard of the Soviet embassy in Tel Aviv. There was never the slightest suspicion that this was anything but an irresponsible private operation. Diplomatic relations were restored after a while, but were broken off again in 1967, this time by the whole Soviet bloc except Rumania.

Even the manner of breaking off diplomatic relations was distinctive. When countries break off diplomatic relations, their interests are normally entrusted to the care of another, friendly country. At the present time, this usually means in practice that each country sends some of its own diplomats, who instead of functioning in their own name act as the interests section of the embassy of the protecting power. Thus, when a number of Arab states broke off diplomatic relations with the United States after the 1967 war, most of them still had diplomatic representatives in Washington, while Washington had representatives in their various capitals, on both sides under the aegis of the protecting powers. The Soviets allowed no Israeli diplomats on Soviet soil, and to achieve this end were willing to pay the price of having none of their own people overtly present in Israel, and no formal line of communication to the Israeli government. This disparity is very striking, and leaves one wondering what peculiar characteristic of Israel, lacking in other countries, has twice required a total rupture of diplomatic relations, and the many inconveniences, practical and of late also political, which this caused to the Soviets. The vocabulary and iconography of Soviet anti-Zionism, with their covert and sometimes overt appeals to old-fashioned racial and even religious prejudice, may indicate an answer.

Besides the Arab and Soviet blocs, there are other governments that have decided, on the basis of a calculation of advantage, to support the Arabs and oppose Israel, for good practical reasons. The Soviet Union possesses immense power, and has shown willingness to use it. Some of the Arab states dispose of immense wealth, and have shown increasing skill in deploying it. Both groups own large and reliable blocs of votes, and have been able to attain a measure of control over the fora of the United Nations and its various agencies. These assets have been used at various times to persuade governments of countries with no strong interests or commitments of their own in the area to adopt anti-Israel and at times even anti-Jewish positions.

The adversary is no longer defined principally as Israel. Increasingly, it is defined as Zionism. As well as adverse interests, adverse ideologies may be involved, and may inspire a principled opposition to the Zionist movement and the Zionist state, without necessarily raising the question of anti-Semitism. For the communist, it is natural and indeed inevitable to oppose Zionism, since there is a fundamental ideological incompatibility between the two. Moscow has its own special reasons, of domestic and imperial policy, to oppose any movement which could affect significant numbers of Soviet citizens and which has its main focus beyond the Soviet frontiers. The Soviets have denounced, condemned, and repressed pan-Islamism, pan-Turkism, and pan-Iranism, because the Muslim, Turkish-speaking, and Iranian-speaking peoples of the Soviet Union could be affected by these movements and have their loyalties turned away from Moscow toward centers in Turkey, Iran, or the Islamic world. Zionism is, so to speak, a form of pan-Judaism, and for that reason alone would be condemned. But again, in dealing with internal opposition movements as in dealing with foreign states, there are significant differences in the degree of hostility and the manner in which it is expressed.

Communism is not the only creed which is ideologically opposed to Zionism. There are some religious believers—Christian and even Jewish as well as Muslim—who oppose Zionism on religious grounds, seeing the establishment of a Jewish state by human agency as something contrary to God's will. This is not at the present time a majority view among either Christians or Jews, but it commands significant support.

The most vocal ideological opposition to Zionism at the present time, however, is concerned not with what Zionism believes and declares itself to be, but rather with what it is accused by others of being. This began with accusations made by propagandists for reasons of expediency, but rapidly acquired a wider significance. The Arab opponents of Zionism and of Israel have usually tried to win support in the Western world by identifying Zionism with the fashionable enemy, at one time defined as bolshevism or communism. When—with growing American influence in the world—the racist became the fashionable enemy, Zionism was reclassified as racist, and a resolution at the United Nations adopted to that effect.[2] The resolution, which was voted on November 10, 1975, was carried by 72 in favor, 35 against, and 32 abstentions. An ideological analysis of the votes for and against and the abstentions gives interesting results. As one might expect, all the communist and Islamic states voted in favor of the resolution. Almost all the surviving liberal democracies in the world voted against the resolution. The countries of the Third World were scattered through all three categories.

In the Soviet bloc, no political opinions may be publicly expressed other than those prescribed by the authorities. In the Arab world, or at least in parts of it, some public debate is possible, but on the question of Israel, even of Jews, it is subject to severe constraints, and it is therefore difficult to judge real attitudes. In the Western world, however, and in some Third World countries, individuals and groups are free to adopt, promote, and argue their different points of view on this as on most other matters. In most Western countries the affairs of Israel and her neighbors receive enormous—indeed, by any reasonable measure, disproportionate—attention. The very magnitude of the debate, as well as the terms in which it is conducted, have led some observers, not all of them Jewish, to suspect that this preoccupation with Israel and Zionism has unwholesome origins, and that criticism may be an expression of hidden anti-Semitism. Clearly, there are many for whom such accusations are false and unjust. The fact must however be faced that there are others—in what proportion it would be difficult to say—for whom the Arabs are in truth nothing but a stick with which to beat the Jews.

There are various reasons, both intellectual and practical, by which the adoption of an anti-Israel position may be explained, without any imputation of prejudice. An obvious example is the honest conviction that the Arabs are right and the Israelis wrong, whether in any particular situation or in the problem as a whole. One may agree or disagree with those who hold this conviction; one cannot simply dismiss their views as prejudiced. One may equally not dismiss the possibility that the formation and expression of such a conviction may be affected by considerations other than the merits of the case.

An easily recognizable group are those who follow the fashionable leftist or progressive line. At one time, this was in general favorable to Israel, and non-Arab leftists usually adopted a pro-Israel position. Since then, the line has turned against Israel, and those who carefully conform to the length of the ideological hemline as decreed by the current arbiters of intellectual fashion have restyled their opinions accordingly. Among some who formulate and express their views in this way, there may perhaps be an element of prejudice, but it can hardly be designated as anti-Semitism, particularly in view of the very large proportion of Jews in this group.

The radical and terrorist left, like the radical and terrorist right, is unanimously and vehemently anti-Israel, in such terms that its statements are sometimes rather difficult to distinguish from old-fashioned anti-Semitism. Thus the celebrated Ulrike Meinhof, as reported in the *Frankfurter Allgemeine Zeitung* of December 15, 1972, observed, speaking of Auschwitz, "The worst thing is that all of us, Communists and others, were agreed on it." She had since recognized that "anti-Semitism in its essence is anti-capitalist. It takes over as its own the hatred of people for their dependence on money as a medium of exchange, and their yearning for Communism. Auschwitz means that six million Jews were murdered and trundled onto the garbage heaps of Europe as that which they appeared to be—as money Jews."

Powerful ideological elements may be involved in the choice of sides. For many outsiders, the decisive factor in determining their choice is the type of regime existing on the two sides. Israel within its 1949 borders is a liberal democracy, with an open press and parliament, an elected government which for long was of social democratic complexion, and a vigorous opposition. Most of the Arab states are authoritarian, with a controlled press, no legal opposition,

and an official program of radical nationalism and revolutionary socialism, blended in varying proportions. Both types of regimes evoke
automatic loyalties and antagonisms, in which political and economic
considerations do not always coincide. Socialists, for example, have
been sharply divided. For some, Gamal Abdel Nasser's nationaliza-
tions atoned for his repressions; for others, Israel's freedoms atone for
its partial capitalism. Support and hostility among the ideologues
seems to be determined very largely by the choice of formulae, the
outward aspect and external alignment of the regimes in question;
they appear to be very little concerned with the real position and
well-being of the people who live under their rule.

Yet another group consists of those who make their choice between the Arabs and Israel for professional or commercial reasons—
a calculation of career needs by individuals in business, in the universities, in the media, and in politics. Many, for good professional,
commercial, or political reasons, decide to support one side or the
other, according to circumstances. One may perhaps question the
good faith of those who make their choice in this way, but prejudice,
though of course always a possibility, is not a necessary component
of their attitude. A public relations consultant improving his client's
image and knocking the competition is not primarily moved by prejudice; he is motivated by the desire to get on in his business and to
make money. Mutatis mutandis, the same may be said of the corpora-
tion executive safeguarding the interests of his stockholders, the
politician responding to the wishes of his electors or contributors, the
newspaperman obeying the directives of his editor or of his hosts,
and the Middle East specialist in the universities, keenly aware of
who controls access and who disposes of funds.

University departments and programs of Middle Eastern studies
may be affected in more than one way. Jews, for sentimental or
religious reasons, because of a knowledge of Hebrew or a concern for
Israel, are often attracted to these studies. They are not the only ones,
and they have long since lost their earlier dominance to others. In
the days when Mao and Maoism reigned supreme in China, Maoist-
minded students were sometimes drawn to Chinese studies, and
some university departments of Chinese or Far Eastern languages
acquired a strong and often intolerant Maoist character. In the same
way, during the vogue of the PLO as the heroes of the radical left,
many students and eventually young teachers of Middle Eastern

studies came to their subject with a strong prior commitment for the Arab cause and against Israel and Zionism.[3] This is not in itself anti-Semitic, but there were some also with avowed or unavowed anti-Jewish feelings who for that reason gravitated toward departments of Arabic studies, in which they hoped to find like-minded company and a congenial atmosphere. They are not always disappointed. Examples of this have been quoted both by Jews and by Arabs, the former often with alarm, the latter sometimes with distaste.

For all these groups, an anti-Israel or anti-Zionist position can be explained without reference to anti-Semitism. But the possibility is of course always there, and even if prejudice does not determine the nature of their opinions, it may well affect the manner in which they express them. Particularly at a time and place where anti-Semitism is considered beyond the pale of decent society, the Palestine problem and the sufferings of the Arabs may provide perfect cover for prejudices which the holders would otherwise be ashamed to reveal.

Some are easy to detect. With a few exceptions who hate Arabs and Jews even-handedly, the openly and avowedly fascist groups still active in various parts of the world are pro-Arab, and their literature makes their real sentiments and purposes abundantly clear. Such are the surviving neofascist and neo-Nazi groups in Europe, and their imitators in North and South America. Some Arabs have disdained the support of such tainted allies; others, including both governments and revolutionaries, have made good use of it; others again have done both at the same time.

In more respectable circles, it is by no means easy to distinguish between those who are pro-Arab and those who are primarily anti-Jewish. There are, however, some symptoms which, though not infallible, are a fairly good indication. One of the characteristics of the anti-Jew as distinct from the pro-Arab is that he shows no other sign of interest in the Arabs or sympathy for them, apart from their conflict with the Jews. He is completely unmoved by wrongs suffered by the Arabs, even Palestinians, under any but Jewish auspices, whether their own rulers or third parties. For him, the hundreds killed at Sabra and Shatila are of far greater concern than the thousands of Arabs slaughtered in Amman, at Tell Za^{c}ātir, in Hama, and in the many wars, in Yemen, Lebanon, the Gulf and elsewhere, that have tormented the long-suffering Arab people. Often, he shows no interest in the history or achievements of the Arabs, no knowledge of their language or culture. On the contrary, he may speak of them in a way which is in reality profoundly disparaging. No one in his right mind would claim to be an expert on, say, France or Germany without knowing a word of French or German. The claims to expertise of many self-styled Arabists without Arabic rests on the assumption that Arabs are somehow different from—and inferior to—Frenchmen and Germans, in that what they say or write in their own language can be safely disregarded. The common attempt to explain away Arab statements and actions by saying, in effect, that the Arabs are not serious, not adult, not responsible, can hardly be taken as an expression of respect or esteem.

To be deeply concerned about the fate of the Arab refugees from Palestine is a natural and humane response. If it is accompanied by total indifference to other refugees in Europe, Asia, Africa and elsewhere, of whom there are countless millions, most of them far worse situated than the Palestinians, this may raise reasonable doubts. In the same way, to support the political cause of the Palestinian Arabs is a legitimate and justifiable political choice. But if it is accompanied by a lack of interest in other causes in the region and elsewhere, questions may arise. The world is full of causes that attract foreign well-wishers and supporters, and many factors may determine an outsider's choice. One of them may be a shared hatred of the adversary.

This raises the general issue of the double standard which, Israelis claim, is applied in judging the actions and more particularly the misdeeds of Israel and of her Arab foes. In part this arises from circumstances unrelated to prejudice or even to taking sides. Israel is an open society, and by the very logic of its own institutions is compelled to allow to reporters and therefore to critics a degree of freedom without parallel anywhere else in the region. This inevitably means that the media have greater detail about Israeli misdeeds and greater opportunity to explore, discuss, and criticize them. The United States suffers from the same fortunate disability, and one American Mylai has attracted more attention and therefore more condemnation than all that the Soviets have done in Afghanistan and in Eastern Europe. Sometimes indeed the disparity in treatment may rise from positive rather than negative feelings—from philo-Semitic rather than anti-Semitic sentiments, and a higher level of expectation of Israeli behavior. Israelis sometimes complain of being held to

an impossibly high standard of virtue. Such complaints may be unreasonable. Israel regards itself and is regarded by most Westerners as
a liberal democracy. Israeli behavior is therefore judged by the same
rigorous standards which, say, Americans, Britons, and Frenchmen
apply in judging their own and each other's actions.

But even allowing for this, there are times when the disparity in
treatment and inequality in judgment raise questions of good faith.
The most obvious example is the affair at Sabra and Shatila. The
performance of the Israeli authorities at Sabra and Shatila, though
they did not themselves perpetrate a massacre, could be a source
only of shame and not of pride to democratic people. That worse
things happen elsewhere is no answer, and it is demeaning for Israelis or their supporters to invite such comparisons. But if comparison
is a poor defense, it is surely a moral and intellectual obligation of
judgment—more specifically, of those whose professional duty it is to
report, to interpret, and to judge. The universal execration of Israeli
behavior at Sabra and Shatila may represent the high moral principles of the outside world and the high standards of behavior expected
from the Israelis. But a comparison between this execration and the
almost total indifference towards other massacres, including more
recent ones carried out by the Shi^{c}a in the same camps at Sabra and
Shatila, raises disquieting questions concerning the sentiments and
motives of the judges.

A characteristic of the anti-Jew as opposed to the pro-Arab is his
tendency to harp on Jewish power and influence, which he usually
greatly exaggerates, and to complain of Jewish double loyalty. The
anti-Jew normally proceeds on the assumptions that: (a) the Jews in
his country are all rich and clever, (b) they are all working for Israel,
and (c) they are committing some offense in doing so.

The question of double loyalty takes different forms. In democratic and open societies like the United States or Britain, Jewish
double loyalty is in the main a problem only for Jews and anti-Jews,
and not for the great mass of the population who are neither. Most
nonpolitical Americans and Britons find it normal that Jews should
sympathize with Israel, and are indeed slightly puzzled or even
disturbed when they do not. It may be significant that while the
charge of dual loyalty is sometimes brought against the Jews, it is
rarely if ever leveled against other American ethnic or religious
minorities, though many of these are actively engaged in political

lobbying. Greek, Armenian, Irish, and of late also Arab American groups for example advocate policies and sometimes even support violent action against governments that are linked by military alliances with the United States. As citizens of a free country, Jews have the same rights as anyone else to be pro-Israel, pro-Arab, or pro whatever they please. A selective restriction of this right, imposed on Jews but not on others, on support for Israel but not for other foreign causes, would put them, in effect, in a separate and inferior category of citizenship. This line of thought has won little support in free countries, though it has made some headway elsewhere.

In countries with an authoritarian tradition, like Russia, or a centralist tradition, like France, the position is somewhat different, and opposition by a group of nationals—Jews or others—to a foreign policy pursued by the government is seen as a form of dissidence verging on treason. In France, in the late sixties and seventies, there were some who saw Zionist Jews as a modern equivalent of the Huguenots and the Ultramontanes. The comparison is far-fetched and its impact very limited, though it caused some concern at the time to French Jews. In Russia and Poland, where this kind of argument is more familiar, the pressures and penalties to which the Jew is subject are incomparably greater. Russian and Polish Jews must not merely refrain from supporting Israel; they must actively oppose her. The point was well made—in private—by a distinguished Polish Jewish writer during the 1967 war. "I agree," he said, "that a man can have only one country to which he owes allegiance—but why does mine have to be the United Arab Republic?"

An important feature of the present time is the rapid development of anti-Zionism, which has acquired a wider range and relevance, often quite unconnected with the Middle East and its problems. In the nineteenth century, religiously expressed anti-Judaism came to be regarded as reactionary and outmoded, and gave way, in more modern and secular circles, to racially expressed anti-Semitism, then regarded as up-to-date and scientific. In our time, racism—especially in the Western world where it is now associated with hostility to blacks rather than to Jews—has also been discredited, and racial anti-Semitism has, for some, been duly succeeded by an anti-Zionism in which politics takes the place previously occupied first by religion and then by race. The change is one of expression and emphasis rather than of substance, since all these elements have been and still are present. Even now, if one wishes to attack or discredit a Jew as such, one may call him an unbeliever, a Semite, or a Zionist, depending on whether the atmosphere and prevailing ideology of the society in which one operates is religious, ethnic, or political.

Racist feelings can work both ways and may underlie non-Jewish goodwill as well as hostility to Israel. One group, the approximate rather than the exact counterpart of the Jew-hating Arabophiles, are those who favor Israel because they hate Arabs. Such motives were at one time prominent in France, where the war in Algeria gave rise to a quasi alliance with Israel against the common Arab enemy, and where the final French withdrawal left a feeling of bitterness for which the Israeli victories provided some solace. This feeling was, however, specific and transitory; it was political and psychological rather than racial, and declined rapidly in importance. More recently, in the United States, the oil crisis, followed by events in Iran, Lebanon, and elsewhere, caused a surge of anti-Islamic and anti-Arab feeling, which sometimes finds expression in the presentation and interpretation of the news, and in the use of hostile stereotypes of Arabs in commentaries, cartoons, anecdotes, films, etc. This sometimes reaches a level of nastiness which, while still permitted when discussing Arabs, is no longer acceptable when dealing with Jews. There is no Holocaust to inhibit the expression of anti-Arab prejudice; there is no anti-Zionism to provide for its sublimation.

In general however this is a minor phenomenon. In the English-speaking countries, hostility to the Arabs as such has not usually been a factor, except perhaps for those who include the Arabs in a generalized dislike of "lesser breeds." For these, the choice between Jew and Arab may present an agonizing dilemma.

European and American attitudes to the dispute are indeed greatly complicated by the fact that one party consists of Jews and the other of Arabs. Both peoples arouse powerful and irrational responses. This can be felt in the obsessiveness, in the note of emotion, even of passion, that affects the public discussion of the problem— a passion and vehemence that have few if any parallels in dealing with other disputes between foreign nations.

The most obvious in their responses are those whom one might term the obverse and reverse racists, two groups who see the problem exclusively as a conflict between races. What matters to them is that the Arabs are an Afro-Asian people and Israel a state created by a population those leadership was predominently European in origin and attitude. For each of these two groups of racists, one of the parties to such a dispute, irrespective of the circumstances, is necessarily right, the other necessarily wrong. The two groups are alike in their passion and their fury; they differ only in their choice. They include some grotesque and sometimes pathetic figures—the Jew driven one way or the other by tribal solidarity or the desire to escape; the Old Guard anti-Semite who becomes a champion of Israel, because he hates the Arabs even more than the Jews; the Anglo-American liberal, who claims a monopoly of sin for his country, as fiercely and as absurdly as his parents claimed a monopoly of virtue; the tortured WASP radical, who sees the Arab–Israeli conflict as ultimately one between Harlem and Scarsdale, and makes a choice determined by his own personal blend of prejudice and guilt.

Two additional groups, who may support Israel for racially influenced reasons, are inverted and repentant anti-Semites. The former are those who basically accept the anti-Semitic myth of secret Jewish world power, but see it with respect and admiration rather than with hatred or fear. The repentant anti-Semites, usually vicarious, are another matter. There can be no doubt that one of the most important sources of support for Israel in the period following the fall of Hitler was guilt, using that word in the modern sense, as a psychological state rather than as a legal fact. The true anti-Semite is rarely repentant, and feelings of guilt for crimes against the Jews are often in inverse proportion to the degree of personal involvement. It is the innocent Germans who feel guilt for what happened; the perpetrators for the most part seem untroubled by any pangs of remorse. Such feelings were, however, a factor of importance in the immediate postwar period, and the response of many Christians to the emergence of Israel, and to the early conduct of Israel, was determined by the feeling that they, their countries, and their churches were accessories to the Nazi crimes, if not by active complicity, then by indifference and inaction.

Such feelings are a dwindling asset to Israel, and must inevitably die away as the memory of Nazi crimes recedes into the past. In the Soviet Union, official propaganda even tries to conceal the fact that the Nazis persecuted Jews, and instead, in a macabre inversion of truth, presents the Jews themselves as Nazis. In the West, especially

in continental Europe, it was with obvious relief that some persons
and institutions, after the long years of unease, abandoned the painful posture of guilt and penitence.

What of the Jews themselves? For the anti-Semite, all Jews are
Zionists and all are pro-Israel, since Jew, Zionist, and Israeli are
interchangeable terms. The reality is somewhat different, and Jews
are by no means unanimous on this or indeed on any subject. The
universal Jewish conspiracy, whether in support of Israel or for any
other purpose, is of course a figment of anti-Semitic imagination and
has never had any reality. Many Jews, by now probably most Jews,
are pro-Israel in varying degrees, the more so when under attack.
There is, however, a by no means insignificant number of others who
are active opponents of Israel.

These are of several kinds. Some, as with non-Jews, are believers
in the justice of the Arab cause; some, again like non-Jews, are moved
by professional, commercial, or career considerations; some again by
Jewish religious beliefs. Of the remainder of the Jewish opponents of
Israel, the most important are supporters of the Old and New lefts,
whose reactions to this as to most other problems are determined by
political decisions not necessarily their own. Many in particular are
guided by fashionable "progressive" assumptions, and find it difficult
to assign any merit to a cause which enjoys American support.

In this, Jewish leftists, both old and new, are no different from
their non-Jewish colleagues. There is, however, an additional factor
which is sometimes overrated but is none the less real—the phenomenon of Jewish self-hate, the neurotic reaction which one finds
among some Jews to the impact of anti-Semitism, by accepting, sharing, expressing, and even exaggerating the basic assumptions of the
anti-Semite. In the nineteenth and early twentieth centuries, this
kind of response could be found in particular among assimilated
German Jews of both left and right. A classic example was Karl Marx's
essay "On the Jewish Question"; another was the posture of some
German Jewish conservatives, who adopted the standards and out-
look, as far as they could, of the German Nationalist right, even
including their accusations against Jews, particularly Jews other than
those of Germany. This did not of course help them in any way when
the Nazis came to power and imposed their own solution of the
Jewish problem. Today the phenomenon of Jewish self-hate is found

chiefly on the far left, where hostility to Israel provides, or appears to provide, an opportunity for freeing oneself from ancestral and, more immediately, parental bonds.

But the most important response to anti-Semitism, far more important than those of the Soviets, the West, or the Jews themselves, is that of the Arabs, whose vast output of anti-Semitic literature raises serious issues, not least concerning the present condition of Arab society.

In the Arab world, as in the West, certain questions arise from an examination of all this anti-Semitic literature. Who reads this stuff, how important is it, what effect does it have? In the Western world, one can answer these questions with reasonable assurance. Since 1945, and in many regions for long before that, explicit anti-Semitic literature was published and read only within the lunatic fringes of society, and its influence has in recent times been minimal. This can no longer be said of the Arab world. The volume of anti-Semitic books and articles published, the size and number of editions and impressions, the eminence and authority of those who write, publish, and sponsor them, their place in school and college curricula, their role in the mass media, would all seem to suggest that classical anti-Semitism is an essential part of Arab intellectual life at the present time—almost as much as happened in Nazi Germany, and considerably more than in late nineteenth and early twentieth century France, where the clamor of the anti-Dreyfusards was answered by at least equally powerful voices in defense of reason and tolerance. There are such voices in the Arab world, too, but there is not a single Arab country at the present time which enjoys a genuinely free press, and these voices have great difficulty in making themselves heard. To condemn anti-Semitism, it is necessary to show that it is harmful to the Arab cause—hence the strange theory, popular in some circles, that anti-Semitism and Zionism are the same thing. By the same reasoning, one might argue that apartheid is a form of African nationalism.

Any opposition to anti-Semitism in the Arab world, even if it is or presents itself as tactical, marks a welcome change from the previously almost unanimous chorus of hate. The enthusiasm with which the first peace moves were received in Egypt, and the warm and friendly welcome given to the first Israelis who went to Cairo, illustrated a genuine desire for peace and good relations, which even affected a limited number of intellectuals. In the years that followed the treaty, the initial euphoria diminished, but did not entirely disappear. The long and often acrimonious negotiations, the failure to make any progress on the Palestinian issue, the settlements on the West Bank, the lack of normalization, the Israeli invasion of Lebanon in 1982, all imposed severe strains on the new and fragile relationship between Israel and the first Arab state to sign a peace treaty or even enter into open negotiations. But despite these difficulties, the Egyptians kept the relationship with Israel alive, albeit as a much reduced level, and permitted the establishment of an Israeli academic center in Cairo. There are even some Egyptian writers who find it possible to discuss Israel in print—if not with sympathy, at least without violent abuse. These are small signs, so far limited to Egypt, and there are even less or none in other Arab countries. Nevertheless, significant changes have taken place. Not all Arab countries broke off diplomatic relations with Egypt after the signing of the peace with Israel, and one which did so, Jordan, has since resumed them. In some countries, Arab politicians and newspapermen now speak of Israel and Israelis, instead of the "so-called state" and "Zionist gangs" of earlier usage. Some—in suitable contexts—even use the previously taboo word peace. Further progress will obviously depend very much on the initiation and the success or failure of peace negotiations. At least these developments leave some glimmer of hope that the anti-Semitic poisoning of Arab thought may not yet be irreversible in this generation.

Another factor, which may yet prove more important, is the absence among even anti-Semitic Muslims—with few exceptions—of the kind of deep, intimate hatred characteristic of the classic anti-Semite in Central and Eastern Europe and sometimes elsewhere. Time and time again, European and American Jews traveling in Arab countries have observed that, despite the torrent of broadcast and published anti-Semitism, the only face-to-face experience of anti-Semitic hostility that they suffered during their travels was from compatriots, many of whom feel free, in what they imagine to be the more congenial atmosphere of the Arab world, to make consciously anti-Semitic and incidentally also antifeminist remarks that they would not make at home. In the same way, Israelis traveling in the West often find it easier to establish a rapport with Arabs than with Arabophiles.

While the public denunciation of anti-Semitism in the Arab lands is virtually unknown, the expression of such prejudice at the personal level, though increasing, is still rare. This may be due to a certain ingrained courtesy in the Arab cultural tradition, which stops even anti-Semites from making overtly anti-Semitic remarks in the presence of Jews. But it must also owe something to the absence hitherto of that kind of visceral, personal hostility that marks the European anti-Semite, and which, even in those only mildly affected, can cause an almost physical discomfort in personal encounters with Jews. Arabs do not seem to be subject to such discomforts. In the Arab lands anti-Semitism is still largely political and ideological, intellectual and literary. Its prevalence in the younger generation is due to the relentless indoctrination of textbooks and media, and the absence of any other information about Jewish history and culture. Despite this, one is constantly surprised to find how the authors of even some of the most violent and Nazi-like anti-Jewish tracts are willing and able to have normal, sometimes friendly relations with Jews or even with Israelis when no one is there to watch and report them. An incident that occurred in Cairo very shortly after the signing of the peace treaty is instructive in this respect. Two Israeli scholars took the newly opened road to Cairo, anxious to meet some of the literary, academic, and political personalities whose work they had for so long studied from afar. Among others they called at the editorial office of a violently anti-Israel, anti-Zionist, even anti-Semitic journal, and asked to see the editor. That gentleman, learning who they were and whence they came, explained that he could not possibly receive them: "We are against you, we are against Israel, we are against Zionism, we are against the peace, and I cannot admit you to my office." However, the editor said, handing them a piece of paper, "If you would like to come and see me in my home after five o'clock, I would be glad to talk to you then and exchange opinions. This is my address."

All unknowingly, the Muslim editor was proposing the exact opposite of the classical American situation known at one time as "the five o'clock shadow"—when the Jew could be received like anyone else in the office, during business hours, but was barred from the social life of the home and the club, the evening and the weekend. In the Western world, the five o'clock shadow is fading, though it has by no means disappeared and could conceivably return. In the world of Islam, it could still go either way.

Which way it goes will in large measure by determined by the further course of the Arab–Israeli conflict. For Christian anti-Semites, the Palestine problem is a pretext and an outlet for their hatred; for Muslim anti-Semites, it is the cause. Perhaps, if that cause is removed or significantly diminished, the hostility too may wane— not disappear, but at least return to the previous level of prejudice. This was not good, but was compatible with human relations and even with the beginnings of political dialogue. At this time there are some signs that the anti-Semitic virus that has plagued Christianity almost since the beginning may at last be in process of cure; by a sad paradox, the same profound religious hatred has now attacked the hitherto resistant body of Islam. It may be that the moment of choice has gone, and that the virus has already entered the bloodstream of Islam, to poison it for generations to come as Christendom was poisoned for generations past. If so, not only Arab but also Jewish hopes will be lost in the miasma of bigotry. The open democracy that is the pride of Israel will be polluted by sectarian and ethnic discrimination and repression, while the free institutions that are the best hope of the Arabs will be forgotten, as the Middle East sinks under the rule of the cynics and fanatics who flourish in the soil of hatred.

But it is more likely that this has not yet happened. Certainly it is easy to identify individual Arab rulers or writers whose hatred of the Jews is as deep and as consuming as that of any classical European or American anti-Semite. But for most, it still seems true that despite its vehemence and its ubiquity, Arab or Muslim anti-Semitism is still something that comes from above, from the leadership, rather than from below, from the society—a political and polemical weapon, to be discarded if and when it is no longer required. If mainstream Arab leaders can bring themselves to follow the example of Sadat and enter into a dialogue with Israel, and if the Israelis can find the strength and courage to respond appropriately, then it is possible that the anti-Semitic campaign will fade away, and be confined, as in the modern West, to fringe groups and fringe regimes. If there is no solution or alleviation, and the conflict drags on, then there is no escape from an unending downward spiral of mutual hate that will embitter the lives of Arabs and Jews alike. An awesome choice now confronts Israelis, Arabs, indeed all of us.

Afterword to the new edition

During the twelve years that have passed since the original edition of this book was sent to press, major changes have taken place in the Middle East, profoundly affecting both the conflict and the prejudice with which it dealt.

Of these, by far the most important is what has come to be known as the "Peace Process"—the developing dialogue between the state of Israel on the one hand and the Palestinians and some Arab governments on the other. In the past, intergovernment communication was limited to Egypt, which had a peace treaty and diplomatic relations with Israel. Communications with other Arab governments, if they occurred at all, were very limited and strictly secret. With the Palestinian organizations there was no formal contact whatever, and even with Egypt both formal and informal relations were minimal and cold.

A new phase began on October 30, 1991 with the convening, under American and Russian auspices, of the Middle East Peace Conference in Madrid. This was followed by the first bilateral peace talks between Israelis and Arabs, which opened in Washington on December 10, 1991 and continued intermittently during the following years. Meanwhile, in the spring of 1992, the first secret contacts began between Israeli and Palestinian representatives. Contacts continued for the rest of the year, and the first round of secret but direct talks was held in Norway in January 1993. In the same month the Israeli parliament repealed the law banning all contacts with the PLO, which was now in effect recognized by Israel as well as by the Arab states as "the sole legitimate representative of the Palestinian people". In the course of a series of discussions in Oslo and later in Washington, an agreement between the government of Israel and the PLO was finally signed on the White House lawn on September 13, 1993.

Mutual recognition between Israel and the PLO opened the way for a number of Arab states to start commercial and to a limited extent diplomatic contacts with Israel. One of them, the Kingdom of Jordan, signed a full peace treaty on October 26, 1994, providing for diplomatic and a wide range of other relations. Other countries, notably China and India, previously inhibited by their support for the Palestinian cause, now felt free to normalize their relations with Israel. Saudi Arabia remained coldly aloof, neither supporting nor opposing the peace process, but avoiding any form of contact with Israel. Syria agreed in principle to negotiate peace, but proved obdurate in the negotiations, refusing even to take "yes" for an answer when it was offered by the Israeli government of the time. Iraq and Libya opposed the peace process as such. A non-Arab state, Iran, emerged as the most implacable opponent not only of the peace process but of any compromise on what its leaders saw as the ultimate objective—the dismantling and elimination of the Israeli state.

Even after the Israeli general election of May 1996 and the replacement of the Labour government by a hard-line coalition government dominated by the Likud, the conflict clearly had now entered a new and less dangerous phase. Full scale conventional war between Israel and any of its Arab neighbours, though not impossible, is much less likely than in the past. Terrorist activities against Israel continue, notably by three organizations—Islamic Jihad and Hamas in the Palestinian territories and the Iranian-sponsored and Syrian-supported Hizballah in Lebanon. But there are signs that the Palestine authority is able to exercise some measure of control over the terrorist organizations. Much will depend on their willingness and ability to use that control.

Hostility remains, and has been exacerbated by some recent Israeli attitudes and policies. This hostility may be specific or general, ideological or political. It is often expressed, especially in the media, with a violence and crudity that are no longer acceptable in democratic countries, though they still persist elsewhere. But neither the hostility as such nor the violence and crudity with which it is expressed constitute anti-Semitism, unless certain other elements are present. They often are.

For a while it seemed that the cooling, perhaps the ending of conflict, would lead to a lessening of anti-Semitism. In some quarters this did indeed occur. But in others the peace process itself aroused a new hostility, among both those who were frustrated by its slowness and those who were alarmed by its rapidity. As a result anti-Semitism has conquered new territory and risen to a new intensity.

The peace process between Israelis and Palestinians began, not because either side had developed any great sympathy or understanding for the other, but because the leaders on both sides realized that they were engaged in wars that were ultimately unwinnable. The PLO was hard hit by the ending both of the Cold War and of the Gulf War. The collapse of the Soviet Union left them, for the first time in more than half a century, without an anti-Western great power patron. Their support for Saddam Hussein antagonized the Arabian kings and princes who had been their principal financial backers. In this situation, they decided, for the time being at least, to abandon their long proclaimed objective of destroying Israel and replacing it with an Arab state ruling all Palestine, and to settle for a form of partition— the solution which they had rejected when it was offered by the British mandatary government and later by the United Nations. Some, including most of the leaders, saw the Oslo process as a lifeline. There were and still are others who saw it as a betrayal.

On the Israeli side too there were some who saw Oslo as a betrayal— as throwing away the moment of victory and wantonly abandoning part of the ancient heritage of the Jews. But on the Israeli as on the Palestinian side, this was not the majority view, and most sober Israelis were coming to realize that their war too, for the whole of Palestine, was unwinnable and that they too would be wise to settle for partition. The moment of truth for the Israelis was the Intifada. This was contained, after a long and bitter struggle in the course of which it became clear that the maintenance of Israeli rule over the Palestinian territories could only be achieved—if at all—at an unacceptable material and moral cost, involving the transformation of the very nature of Israeli government and society. A dramatic example of what this transformation might mean was given by the assassination of the Israeli prime minister Yitzhak Rabin by an Israeli extremist.

Arab opposition to the peace process as such or to the manner in which it is being conducted is of three major types.

The first is basically a continuance of what went before—ideological polemic against Zionism, political warfare against the state of Israel. Ideological or political opposition as such is not based on prejudice, but, as before, it affects and is affected by prejudice. This kind of opposition, and the prejudice associated with it, continue to flourish and even to spread in spite of, and in some quarters because of, the peace process. It has been aggravated by some of the actions of the new Israeli government and still more the utterances of some of its followers. Israeli extremists cannot really be blamed for the anti-Semitic propaganda in the Egyptian and other Arab media, which had already reached high levels of scurrility before the change of government and policy in Israel. They have, however, undermined the efforts of some well-meaning Arabs to counter these campaigns.

An example of reporting and comments on the news may be seen in the suicide bombing in Ramat Gan on July 24, 1995. This was disclaimed, even denounced, by responsible Palestinian and other Arab leaders. It was acclaimed by many others, from the centre and the left as well as in the fundamentalist press. A leading article in the Jordanian leftist weekly, *Al-Majd*, of July 31, 1995, by its editor, Fahd al-Rimāwī, acclaims the heroism of the Hamas bomber who "sent seven Zionist settlers to hell and thirty others to the casualty wards" and goes on to denounce those who had condemned the attack as hypocrites or worse. Ramat Gan is near Tel Aviv, part of Israel since the foundation of the state. The description of its inhabitants as "Zionist settlers" is the more noteworthy. The Jordanian fundamentalist Ziyād Abū Ghanīma, in the weekly *Shīhān* of July 29, 1995, rails against those who "shed torrents of tears in mourning for filthy Jewish blood while sparing their tears when Palestinian or Lebanese blood is shed by the hands of the Jews, may God curse them".

More dangerous than the old guard resistance to the peace process is the new active opposition arising from the process itself, and the fear that the prowess which the Israelis had demonstrated in the battlefield would be equalled or even exceeded in activities with which Jews are more traditionally associated—in the factory, the countinghouse, and the marketplace. Such fears have often been exacerbated by a certain Israeli brashness and lack of understanding of the courtesies and sensitivities of Middle Eastern society. According to this perception Israel has changed its tactics. It has now switched from warlike to peaceful methods to pursue its nefarious design of penetrating and dominating the Arab world. Some see dark menace in every Israeli attempt at communication and cooperation. The expansion of trade links means economic exploitation and subjugation; the development of cultural links means the subversion and destruction of Arab-Islamic culture; the quest for political relations is a prelude to imperial domination. These fantasies, absurd as they may seem to the outsider or indeed to any rational observer, nevertheless command wide support in the Arab media and particularly in Egypt. For exponents of this view, European anti-Semitism provides a rich reservoir of themes and motifs, of literature and iconography, on which to draw and elaborate.

A few examples may suffice. Shimon Peres' book, *The New Middle East*, containing a somewhat idyllic view of future peaceful cooperation between Israel and the Arab states for economic improvement and cultural advancement, has appeared in several Arabic translations. The purpose of these translations is indicated in the preface to one of them, published in Cairo by the semi-governmental Al-Ahrām press: "When *The Protocols of the Elders of Zion* were discovered about two hundred years ago [sic] by a Frenchwoman [sic] and disseminated in many languages including Arabic, the international Zionist establishment tried its best to deny the plot. They even claimed that it was fabricated and sought to acquire all the copies in the market in order to prevent them from being read. And now, it is precisely Shimon Peres who brings the decisive proof of their validity. His book confirms in so clear a way that it cannot be denied that the *Protocols* were true indeed. Peres' book is yet another step in the execution of these dangerous plots."

The *Protocols* remain a staple not just of propaganda but even of academic scholarship. Thus, according to an article published in the Egyptian paper *Ākhir Sā`a* in November 1996, an important "scientific treatise" dealing with the economic role of the Jews in Egypt in the first half of the twentieth century was accorded the degree of MA from the University of Alexandria. From the description it is clear that the writer of this dissertation relied very heavily on the *Protocols* and on the methodology of research that they provided. The *Protocols* also form the basis of an interview published in the Egyptian popular magazine *Al-Muṣawwar* on December 27, 1996. The article opens with a statement by the interviewer, who introduces the *Protocols* as an authentic historical record and then proceeds to question the patriarch Shenouda, head of the Coptic church. The patriarch's comments on Jews and Judaism seem to be based on the information supplied to him by the interviewer, and derived from the *Protocols* and from another popular anti-Semitic forgery, the Pseudo-Talmud.

The argument that "we cannot be anti-Semitic because we ourselves are Semites" may still occasionally be heard in Arab countries, though not of course in Turkey or Iran. But some of the more sophisticated spokesmen have become aware that to most outsiders this argument looks either silly or disingenuous. There is however a serious, though not always consistent, effort to maintain the distinction between hostility to Israel and Zionism and hostility to Jews as such. Spokesmen of the government of Iran disclaim anti-Semitism; they usually refrain from anti-Semitic phraseology and proclaim their readiness to tolerate Jews—of course within the limits prescribed by the Sharī'a. This however does not prevent them from embracing the *Protocols*. These are frequently reprinted in Iran and in 1995 were published serially in the daily paper *Ettelā'āt* in more than one hundred and fifty installments "as a reminder to the reader". Copies of the *Protocols* in various languages are also distributed internationally through Iranian networks.

Some of the accusations are sexual. The Israelis are accused of infecting girls with AIDS and syphilis and sending them to Egypt to spread these diseases. They are also accused of supplying Egyptian women with hyper-aphrodisiac chewing gum which drives them into a frenzy of sexual desire, while at the same time selling hormonally altered fruit that kills male sperm. This is part of a series of attacks on Israeli agricultural techniques and products—the one area in which there has been real cooperation. Other stories accuse the Israelis (or simply "the Jews") of supplying Egyptian farmers with poisoned seeds and disease-bearing poultry "like time bombs" (*Al-Sha'b*, March 14, 1997), of deliberately spreading cancer among the Egyptians and other Arabs by devising and disseminating carcinogenic cucumbers and shampoos; of promoting drug-taking and devil-worship, and organizing a campaign to legalize homosexuality in order to undermine Egyptian society. A Syrian paper (*Al-Thawra*, October 4, 1995) even claims that Arafat made peace because he himself is a Jew.

Even these however do not qualify as anti-Semitic in the strict sense. They do however exemplify the emotional and intellectual context in which anti-Semitic accusations can be swiftly disseminated and readily believed.

Some accusations are clearly transference or projection. An example is the statement that Israelis are told by their rabbis that if they are killed while killing Palestinians they will go straight to Paradise. Some are traditional Islamic accusations against the Jews, based on well-known passages in the Qur'an and traditions; some are borrowed or adapted from the standard armory of European anti-Semitism. Increasingly, they represent a combination of the second and third.

The strongest, most principled, and most sustained opposition to the peace process is offered in the name of Islam, especially by the government of Iran and its various agencies, and by other Islamic parties and organizations. This opposition has the considerable advantage of being ideologically formulated and logically consistent, and of using familiar language to appeal to deep-rooted sentiments. This gives to arguments based on Islam far greater cogency and power than those based on nationality and race. Nevertheless, spokesmen for Islamic movements do not disdain to use racist arguments, and specifically, to draw on the rich resources of hatred provided by European anti-Semitism. Standard anti-Semitic themes have become commonplace in the propaganda of Arab Islamic movements like Hizballah and Hamas, in the pronouncements of various agencies of the government of Iran, and even in some newspapers and other publications of the Turkish Islamic party, the leading member in the governing coalition of 1996–1997.

Most of these accusations are familiar and can be traced to their European sources. Others arise from local circumstances. Thus, for Turkish anti-Semites, the misdeeds of the Jews include the downfall of the Ottoman Empire and the recent troubles in Bosnia. In Iran it is American sanctions and the resulting economic hardships that are ascribed to sinister Jewish influences in Washington.

European anti-Semitism, in both its theological and racist versions, was essentially alien to Islamic traditions, culture and modes of thought. But to an astonishing degree the ideas, the literature, even the crudest inventions of the Nazis and their predecessors have, so to speak, been internalized and Islamized. The major themes—the *Protocols*, the invented Talmud quotations, ritual murder, the hatred of mankind, the masonic and the rest of the conspiracy theories, poisoning the wells and taking over the world—remain; but they are given an Islamic, even a Qur'ānic twist. Thus, the classical Islamic accusation, that the Old and New Testaments are superseded because the Jews and Christians had falsified the revelations which had been vouchsafed to them, is given a new slant—that the Bible in its extant form is not authentic but is a version distorted and corrupted by the

Jews in order to show that they are God's chosen people and that Palestine belongs to them.[1] Various current news items, such as the scandal over the Swiss gold, the appointment of Madeleine Albright as Secretary of State, even the collapse of BCCI, are given an anti-Semitic slant. Jewish world plots, against mankind in general, against Islam, against the Arabs—have become commonplace. In an article published on December 20, 1996 in the Egyptian newspaper *Al-Ittiḥād*, a preacher from Al-Azhar University explains why he hates the Jews. Briefly, it is because they are the worst enemies of the Muslims and have no moral standards. Instead they have chosen evil and villainy. He concludes: "I hate the Jews so as to earn a reward from God."

One of the crimes of Israel and of the Zionists in these writings is that they are a bridgehead or instrument of American or, more generally, of Western penetration. For such, America is the Great Satan, Israel the Little Satan, and it is as a spearhead of Western corruption that Israel is dangerous. An alternative view is provided by the more consistent European-type anti-Semites. For these, it is America that is the tool of Israel rather than the reverse. This argument is backed with a good deal of Nazi-style or original Nazi documentation. In much of the literature produced by the Islamic organizations the enemy is no longer defined as the Israeli or the Zionist. He is simply the Jew, and his evil is innate and genetic, going back to remote antiquity.

A technique shared by all these different kinds of propaganda is the rewriting or obliteration of the past and in particular the removal of anything which might either arouse compassion or evoke respect for the Jew. One standard theme is Holocaust denial. Either the Holocaust never happened, or if it did, it was on a small scale and—some add—the Jews brought it on themselves. The Zionists were the collaborators and successors of the Nazis. This remarkable version of history commands increasing Arab support, as was evidenced by the reception accorded to Roger Garaudy. A French ex-Communist convert to Islam, he had just published a book entitled *The Founding Myths of Israeli Politics*. These are three: the religious myth of the Chosen People and the Promised Land; the Holocaust myth of Jewish extermination and Zionist anti-fascism, and the new myth of the modern Israeli miracle, actually due to foreign money procured by Jewish lobbyists. His sources include apologists for Hitler, post-Zionist Israeli revisionists, and current European anti-Americanism. His mid

East tour in the summer of 1996 was a triumph. In Lebanon he was received by the Prime Minister and the Minister of Education, in Syria by the Vice President and several other ministers. In both countries he gave a number of highly publicized lectures and interviews and was welcomed by major literary and other intellectual bodies. In Jordan and Egypt he was not officially received but was welcomed with the same or greater acclaim in literary circles. He was invited to Cairo by the government-sponsored Arab Artists Union with the support of the Egyptian Writers Federation, which elected him an honorary member—the first since the Federation was established more than twenty years ago. Among many honours, he was given the "Egyptian Writers Award". The editor-in-chief of the semi-official *Al-Ahrăm* newspaper conferred a press prize on Garaudy in recognition of the "fresh air" that he had contributed to the debate. Garaudy's welcome was not unanimous. Some fundamentalists, while approving his views on Israel, questioned his understanding of Islam. In Morocco he was acclaimed by some newspapers, but his public appearances were cancelled. "The universities," said the Minister of Higher Education, "will not open their gates to anti-Semites." Curiously, in May 1997, Mr Garaudy was invited to contribute a series of articles to an Arabic weekly published in London by the BBC Arabic service.

Denying or minimizing the Holocaust facilitates another favourite theme—that far from being victims of the Nazis, the Jews were their collaborators and carry on their tradition. The use of Nazi as a term of abuse in the Arab world dates from the beginnings of Soviet influence in the mid-1950s—before that it would have been seen rather as a compliment. Cartoons depicting Israelis and other Jews with Nazi-style uniforms and swastikas have now become standard. These complement the Nazi-era hooked noses and blood-dripping jagged teeth. The memory of both the Jewish victims and Arab admirers of the Third Reich is totally effaced. To maintain this interpretation of history, some measure of control is necessary, extending even to entertainment. *Schindler's List*, a film portraying the suffering of the Jews under Nazi rule, is banned in Arab countries. Even *Independence Day*, which has nothing to do with either the Nazi regime or the Middle East, was denounced because it has a Jewish hero, and that is unacceptable. It was approved for release in Lebanon only after the censors had removed all indications of the Jewishness of the hero—the skullcap, the Hebrew prayer, the momentary appearance of Israelis and Arabs

working side by side in a desert outpost. In November 1996, a Hizballah press liaison officer explained his objection to the film. "This
film polishes and presents the Jews as a very humane people. You are
releasing false images about them."

The rewriting of the past extends even to ancient history. The
historical museum in Amman, for example, tells through objects and
inscriptions the history of all the ancient peoples of the region—with
one exception. The kings and prophets of ancient Israel are entirely
missing. I was able to find only three references. The first explains the
inscription on the Mesha Stele as "thanking the Moabite god Chemosh
for deliverance from the Israelites". Thus the English text; the Arabic
reads "from the tyranny of the Israelites". The second appears in an
alcove containing the Dead Sea scrolls produced by a "Jewish sect".
The third is a reference to "the militant Hasmonean Jews [who] …
established their own reign in Palestine and the northern part of
Jordan. Most of the Greek cities welcomed the Roman army headed
by General Pompey as a liberator from Jewish oppression".

Even these few allusions are missing in the textbooks used in schools
under the Palestine authority. For them, the history of Palestine begins
with the retroactively Arabized Canaanites and jumps from them to
the Arab conquest in the seventh century C.E., entirely omitting the
Old Testament, its people and their history.

Visits to Arab bookshops, or to religious bookshops in Turkey, reveal
a wide range of anti-Semitic literature of many kinds. What is lacking
is any kind of corrective. The Arab reader seeking guidance on such
topics as Jewish history, religion, thought and literature will find
virtually nothing. There is some material on modern Israel, the best
of which, produced by the former Palestine Research Center in Beirut,
is reasonably factual. But most of what is available is lurid propaganda
or used as such. Translations from Hebrew are few and fall mainly
into three categories: 1. Accounts of Israeli espionage. 2. Memoirs by
Israeli leaders including Rabin, Peres, and Netanyahu, with explana-
tory introductions and annotations and 3. Writings by anti-Zionist and
anti-Israel Jews.

Peace is negotiated and signed between governments, but it will
remain cold and formal, meaning little more than a cessation of hostilities, until it is made between peoples. As long as a high-pitched
scream of rage and hate remains the normal form of communication,
peace between peoples is unlikely to make much progress. But there

are some signs of improvement, of the beginnings of a dialogue. Statesmen, soldiers and businessmen have been in touch with their Israeli opposite numbers, and some of these contacts have so far survived even the change of government in Israel. Intellectuals have proved more recalcitrant, but even among them, there have been signs of change. A few courageous souls have braved the denunciation of their more obdurate colleagues to meet publicly with Israelis and even on rare occasions to visit Israel.

An incident in the spring of 1997 evoked disquieting memories of the rampage of the Egyptian gendarme Sulaymān Khāṭir in 1985. It also provided an encouraging contrast. On March 13, 1997 a Jordanian soldier, Aḥmad Daqāmsa, suddenly started firing at an Israeli girls' school outing, killing seven girls and wounding several more before he was overpowered by his comrades. A few days later King Hussein, in a gesture of contrition and compassion, crossed into Israel and called in person to offer his condolences to the bereaved families. Reactions among his people were mixed. Some joined the Israelis in acclaiming this act of courage, human decency and generosity of spirit. Others, while condemning the murders, thought the King's reponse excessive. Others again made the murderer's home a place of pilgrimage. But there was nothing comparable with the outpouring of support that, for a while, made Sulaymān Khāṭir a national, popular and even intellectual hero in Egypt. Sulaymān Khāṭir was reported to have committed suicide in prison in Cairo. Aḥmad Daqāmsa was tried by court-martial in Jordan, and sentenced to life imprisonment. As before, opinions were divided. Some found the sentence too light, some too heavy. Some thought he should have been honoured, not punished.

Closer contact between the two societies may bring interesting, perhaps even valuable results. Israel, with all its faults, is an open, democratic society. A million Arabs are Israeli citizens; two million Palestinians have lived or are living under Israeli rule. Although this rule has often been harsh and arbitrary, it has on the whole been benevolent by the standards of the region. Two contrasting incidents illustrate a direction of possible change. During the Intifada, a young Arab boy had his wrist broken by a baton-wielding Israeli soldier. He appeared next day, bandaged and in hospital, denouncing Israeli oppression—on Israeli television. In 1997 a lawyer in Gaza submitted an article to a journal describing the investigation by the Israeli police of the Prime Minister and other members of the Israeli government, and suggesting that similar procedures might be adopted by the Palestine Authority. The editor of the journal did not publish the article but instead referred it to the attorney general who ordered the arrest and imprisonment of its author.

Growing numbers see—and some even make—the point. The election for the Palestine authority held in January 1996 was acclaimed as the freest and fairest held in the Arab world. It contrasted the more sharply with the show election held a little earlier in Lebanon in the presence of a different neighbour. It did not pass unnoticed that the only public investigation of the Sabra and Shatila massacre was a judicial inquiry held in Israel. No such inquiry was held in any Arab country, and the principal perpetrator of the massacre, a Lebanese Christian militia leader who was at that time an ally of Israel, subsequently went over to the Syrian side and has for some years past been a respected member of the Syrian-sponsored government in Beirut.

Latterly there have been some signs of change. The Royal Institute for Interfaith Studies in Amman is concerned with Judaism as well as with Islam and Christianity. It has invited Jewish scholars from Israel and elsewhere to contribute to its activities and to its English-language journal.[2] This attempt to present Jewish beliefs and culture in objective terms, even to allow Jews to speak for themselves, is rare if not unique in the Arab, perhaps even in the Islamic world.

On a more political level, a number of Arab intellectuals abroad and some even in Arab countries have expressed disquiet and distaste with the vicious anti-Semitism that colours so much debate on the Arab–Israel conflict. In January 1997 a group of Egyptians, Jordanians, and Palestinians, including intellectuals, lawyers, and businessmen, met with a similar group of Israelis in Copenhagen and agreed "to establish an international alliance for Arab–Israeli peace". Their declaration is not confined to pious generalities but goes into detailed discussion of some of the specific issues at stake. Needless to say, the participants in this enterprise were denounced and reviled by many of their colleagues as dupes, traitors or worse.

The last word may be left to ʿAlī Sālim, one of the first Egyptian intellectuals who dared to visit Israel. He said: "I found that the agreement between the Palestinians and Israelis was a rare moment in history. A moment of mutual recognition. I exist and you also exist.

Life is my right; it is also your right. This is a hard and long road. Its final stage is freedom and human rights. It will not be strewn with roses but beset with struggle and endurance. One cannot make peace just by talking about it. There is no way to go but forward, to achieve peace with deeds and not just with words".[3]

Notes

Introduction

1. Alain Finkielkraut, *La Réprobation d'Israël* (Paris: 1983), pp. 14 ff.
2. See for example the figures cited by Joshua Muravchik, "Misreporting Lebanon," *Policy Review* (Washington D.C.), 23: 11–66, and Edward Alexander, "The Journalists' War Against Israel," *Encounter*, September–October 1981.
3. ᶜAbd al-Raḥmān Sāmī ᶜIṣmat, *Al-Ṣahyūniyya wa'l-Māsūniyya* (Alexandria, 1950), pp. 45 and 50.
4. The point is made by Yehoshafat Harkabi, *Arab Attitudes to Israel* (Jerusalem, 1972), p. 223.
5. See for example Khomeini's book on Islamic government: Persian text, *Vilāyat-i Faqīh* (Tehran, n.d.), p. 175; French translation, *Pour un gouvernement islamique* (Paris, 1979), p. 114. Correct translation in *Islam and Revolution: Writings and Declarations of Imam Khomeini*. Translated by Hamid Algar (Berkeley, Ca., 1981), pp. 127, 128. More recently, the extension of meaning has, in some quarters, gone even further, and "Zionist" has become a term of abuse without any specific meaning whatsoever. Thus, in the Gulf War the governments of Iraq and Iran, both implacable enemies of Israel, denounce one another as Zionists. An even more bizarre example occurred in the Far East, where the radio service of the Soviet dominated Mongolian Republic accused the Chinese in Sin Kiang of "Zionist activities."
6. English translation in *Documents on British Foreign Policy 1919–1939*, ed. E. L. Woodward and Rohan Butler, 3rd series, 7: 1939 (London, 1954), p. 258; German text in *Akten zur deutschen Auswärtigen Politik 1918–1945, Aus dem Archiv des Deutschen Auswärtigen Amtes* (Imprimerie Nationale: Baden-Baden, 1956), p. 171. On the provenance of this document, see Gerhard L. Weinberg, *The Foreign Policy of Hitler's Germany* (Chicago, 1980), 2: 610–611.
7. See Rochelle Saidel Wolk, "Anti-Semitism in America: Prophecy or Paronoia?" in *Lilith* (1980), 7: 8–11, and Judith Plaskow, "Blaming Jews . . . For the Birth of Patriarchy," in *Lilith* (1980) 7: 11–13. In Wilhelminian Germany, anti-Semitism and antifeminism were closely linked, and Jewish responsibility for the feminist movement was a frequent theme in anti-Semitic propaganda. See P. G. J. Pulzer, *The Rise of Political Anti-Semitism in Germany and Austria* (London, 1964), pp. 221 ff.
8. Norman Cohn, *Warrant for Genocide: The Myth of the Jewish World-Conspiracy and the Protocols of the Elders of Zion* (London, 1967).

CHAPTER ONE
The Holocaust and After

1. There is an extensive literature on the Holocaust. The most recent and most authoritative study is Raul Hilberg, *The Destruction of the European Jews*, revised and definitive edition (New York, 1985). A briefer but valuable account will be found in Lucy Dawidowicz, *The War against the Jews, 1933-1945* (New York, 1975). The attitudes and policies of the Western allies have been examined by a number of scholars, most recently by David S. Wyman, *The Abandonment of the Jews: America and the Holocaust, 1941-1945* (New York, 1984), and Bernard Wasserstein, *Britain and the Jews of Europe 1939-1945* (Oxford, 1979).
2. *Mein Kampf*, ed. John Chamberlain et al (New York, 1939), pp. 448-449.
3. W. Erbt, *Weltgeschichte auf rassischer Grundlage* (Leipzig, 1934), p. 76.
4. Rolf Beckh, *Der Islam* (Munich, 1937).
5. Alfred Rosenberg, *Mythus des XX Jahrhunderts* (Munich, 1934), p. 665.
6. On Kielce and other outbreaks in Poland, see Yehuda Bauer, *Flight and Rescue: Brichah* (New York, 1970), especially pp. 208 ff.
7. Michael J. Cohen, *Palestine and the Great Powers 1945-1948* (Princeton, 1982), pp. 66-67; cf. J. C. Hurewitz, *The Struggle for Palestine* (New York, 1950), pp. 237-238.
8. For a comprehensive survey of Soviet policies toward the Jews, see Benjamin Pinkus, *The Soviet Government and the Jews 1948-1967: A Documented Study* (Cambridge and Jerusalem, 1984).
9. Pinkus, pp. 147 ff, 181 ff.
10. Pinkus, pp. 300-301.
11. See Maxime Rodinson, *Peuple juif ou probleme juif?* (Paris, 1981), pp. 23 ff. On this question in general, see the useful collection of essays edited by Robert S. Wistrich, *The Left Against Zionism: Communism, Israel, and the Middle East* (London, 1979).
12. Pinkus, p. 58.
13. On economic crimes, see Pinkus, pp. 197-198, 201-207.
14. On Kichko see William Korey in Nathan Glazer et al., *Perspectives on Soviet Jewry* (New York, 1971), pp. 45-46.

CHAPTER TWO
Semites

1. G. W. von Leibniz, *Nouveaux Essais sur l'entendement humain*, book 3, chapt. 2, par. 1, cit. Renan.
2. August Ludwig Schlözer, in J. G. Eichhorn, ed., *Repertorium für Biblische und Morgenländische Litteratur* (Leipzig, 1777-80), 8: 161-163.
3. Ernest Renan, *Histoire générale et système comparé des langues sémitiques*, (Paris, 1863), 1: 40-41.
4. Theodor Nöldeke, *Sketches from Eastern History* (London and Edinburgh, 1892), p. 4.
5. Edward Ullendorff, "The Knowledge of Languages in the Old Testament," in *Bulletin of the John Rylands Library* (March 1962), 44(2): 455-465.

CHAPTER THREE

Jews

1. S. Dubnov, *History of the Jews in Russia and Poland from the Earliest Times until the Present Day* (Philadelphia, 1916), 1: 260. The term *zhid* in Russian is considered offensive, as contrasted with the neutral term *evrei*. It might therefore be more accurately translated as Yid or Kike.
2. Ibid., 1: 257.
3. On the *millets*, see Benjamin Braude and Bernard Lewis, eds., *Christians and Jews in the Ottoman Empire*, 2 vols. (New York, 1982).
4. For a masterly study of these events and of their significance in Jewish history, see Gershom Scholem, *Sabbatai Sevi, the Mystical Messiah 1626–1676* (Princeton, N. J., 1973; Hebrew original, Tel Aviv, 1957). On the *dönme*, see *Encyclopaedia of Islam*, 2nd ed. *s.v.* (by M. Perlmann), where further references are given.
5. For demographic data see Jakob Lestschinsky, "Die Umsiedlung and Umschichtung des jüdischen Volkes im Laufe des letzten Jahrhunderts," in *Weltwirtschaftliches Archiv* (1929), 30: 123–156, idem, "Jewish Migrations, 1840–1956," in Louis Finkelstein, ed., *The Jews, Their History, Culture, and Religion*, 3rd ed. (New York, 1960), 2: 1536–1596; Arthur Ruppin, *Jewish Fate and Future* (London, 1940) pp. 24 ff; and articles in *Encyclopaedia Judaica*, svv. "Demography" and "Population."
6. Cited in Arthur Hertzberg, *The Zionist Idea: A Historical Analysis and Reader* (Cleveland and New York, 1959), pp. 102 ff.
7. Rabbi Zvi Hirsch Kalischer, in Hertzberg, p. 114.
8. Quoted in Lucy Dawidowicz, *The Golden Tradition: Jewish Life and Thought in Eastern Europe* (New York, 1967), p. 335.

CHAPTER FOUR

Anti-Semites

1. On Marr, see P. G. J. Pulzer, *op. cit.*, pp. 47, 49–52; and Léon Poliakov, *Histoire de l'antisémitisme*, 4 vols. (Paris, 1961–77), 3: 432, 466, 4: 29–30. On the history of anti-Semitism, see further Jacob Katz, *From Prejudice to Destruction: Anti-Semitism, 1700–1933* (Cambridge, Mass., 1980), and Samuel Morag, ed. *Sinat Yisra'el le-doroteha* (Jerusalem, 1980).
2. See Albert Sicroff, *Les Controverses des statuts de "Pureté de sang" en Espagne du XV au XVII siècle* (Paris, 1960), pp. 223 ff; and S. W. Baron, *A Social and Religious History of the Jews*, 2nd ed. (New York, 1952–vol. 8, 1969), p. 85.
3. Sicroff, pp. 90 ff; Baron, 8: 88–89.
4. John Locke, *A Letter Concerning Toleration with the Second Treatise of Civil Government*, ed. J. W. Gough (London, 1946), p. 160; cit. Arthur Hertzberg, *The French Enlightenment and the Jews* (New York and London, 1968), pp. 46–47, n. 3.
5. On anti-Semitic and antiblack sentiments and ideologies in eighteenth-century France, see Pierre Pluchon, *Nègres et juifs au XVIII siècle* (Paris, 1984).
6. Poliakov, 3: 233.
7. Poliakov, 3: 234.
8. Poliakov, 3: 107.

9. *Voltaire's Notebooks*, ed. Theodore Besterman (Geneva, 1952), pp. 31 and 233; Poliakov, 3: 114.

10. *Essai sur les moeurs*, ed. René Pomeau (Paris, 1963), 1: 478; Poliakov, 3: 106.

11. *Traité de métaphysique*, ed. Temple Patterson (Manchester, 1937), p. 33, cf. Ibid., p. 4.

12. Poliakov, 3: 115.

13. Karl Wilhelm Friedrich Grattenauer, *Wider die Juden: Ein Wort der Warnung an alle unsere christliche Mitbürger* (Berlin, 1803), 3: 29; cit. Poliakov, 3: 158.

14. Cited in Léon Poliakov, *Le Mythe aryen: Essai sur les sources du racisme et des nationalismes* (Paris, 1971), pp. 172–173.

15. Baron, 9: 32.

16. Poliakov, *Histoire*, 3: 243.

17. Poliakov, *Histoire*, 3: 242–243.

18. Lessing, *Die Juden* (1749), scene 22, cf. Poliakov, *Histoire*, 3: 69, who interprets this remark differently.

19. T. S. Eliot, "Burbank with a Baedeker, Bleistein With a Cigar," in *Poems 1909–1925* (London, 1925), p. 55. See further Edgar Rosenberg, *From Shylock to Svengali; Jewish Stereotypes in English fiction* (London, 1961); Moses Debré, *Der Jude in der französischen Literatur von 1800 bis zur Gegenwart* (Ansbach, 1909); Montagu Frank Modder, *The Jew in the Literature of England to the end of the 19th century* (New York-Philadelphia, 1939).

20. Solomon Rappaport, *Jew and Gentile, the Philo-Semitic Aspect* (New York, 1980).

21. Text in Pulzer, pp. 337–338.

22. Poliakov, *Histoire*, 4: 29–30.

23. Pulzer, p. 204. See further Robert S. Wistrich, *Socialism and the Jews; the Dilemmas of Assimilation in Germany and Austria-Hungary* (London and Toronto, 1982).

24. The curious reader may note that some of the more striking anti-Semitic phrases found in the English editions of Miss Christie's detective stories were omitted from the American editions.

25. Poliakov, *Histoire*, 3: 336.

26. Mark Twain, *Concerning the Jews* (Philadelphia, 1985), reprinted from *Harper's New Monthly Magazine*, September 1898.

27. William F. Moneypenny and George E. Buckle, *Life of Disraeli* (London, 1929), 1: 885; Poliakov, *Histoire*, 3: 345.

28. Poliakov, *Histoire*, 3: 301.

29. St. John Chrysostom, cit. James Parke in *Conflict of the Church and the Synagogue* (London, 1934), pp. 163–166; John G. Gager *The Origins of Anti-Semitism* (New York, 1983), pp. 118–120; Norman Cohn, "The Myth of the Demonic Conspiracy of Jews in Medieval and Modern Europe," in Anthony de Reuck and Julie Knight, eds., *Caste and Race: Comparative Approaches* (London, 1967), pp. 240 ff. See further Jeremy Cohen, *The Friars and the Jews: The Evolution of Medieval Anti-Judaism* (Ithaca and London, 1982).

30. Father Barruel, pp. 58–62, cit. Poliakov, *Histoire*, 3: 296.

31. From a German pamphlet of 1816, *Das Judenthum in der Maurerey* (Judaism in Freemasonry). This pamphlet was much used in later Nazi literature. Poliakov, *Histoire*, 3: 297–298.

32. Poliakov, *Histoire*, 3: 298.

33. Poliakov, *Histoire*, 3: 299.

34. Jacob R. Marcus, *The Jew in the Medieval World: A Source Book 1315–1791* (New York and Philadelphia, 1960), pp. 145 ff, 161 ff, 170 ff.

35. Poliakov, *Histoire*, 4: 38, 39.

36. Rappoport, p. 180; S. Zeitlin in *Jewish Quarterly Review* (July 1968), pp. 76–80, review of *The Strange History of the Beiless Case* by Maurice Samuel.

37. Norman Cohn, *Warrant for Genocide.*

38. Anîs Manṣūr, an Egyptian journalist specializing in anti-Jewish polemics, has his own way of explaining the discoveries of the *Times* correspondent: "Anti-Semitism reached its peak with the publication of the secret plan to rule the world. The *Times* correspondent in Istanbul revealed in 1929 that the Jews had composed a book called the *Protocols of the Elders of Zion*, when their first Zionist Congress met in Bâle in Switzerland, and that at this Congress they had agreed on their devilish plan to rule the whole world. This book was translated in all the countries of the world. It was translated four times in Egypt, and I myself was the first to draw attention to it and translate parts of it 25 years ago" (Anîs Manṣūr, *Wajᶜ fī qalb Isrāʾīl*, Cairo, 1977, p. 140).

    Mr. Manṣūr is wrong in every particular. The achievement of Philip Graves, the *Times* correspondent in Istanbul, was not to "reveal" the *Protocols*, which were already widely circulated at the time, but to expose them as a forgery. The year was not 1929 but 1921. (Philip Graves's *Times* articles were reprinted in his little book *The Truth about the Protocols*, [London: 1921].) Even Mr. Manṣūr's own claim to have been the first to draw attention to them in Arabic is unfounded. Arabic translations appeared in Palestine in 1926 and in Egypt in about 1927.

    On the role of Eastern Christians in introducing anti-Semitism to the Middle East, Elie Kedourie aptly observes that they "had easier access to Western literature but not enough judgment to exercise critical and discriminating choice" (Kedourie, *The Chatham House Version*, London, 1970, p. 338).

39. Pierre-Joseph Proudhon, *Césarisme et christianisme* (Paris, 1883), 1: 39; Poliakov, 3: 386; Edmund Silberner, *Sozialisten zur Judenfrage* (Berlin, 1962), pp. 56 ff.

40. Johann Gottlieb Fichte, *Sämmtliche Werke* (Berlin, 1845), 6: 150; Silberner, pp. 382–383; Poliakov, *Histoire*, 3: 198.

41. Article in New York *Daily Tribune*, cit. *Commentary*, April 1985, p. 39. On Marx, Engels and the Jews see further Wistrich, *Socialism.* pp. 25 ff.

42. Wistrich, loc. cit.

43. Silberner, p. 390.

44. Silberner, p. 391.

45. Silberner, p. 393; Pulzer, p. 265.

46. *Mein Kampf*, pp. 73 ff.

CHAPTER FIVE

Muslims and Jews

1. For a survey of Jewish–Muslim relations see B. Lewis, *The Jews of Islam* (Princeton, N.J., 1985), where earlier literature is cited.

2. Ibn Khaldūn, *al-Muqaddima.* Translated by Franz Rosenthal. (New York, 1958); Charles Issawi, *An Arab Philosophy of History: Selections from the Prolegomena of Ibn Khaldun of Tunis (1332–1406)* (London, 1950), p. 61, repeated on p. 161.

3. A. S. Tritton, *The Caliphs and Their Non-Muslim Subjects* (London, 1930), pp. 174 ff.
4. On the origins and development of anti-Semitic literature in Arabic, see Sylvia G. Haim, "Arabic Antisemitic Literature," in *Jewish Social Studies*, 17(4): 307–312; Yehoshua Ben-Hananyah, "Sifrut Caravit anti-tsiyonit," in *Ha-Shiloah*, 43: 272–279; Yehoshafat Harkabi, *Arab Attitudes to Israel* (Jerusalem, 1972); idem., "La'anti-shemiyut ha-Caravit mehadash," in *Sinat Yisra'el ledoroteha* (Jerusalem, 1980), pp. 247–259; Yehoshua Porat, "Ideologia anti-tsiyonit ve-anti-yehudit ba-hevra ha-le'umit ha-Caravit be-Eretz-Yisrael," in *Sinat Yisra'el*, pp. 237–246; Moshe Maoz, "The Image of the Jew in Official Arab Literature and Communications Media," in *World Jewry and the State of Israel* (New York, 1977), pp. 33–51; Shimon Shamir, "The Attitude of Arab Intellectuals to the Six-Day War," in *The Anatomy of Peace in the Middle East* (New York, 1969), pp. 5–24; Norman A. Stillman, "New Attitudes toward the Jew in the Arab World," in *Jewish Social Studies* (1975), 38(3–4): 197–204; Dafna Alon, *Arab Racialism* (Jerusalem, 1969); Raphael Israeli, "Anti-Jewish Attitudes in the Arabic Media, 1975–1981," in *Research Report* (September 1983), 15: 1–18; Daniel Pipes, The Politics of Muslim Anti-Semitism," *Commentary*, August 1981, pp. 39–45; Ronald L. Nettler, "Islam vs. Israel," *Commentary*, December 1984, pp. 26 ff. Hava Lazarus Yafeh, "An Inquiry into Arab Textbooks," in *Asian and African Studies* (1972), 8(1): 1–20; Rivka Yadlin and Amazia Baram, "Egypt's Changing Attitude Towards Israel," in *The Jerusalem Quarterly* (Spring, 1978), 7: 68–87; Stefan Wild, "Judentum, Christentum und Islam in der Palästinensischen Poesie," in *Die Welt des Islams* (1984), 23–24: 265 ff. Of particular interest is AsCad Razzūq, *Al-Talmūd wa'l-Sahyūniyya* (Beirut, 1970). This book, published by the PLO Research Center, is the first and probably the only monograph which attempts to deal in a scholarly way with the Talmud and with its defenders, critics and slanderers.
5. Nāfiṭūs, *al-Sahāfa al-Radiyya al-lamāCiyya fī inhidām al-diyāna al-Cibriyya* (Beirut, 1869; (not seen), cit. Harkabi, *Arab Attitudes to Israel*, pp. 273–275, and, in greater detail by Razzūq, pp. 71 ff.
6. *Fi'l-zawāyā khabāyā, aw kashf asrār al-Yahūd* (Cairo, 1893). An anonymous refutation was published in Cairo shortly after.
7. Abraham Galante in *Archives Israelites*, 45: 29 (Paris, 1899), pp. 232–233.
8. Sylvia G. Haim, "The Palestine Problem in al-Manar," in Amnon Cohen and Gabriel Baer, eds., *Egypt and Palestine: A Millennium of Association (868–1948)* (Jerusalem and New York, 1984), pp. 300 ff.
9. Muhammad Bakir Alwan, "Jews in Arabic literature 1830–1914," *Al-CArabiyya* (1978), 2: 51–53; Salih J. Altoma, "The Image of the Jew in Modern Arabic Literature," ibid., p. 62.
10. Cevdet Pasa, *Tezakir*, ed. Cavid Baysun (Ankara, 1963), 3: 236–237; translated in Braude and Lewis, 1: 30.
11. Ignaz Goldziher, *Muslim Studies* (London, 1967; German original, Halle, 1889), 1: 186–188 (German pp. 203–205), cf. Lewis, *Jews of Islam*, p. 103.

CHAPTER SIX

The Nazis and the Palestine Question

1. The English translation of this document was published in *Documents on British Foreign Policy 1919–1939*, ed. E. L. Woodward and Rohan Butler, 3rd series, 7:

1939 (London, 1954), pp. 257 ff. The German original was published in *Akten zur Deutschen Auswärtigen Politik 1918–1945, Aus dem Archiv des Deutschen Auswärtigen Amtes* (Imprimerie Nationale: Baden-Baden, 1956).

2. U.S. Department of State, *Nazi–Soviet Relations, 1939–1941. Documents from the Archives of the German Foreign Office*, ed. R. J. Sontag and J. S. Beddie, Dept. of State publication 3023, (Washington, D.C., 1948, p. 259; cf. ibid., pp. 244–245 and 270.

3. Cited in David Yisraeli, "The Third Reich and Palestine," in *Middle Eastern Studies* (October 1971), 7: 344 and n. 9.

4. David Yisraeli, "The Third Reich and Palestine," p. 346, n. 18, citing letter from Schwartz von Berk to Dr. von Hentig, dated July 9, 1937.

5. Lukasz Hirszowicz, *The Third Reich and the Arab East* (London, 1966), p. 30, cf. David Yisraeli, *Ha-Reich ha-Germani ve-Eretz Yisrael: Ba^c ayot Eretz Yisrael ba-mediniut ha-Germanit ba-Shanim 1889–1945* (Ramat Gan, 1973).

6. Hirszowicz, p. 30, cf. Yisraeli, *Ha-Reich*, p. 300.

7. The first serious study of Nazi–Arab relations was the work of the Polish scholar Lukasz Hirszowicz. Originally published in Warsaw in 1963, it appeared shortly after in an English translation, *The Third Reich and the Arab East* (London, 1966), and still remains the only monograph on the subject in English. Later works include: Heinz Tillman, *Deutschlands Araberpolitik im Zweiten Weltkrieg* ([East] Berlin, 1965); Bernd Philipp Schröder, *Deutschland und der Mittlere Osten im Zweiten Weltkrieg* (Göttingen, 1975); Josef Schröder, "Die Beziehungen der Achsenmächte zur Arabischen Welt," in *Zeitschrift für Politik,* 1971; David Yisraeli, "The Third Reich and Palestine" and *Ha-Reich ha-Germani ve-Eretz Yisrael*). All of these are based mainly on unpublished German archival material. Some of the relevant German documents were published later in the original and in English translation in the standard series; others are included in various volumes of memoirs by German officials engaged in Arab affairs, notably: Fritz Grobba, *Männer und Mächte im Orient* (Göttingen, 1967). Italian documents were used by Daniel Carpi, "The Mufti of Jerusalem, Amin el-Huseini, and His Diplomatic Activity during World War II (October 1941–July 1943)," in *Studies in Zionism*, No. 7 (Spring 1983). Arabic documents have been less used. Some of them, selected for political purposes, were published in *The Arab Higher Committee: Its Origins, Personnel and Purposes, The Documentary Record*, submitted to the United Nations May 1947 by the Nation Associates, Inc., New York, 1947. A number of these, with other documents, also appeared in the mufti's memoirs, published in installments in the Beirut monthly *Falastīn*, No. 112 (July 1970), and in Bayān al-Hūt, *Al-Qiyādāt wa'l-mu'assasāt al-siyāsiyya fī Falastīn 1917–1948* (Beirut, 1981), pp. 462 ff. The mufti himself was the subject of two books, both highly critical, both using captured German documents, by Maurice Pearlman, *Mufti of Jerusalem* (London, 1947), and Joseph B. Schechtman, *The Mufti and the Fuehrer* (London and New York, 1965). For a more sympathetic account with further bibliography, see D. Hopwood's article in *Encyclopedia of Islam*, 2nd ed., supplement, 1: 67–70.

8. Yisraeli, *Ha-Reich*, p. 210, citing a review of Bertram Thomas's book, *The Arabs*, in the Nazi newspaper *Völkischer Beobachter*, December 4, 1933. For a similar comment by Hitler himself in 1942, see Hirszowicz, p. 263 or n. 72 on p. 358, citing *Hitler's TableTalk 1941–1942*, p. 547 (English translation, London, 1953; German original, Bonn, 1951).

9. Sāmī al-Jundī, *Al-Ba^cth* (Beirut, 1969), pp. 27 ff; Elie Kedourie, *Arabic Political Memoirs and Other Studies* (London and Portland, 1974), pp. 200–201. Dr. Carmen Ruiz Bravo, *La controversia ideologica: nacionalismo arabe/nacionalismos locales, oriente, 1918–1952* (Madrid, 1976), pp. 89 and 175 ff, offers a highly original explanation of this trend. While conceding some Nazi and Fascist elements in the Arab nationalism of the time, she attributes it to indirect influence via Zionism, "which inherited from fascism some of its charactersitics: the same concept of nationalism, racism, and aggressiveness." This, it will be recalled, was ten years before the birth of Israel, and at a time when hostility to Jews was a main theme in the policies of the Nazis, the Fascists, and their disciples.
10. Daniel Carpi, "The Mufti of Jerusalem," pp. 104–105.
11. Grobba, p. 255.
12. Grobba, pp. 255–256, cf. Carpi, p. 108, and Hirszowicz, pp. 214 ff.
13. Yisraeli, *Ha-Reich,* p. 309; Carpi, p. 110.
14. Yisraeli, *Ha-Reich, pp. 309–311* (document in German); Carpi, *p. 110; cf.* Grobba, *pp. 256–257;* Hirszowicz, *pp. 218 ff;* Schröder, *Deutschland,* p. 199; Tillmann, pp. 324 ff.
15. Carpi, pp. 112–113; Yisraeli, pp. 246–247; Grobba, pp. 264–267; Hirszowicz, pp. 226 ff.
16. Hirszowicz, p. 227.
17. A brief account of the *Orientlegionen* in Schröder, pp. 215–231. See also Tillmann, pp. 313 ff.
18. Ettore Rossi, *Documenti sull'origine e gli sviluppi della questione Araba (1875–1944)* (Rome, 1944), pp. 228–231, citing *Oriente Moderno,* (1942), 22: 453–455.
19. "Une surveillance active . . . de facon à se garder de leurs dangers et en eviter les dommages," French text in *The Arab Higher Committee,* 1947; this and other texts were also published in the mufti's memoirs, *Falasṭīn,* Beirut, No. 112 (July 1970), pp. 4 ff. The mufti also records that he wrote to the Turkish authorities, urging them not to allow Jewish refugees from Axis-ruled Europe to travel through Turkey to Palestine.
20. *Falasṭīn* (Beirut, July 1970), 112: 8–9.
21. Translated from the German documents in Fritz Grobba, *Männer und Mächte im Orient.* English translation in *Documents on German Foreign Policy,* series D (London and Washington, 1950–1964), 10(403): 559–560, and 11(680): 1151–1155. Cf. Lukasz Hirszowicz, *The Third Reich,* pp. 82–84, 109–110, and Bernd Phillipp Schröder, *Deutschland und der Mittlere Osten,* pp. 44–48, 53, 65–66, where, however, the references to "solving the Jewish problem" are not mentioned.
22. Grobba, p. 208.
23. Somerset de Chair, *The Golden Carpet* (London, 1943), p. 118; (New York, 1945), p. 127.
24. Anwar Sadat, *Revolt on the Nile.* Translated by Thomas Graham. (London, 1957), pp. 34–35.
25. Sadat, pp. 34–51; A. W. Sansom, *I Spied Spies* (London, 1965), pp. 75–76, 103–132; J. W. Eppler, *Rommel ruft Kairo* (Bielefeld, 1959), pp. 151, 164–165, 186–187, 201–204, 232.
26. Majid Khadduri, "General Nuri's Flirtations with the Axis Powers," in *Middle East Journal* (1962), 16: 328–336.
27. *Al-Muṣawwar,* September 18, 1953.

CHAPTER SEVEN

The War Against Zionism

1. Norman A. Stillman, *The Jews of Arab Lands, A History and Source-Book*, 37: 3–4, pp. 197–204 (Philadelphia, 1979), p. 356.
2. On the policies of the Ottoman government concerning Zionism, see Neville Mandel, *The Arabs and Zionism before World War I* (Berkeley and Los Angeles, 1976); Mim Kemal Öke, *Osmanli Imparatorlugu, Siyonizm ve Filistin Sorunu* (Istanbul, 1966); idem, *Abdülhamid, Siyonistler ve Filistin Meselesi* (Istanbul, 1981); Jacob M. Landau, "The 'Young Turks' and Zionism: Some Comments," in *Fields of Offerings; Studies in Honor of Raphael Patai* (Rutherford, N.J., 1983), pp. 197–205; David Farhi, "Documents on the Attitude of the Ottoman Government towards the Jewish Settlement in Palestine after the Revolution of the Young Turks (1908–1909)," in Moshe Ma'oz, ed., *Studies on Palestine during the Ottoman period* (Jerusalem, 1975), pp. 190–210. On the Arabic press in Ottoman Palestine see Ya^{c}qūb Yehoshua, *Ta'rīkh al-Ṣiḥāfa al-^{c}Arabiyya fī Filasṭīn fi'l-^{c}ahd al-^{c}Uthmānī 1908–1918* (Jerusalem, 1974).
3. See B. Lewis, "Palestine: On the History and Geography of a Name," in *International History Review* (1980), 2: 1–12.
4. Najīb al-Khūrī Naṣṣār, *Al-Ṣahyūniyya-Ta'rīkhuhā-Ghardụhā-Ahammiyyatuhā* (Haifa, 1911). On Naṣṣār, see Khayriyya Qāsimiyya, "Najīb Naṣṣār fī jarīdatihi al-Karmal (1909–1914), aḥad ruwwād munaḥāḍat al-ṣahyūniyya," in *Shu'ūn Filasṭīniyya* (1973), 23: 101–123, and Yehoshua, pp. 130–142.
5. Mandel, p. 101; Öke, *Osmanli Imparatorlugu*, pp. 109–110.
6. Mandel, p. 53.
7. Négib Azoury, *Le Réveil de la Nation Arabe dans l'Asie Turque* (Paris, 1905), p. v; Mandel, p. 52; Kedourie, pp. 111 ff.
8. Farid Kassab, *Le nouvel Empire Arabe: La Curie Romaine et le prétendu péril juif universel—Réponse à M. N. Azoury bey* (Paris, 1906), pp. 39–40, cit. Mandel; Mandel, pp. 50–51.
9. "The Return to Palestine," in *New Liberal Reivew* (London), II, December 1901, p. 627. My thanks are due to Professor Michael Curtis for this reference.
10. V. Jabotinsky, *Poems* (Jerusalem, 1947), p. 201.
11. Theodor Herzl, *Old-New-Land*. Translated by Lotta Levensohn. (New York, 1960), pp. 169–170; cf. pp. 66, 68–69, 74–75, 97, 121–124, 152, 175.
12. For details, see Kenneth W. Stein, *The Land Question in Palestine, 1917–1939* (Chapel Hill and London, 1984).
13. A good example of this form of persuasion may be found in a memorandum presented to the British secretary of state for the colonies, Mr. Winston Churchill, on behalf of the Executive Committee of the Arab Palestine Congress by its president, Mūsā Kāzim al-Ḥusaynī, on March 28, 1921. The memorandum, after observing that "the fact that a Jew is a Jew has never prejudiced the Arab against him," and that the Jews "in Germany are Germans, in France Frenchmen, and in England Englishmen," goes on to present what it calls a "moral point of view." According to this, "Jews have been amongst the most active advocates of destruction in many lands, especially where their influential positions have enabled them to do more harm. It is well known that the disintegration of Russia was wholly or in great part brought about by the Jews, and a large proportion of the defeat of Germany and Austria must also be put at their door. When the star of the Central Powers was in the ascendant Jews flattered them, but the moment

the scale turned in favour of the Allies Jews withdrew their support from Germany, opened their coffers to the Allies, and received in return that most uncommon promise.

"We have seen a book entitled 'The Jewish Peril' which should be read by everyone who still doubts the pernicious motives of the Jews towards the Powers that be and towards civilisation. It is a collection of the minutes of a secret society of prominent Jews who meet from time to time to discuss world affairs in relation to Judaism. The book is replete with an overflowing hatred of mankind, and Christendom in particular. It points out in detail ways and means for upsetting the present order of things, so that out of the ensuing chaos Jews might come out masters of the world.

"Looking into the ranks of socialism, we find Jewish names such as Carl [sic] Marx, Becknin [sic—recte Bakunin?] and Trotsky topping the list, besides a host of others as pernicious, if not as renowned."

The document is given in full in Aaron S. Klieman, *Foundations of British Policy in the Arab world: The Cairo Conference of 1921* (Baltimore, 1970), pp. 259–267, and discussed pp. 127 ff. The book on the "Jewish Peril" is of course the *Protocols*. This citation, and the whole tenor of this section of the document, suggest a foreign, probably a Western, hand.

14. See for example the memoirs of Khālid al-ᶜAẓm, prime minister of Syria in 1948–49. Enumerating the factors which led to the success of Israel, he says: "Fifth; the summons of the Arab governments to the population of Palestine to leave the country and take refuge in the neighboring Arab countries . . . this collective flight served the Jews and strengthened their position without effort. . . . Since 1948 we have been demanding the return of the refugees to their homes, when we ourselves were the ones who induced them to leave them. . . . We doomed a million Arab refugees, by calling on them and insisting that they abandon their land, their homes, their work and their occupations, and we made them unemployed and homeless." *Mudhakkirāt Khālid al-ᶜAẓm* (Beirut, 1973), 1: 386–387. For an indication, from an Israeli source, about the expulsion of Arab civilians from Lydda and Ramla, see Tom Segev, *1949: ha-Yisraᴄlim ha-Rishonim* (Jerusalem, 1984), p. 41.

15. Shimon Ballas, *La littérature arabe et le conflit au proche-orient (1948–1973)* (Paris, 1980), p. 140.

CHAPTER EIGHT

The War Against the Jews

1. "It may happen that a man lies or falls into error, but for a people to build their society on lies, that is the speciality of the children of Israel alone! . . . Such are the Jews, my brother, Muslim lion cub, your enemies and the enemies of God, and such is the truth about them as told in the Book of God. . . . Such is their particular natural disposition, the corrupt doctrine that is theirs . . . they have never ceased to conspire against their main enemy, the Muslims. In one of their books they say: 'We Jews are the masters of the world, its corrupters, those who foment sedition, its hangmen!' They do not like you, Muslim lion cub, you who revere God, Islam, and the Prophet Muhammad. . . . Muslim lion cub, annihilate their existence, those who seek to subjugate all humanity so as to force them to serve their satanic designs." *al-Daᶜwa* (Cairo), October 1980. Translated and

discussed in Gilles Kepel, *The Prophet and Pharoah; Muslim Extremism in Egypt* (London, 1985; French original, Paris, 1984), pp. 110 ff.

2. Speech to United Nations seminar on religious tolerance and freedom, delivered in Geneva on December 5, 1984. Dr. Dawālibī spent the war years in German-occupied Europe, and was described as "our man of confidence" (Unser Vertrauensmann) in a secret letter from SS Obergruppenführer Erwin Ettel, writing from the Foreign Ministry in Berlin to the German Embassy in Paris, dated October 21, 1943 (German Foreign Ministry Archives A, b 21/w).

3. Official English translations of the Proceedings of the Fourth Conference of the Academy of Islamic Research, Cairo, 1970, pp. 458–459.

4. Porat, "Ideologia," p. 241; idem, *The Emergence of the Palestinian National Movement 1918–1929* (London, 1974), pp. 60 ff; cf. Ann Mosely Lesch, *Arab Politics in Palestine, 1917–1939: The Frustration of a Nationalist Movement* (Ithaca and London, 1979), pp. 60 ff.

5. Daphne Tsimhoni, "The Arab Christians and the Palestinian Arab National Movement during the Formative Stage," in Gabriel Ben-Dor, ed., *The Palestinians and the Middle East Conflict* (Ramat Gan, 1978), p. 79.

6. See Trevor LeGassick, "The Image of the Jews in Post–World War II Arabic Literature," *Al-ᶜArabiyya* (1978), 2: 74–89; S. Ballas, op. cit.; Pierre Cachia, "Themes Related to Christianity and Judaism in Modern Egyptian Drama and Fiction," *Journal of Arabic Literature* (1971), 2: 178–194; Werner Ende, "The Palestine Conflict as Reflected in Contemporary Arabic Literature," in Gustav Stein and Udo Steinbach, eds., *The Contemporary Middle Eastern Scene: Basic Issues and Major Trends* (Opladen, 1979), pp. 154–167.

7. *Dīwān al-Ruṣāfī* (Cairo, 1956), pp. 431–432; also (Beirut, 1931), pp. 408–409; cf. Ṣafā Khulūsī, "Maᶜrūf ar-Ruṣāfī in Jerusalem," in *Arabic and Islamic Garland . . . presented to Abdul-Latif Tibawi* (London, 1977), pp. 147–152; Stefan Wild, "Judentum," pp. 267–269.

8. Tsimhoni, p. 92, n. 29.

9. Wild, pp. 271–272.

10. *Maᶜrakatunā maᶜ al-Yahūd.* Republished in Saudi Arabia in 1970, in a collection of essays on various subjects, but with this as title of the book.

11. H. J. Cohen, "The Anti-Jewish *Farhud* in Baghdad, 1941," *Middle Eastern Studies* (1966), 3: 2–17.

12. Robert St. John, *The Boss* (New York, 1960), 153. For a sample of his work, see Johann von Leers, *Juden sehen Dich an,* 5th ed. (Nuremberg, n.d.), pp. 163–166.

13. Ṣādiq Jalāl al-ᶜAẓm, *Al-Naqd al-Dhātī baᶜd al-hazīma* (Beirut, 1972), pp. 53 ff.

14. Asᶜad Razzūq, *Al-Talmūd wa'l-Ṣahyūniyya,* pp. 15–16, 18.

15. Ṣalāḥ Dasūqī, in *al-Majalla* (Cairo), (November 1960), 4(47): 7–11; cf. ibid., (January 1961), 5(49): 134–136. Mr. Dasūqī was military governor of Cairo, and later ambassador to Finland.

16. Ṣalāḥ Dasūqī, *Amrīkā Mustaᶜmara Ṣahyūniyya* (Cairo, 1957).

17. Abdelwahab M. Elmessiri, "Arab views on the Protocols," *Foreign Affairs* (April 1977), 55: 641–642.

18. The press reported such gifts to the entourage of several visiting foreign ministers, e.g., Michel Jobert of France (January 29, 1974), and Aldo Moro of Italy (February 13, 1974).

19. London press reports of proceedings at the Central Criminal Court against Colin Jordan and John Tyndall, then respectively leader and deputy leader of the British National Socialist movement, in early October 1962; cf. an interview with

Tyndall in the *Sunday Telegraph* of March 10, 1963. For a later example see the *Daily Telegraph*, January 13, 1970, on the trial of T. O. Williams.

A sympathetic visitor to a Fatah training camp noted the literature in use by them: "There are political books available: Castro, Guevara, Mao Tse-tung, Giap, Rodinson; General de Gaulle's memoirs; and also *Mein Kampf*. When I expressed surprise at the presence of this last volume, the political commissar replied that it was necessary to have read everything, and that since the Israelis behaved like Nazis it was useful to know precisely what Nazism was." Gerard Chaliand, *The Palestine Resistance* (London, 1972), p. 10. M. Chaliand does not comment on this reply.

20. "Was Kennedy the Victim of a Zionist-Armed Hand?" in *The Scribe* (April 1964), 8(3): 8 ff.

21. Ṣabrī Jirjis, *al-Turāth al-Yahūdī al-Ṣahyūnī wa'l-Fikr al-Freudi* (Cairo, 1970).

22. Ibrahim al-Hardello, *Anti-Semitism: A Changing Concept* (Khartoum, 1970), p. 9.

23. Anîs Manṣūr, *Al-Ḥā'iṭ wa'l-dumūᶜ* (Cairo, 1972), pp. 15 ff.

24. Hava Lazarus-Yafeh, "An Inquiry into Arab Textbooks," p. 17, n. 43.

25. *Al-Jumhūriyya* (Baghdad), May 23, 1978; *Baghdad Observer*, May 24, 1978; *New York Times*, April 14, 1979; *al-Wafd* (Cairo), March 29, 1984.

26. ᶜAbbās Maḥmūd al-Sharīf and Yūsuf Aḥmad Maḥmūd al-Qūsī, *Al-Ta'rīkh al-ᶜArabi al-Islāmī: al-Ṣaff al-Thālith* (Cairo, n.d.), p. 47; Muḥammad Yūsuf al-Mahjūb et al., *Al-Tarbiya al-Dīniyya*, (Cairo, 1966), 1: 93. For more recent treatments, see Hava Lazarus-Yafeh, pp. 1–20; Avner Giladi, "Israel's Image in Recent Egyptian Textbooks," *Jerusalem Quarterly* (1978) pp. 88 ff. A book on "The Jews, Judaism and Islam," written by a professor at the College of Education of ᶜAyn Shams University in Cairo, explains that the "three main basic sources" for the study of the Jews must necessarily be the Torah, the Talmud, and the Protocols (p. 5). The author declares his intention of basing himself in the first. This limitation in no way confines his anti-Jewish fervor. (ᶜAbd al-Ghanī ᶜAbbūd, *Al-Yahūd wa'l-Yahūdiyya wa'l-Islām*, Cairo, 1982.)

27. Khomeini, *Vilāyat-i Faqīh*, p. 6; English version (Algar), p. 27.

28. *Arabische Korrespondenz* (Bonn), October–November, 1964.

29. Text in *al-Bilād*, November 29, 1964; translated from the Italian version in *Oriente Moderno*, 1964, p. 703.

30. According to a letter in the *New York Times* of May 31, 1985, a Malaysian law forbids the "screening, portrayal or musical presentation of words of Jewish origin"; *New York Times*, August 10 and 11, 1984. On the *Protocols* in Malaysia see *Asiaweek*, December 8, 1978, pp. 4–5.

31. *Egyptian Gazette*, June 11, 1979.

32. Muhammad Bakir Alwan, "Jews in Arabic Literature," p. 50, rightly describes this as ludicrous.

33. *New York Times*, September 26, 1979.

34. Yūsuf Rizqallāh Ghanīma, *Nuzhat al-Mushtāq fī Ta'rīkh Yahūd al-ᶜIrāq*, (Baghdad, 1924).

35. Ghassān Kanafānī, *Fi'l-Adab al-Ṣahyūnī* (Beirut, 1967).

36. *Cairo Today*, June, 1984, p. 53. According to the statistics for 1983 published there, the largest number of tourists came from the USA (183,600), the second largest from Saudi Arabia (162,000), and the third largest from "Palestine" (117,000). The next four, in order, are France, Germany, Italy, and the United Kingdom.

37. For these and other similar statements in praise of Sulaymān Khāṭir and his action, by Egyptian writers artists, and intellectuals, see *Al-Ahālī*, December 25, 1985.
38. *Al-Muṣawwar*, December 28, 1985. For another article protesting against the misrepresentation and glorification of Sulaymān Khāṭir, see Ibrāhīm Saᶜduh in *Akhbār al-Yawm*. December 28, 1985.

CHAPTER NINE

The New Anti-Semitism

1. The point is vividly made in an article by Ṣabrī Abu'l-Majd in *al-Muṣawwar*, annual special issue, December, 1972: "The proud Arab spirit could endure the Ottoman, or British, or French occupation, because Turkey or Britain or France are states, each with its history and its forces; but the Arab spirit cannot endure occupation by gangs and cliques who came from various parts of the world and know no law but that of the jungle."
2. B. Lewis, "The Anti-Zionist Resolution," in *Foreign Affairs* (October 1976), 55(1): 54–64.
3. B. Lewis, "The State of Middle Eastern Studies," in *American Scholar* (Summer 1979), 48(3): 365–81.

Afterword to the new edition

1. *Al-Shaʿb* (Cairo), January 3, 1997; *Al-Waṭan* (Muscat), February 12, 1997.
2. *Interfaith Newsletter*, March–September, 1995; *Interfaith Monthly*, September, 1995.
3. `Alī Sālim, *Riḥla ilā Isrāʾīl*, Cairo 1994, p. 8.

Index